Strategy Savvy

With the COVID-19 pandemic, many business leaders question the need for strategy and the value of strategic planning and management in today's environment. This book will demonstrate that our approach to strategy development and implementation needs to change to be able to help organizations change. The proposed new approach in this book can provide insights and perspectives to keep strategy relevant by "Putting Strategy in Action" through developing a "Making the Future Happen Today" way of thinking and living.

Many strategy books focus on the perspective of large multinational corporations that have the capacity and capabilities to develop and implement a strategy using very structured methodologies and tools. This book will add a new dimension by focusing on the use of Strategy-as-Practice (SaP), intuition, and serendipity as important complements that can be used by large corporations as well as small- and medium-sized enterprises (SMEs) and entrepreneurs to develop and implement winning strategies. This is an important dimension to support the strategic decision-making process that is frequently undermined in traditional strategic planning and management-focused books.

The author theorizes that developing into a Strategy Savvy professional is about embracing two of the most important concepts in strategy development—Proactivity and Sustainability. This book addresses the opportunities and threats presented by VUCA (Volatility, Uncertainty, Complexity, and Ambiguity) and how we can capitalize on those opportunities to create unprecedented growth opportunities in Society 5.0 that is shaping new economies, such as the Digital Economy, the Experience Economy, the Sharing Economy, the GIG Economy, the Purpose Economy and the Circular Economy. The author also proposes a new approach to strategy development and implementation that mixes formal planning with practice and intuition that is helped by serendipity. He presents a strategy that is driven by four propellers—insights, culture, operations, and digitization—to ensure arrival at a better future.

Strategy Savvy

Balanced Strategy Development Approach Using Insights, Culture, Operations, and Digitization

Hesham O. Dinana, PhD

Routledge
Taylor & Francis Group

A PRODUCTIVITY PRESS BOOK

First Published 2023
by Routledge
605 Third Avenue, New York, NY 10158

and by Routledge
4 Park Square, Milton Park, Abingdon, Oxon, OX14 4RN

Routledge is an imprint of the Taylor & Francis Group, an informa business

ISBN: 978-1-032-24967-4 (hbk)
ISBN: 978-1-032-24964-3 (pbk)
ISBN: 978-1-003-28094-1 (ebk)

DOI: 10.4324/9781003280941

Typeset in Garamond
by Deanta Global Publishing Services, Chennai, India

This book is dedicated to my family—my wife, Noha, my son, Mahmoud, my daughter, Engie, and my brother, Walid. They gave me the inspiration to embark on this journey and provided much support, encouragement, and understanding throughout the process. I would not have been able to do this without them.

I would like to also dedicate this book to the memory of my parents—my father, Osama, and my mother, Nawal—for teaching me to continuously challenge myself to add values and uphold them. My final dedication goes to the memory of my father-in-law, Mohamed, and my mother-in-law, Samia, for their love and belief in me.

Contents

SECTION 3 *WHAT* DOES THE FUTURE HOLD?

SECTION 4 *WHAT* TO DO TO PUT STRATEGY IN ACTION

Preface

Many years ago, I heard a very interesting definition for the word strategy—it simply stated that strategy is about **Making the Future Happen Today**. This definition got me to think that strategy is not only about planning—it really is also about making things happen. Strategy is not only about the Future but also about Today. It is a bridge that connects today with the future. Since the future becomes the new today, building those bridges is not an act but a continuous way of living. Building on that thought, I completely changed my way of teaching and advising corporate leaders on strategy.

Pushed by many of my students and my customers to document my approach and research on strategy, I decided to write this book to inspire corporate leaders, government officials, and academicians who are trying to proactively shape the future.

Over the years, my firsthand experience with the impact of Volatility, Uncertainty, Complexity, and Ambiguity (VUCA) on the business world made me question the relevance and validity of many of the strategy development and execution concepts and models that were available then. With COVID-19, VUCA became part of the day-to-day life of every soul on the planet. Hence, the need to develop a new approach to strategy became a more pressing need to ensure future sustainability.

This book will guide you through a comprehensive and balanced strategy development approach that is driven by insights, culture, operations, and digitization. It will provide a new approach to integrating and using existing strategy tools to deliver better results that can help you put your strategy into action. It will help you prepare your organization for Society 5.0 and the future economies (such as the Sharing Economy, the GIG economy, the Purpose Economy, and the Circular Economy). Finally, it is meant for all kinds of organizations (e.g., public/private, multinationals/small-medium enterprises, etc.) because it combines formal and informal approaches to strategy development including the use of intuition and serendipity.

Reading this book will make you Strategy Savvy and will help you truly Make the Future Happen Today.

Preface

Acknowledgments

A book like this does not happen without a lot of support. First and foremost, I would like to thank Taylor & Francis Sr. Editor Ms. Kristine Mednansky for believing in my book and guiding me to bring it to this level. I also like to thank Mr. Shehroz Ahmed for his amazing support and great efforts in researching the different topics covered, Mr. Diaa El Sayed for helping me logically structure the text from a professional practitioner and critical reader perspective, and Dr. Shams Al Batrawy for supporting my book proposal development.

Thanks also go to my EFESO Consulting team and customers that provided me with great opportunities to validate and test my model and approach. My colleagues at the American University in Cairo inspired me with their dedication and passion to excel. Finally, thanks to all my students who believed in me and continuously pushed me to embark on this journey to try to leave a mark with this book.

About the Author

Dr. Hesham O. Dinana has over 30 years of working experience in strategy, marketing, information technology, customer care, and hi-tech manufacturing. In addition, he has more than 15 years of teaching experience both at undergraduate and graduate degree levels.

His industry experiences include healthcare, ICT, real estate, food and agribusiness, oil and gas, furniture, and Fast Moving Consumer Goods (FMCG). Through his various managerial positions at Philips Medical Systems—North America and his consultancy work in the United States, Europe, and the Middle East, his experience and expertise evolved to cover a wide spectrum of business and technical areas with hands-on specialization in strategic management, marketing, healthcare planning, corporate governance, IT management, and Customer Relationship Management (CRM).

Dinana is an assistant professor of integrated marketing communications (IMC) at the American University in Cairo and has taught MBA and DBA courses in strategic and international marketing at Arab Academy Graduate School of Business.

Dinana has an active research agenda in various marketing areas with a focus on digital marketing, entrepreneurship, and SME's marketing and the use of the Internet of Things in marketing. He has supervised many MBA theses and DBA dissertations in those areas.

Dinana has given numerous interactive talks/training courses to senior and middle managers and served as a speaker at numerous international conferences focusing on strategic and international management, healthcare marketing, and information technology management, especially e-marketing and e-health. As the vice president and regional managing director of a leading international consulting group, his consulting projects' engagement level span from one-on-one executive coaching to national-level strategy development initiatives.

He is a certified management consultant (CMC) by the UK Institute of Management Consultancy, a certified board director by the Egyptian Institute of Directors, a certified Balanced Scorecard consultant, a certified management simulation trainer, and a member of the American Management Association, Academy of Management, Association for Service Managers, American College of Healthcare Executives, Egyptian Engineers Syndicate, and the Egyptian Society for Quality in Healthcare. As an active member of his community, Dinana has served as a board member at the Grand Egyptian Museum (GEM), Egyptian Junior Businessmen Association and the Management Consultants Association, and has been advising the Board of Children Cancer Hospital Foundation 57357 and actively leading the development of its projects since 1998.

About the Author

WHY DO WE NEED STRATEGY?

Chapter 1

Do We Really Need to Have a Strategy?

1.1 Making the Future Happen Today

Many practitioners and academicians preach the need for change as the way to manage the **VUCA** (**V**olatile, **U**ncertain, **C**omplex, and **A**mbiguous) business environment we live in. Hundreds of books have been written over the last few decades about strategy and strategic management as the way to win in the ever-changing environment.

With the COVID-19 pandemic—that I describe as the **Super VUCA**—many business leaders today question the need for strategy and the value of strategic planning and management in today's environment. This book will demonstrate that our approach to strategy development and implementation needs to change to be able to help organizations change. The proposed new approach in this book can provide insights and perspectives to keep strategy relevant.

I would begin this book by referring to a simple but powerful model proposed by Simon Sinek [1], who once said if you want to lead the change, you have to answer three questions as an organization: First, **Why** do we do what we do? Second, **How** do we get things done?, and, finally, **What** do we offer to our stakeholders? In this book, we will follow the same three-step approach.

In order to be Strategy Savvy, we need to answer three questions: **Why** do we need a strategy (Chapters 1), **How** does strategy emerge and get formulated (Chapters 2 and 3), **What** does the future hold (Chapter 4), and, finally, **What** to do to put the strategy in action to ensure arrival (Chapters 5–8)—see Figure 1.1.

Many strategy books focus on the perspective of large multinational corporations that have the capacity and capabilities to develop and implement a strategy using very structured methodologies and tools. This book will add a new dimension focusing on the use of **Strategy-As-Practice (SaP)**, **Intuition**, and **Serendipity**, as important complements that can be used by large corporations as well as SMEs and entrepreneurs to develop and implement winning strategies. This is an important dimension to support the strategic decision-making process frequently undermined in traditional strategic planning and management-focused books.

In fact, the main theme of this book is "**Making the Future Happen Today**". So, it is about taking actions *Today* to shape the organization's *Future*. It tries to break the myth that strategy is

DOI: 10.4324/9781003280941-2

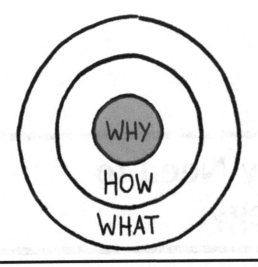

Why: Why do we need strategy?

How: How does strategy emerge?

What: What does the future hold, and **What** to do to put strategy in action?

Figure 1.1   Start with Why model by Simon Sinek [1]

only about the future and is focused on rigorous planning. It emphasizes the need for anticipation and action and the use of strategy as the **bridge between today and tomorrow**.

This can happen by developing **Strategy Savvy** organizations/professionals that are embracing two of the most important concepts in strategy—**Proactivity and Sustainability**.

Strategy is all about proactive; there is an American saying about three types of companies:

- Ones that **make** things happen
- Ones that **watch** things happen
- Ones that **wonder** what happened

The ones that make things happen are the companies that are proactive, and, in the process, they enable their sustainable future. This brings us to the second most important concept "**Sustainability**". The word sustainability has been a buzzword for quite some time now, and the key reason behind it is the rapidly changing business environment or more precisely, in business terms, "**The VUCA World**". This term has been widely used to describe an environment which defies confident diagnosis and befuddles executives so much that it has been a major source of disruption and has resulted in the demise of the likes of Nokia, Kodak, Sears, and Hertz to name a few.

This book will address the opportunities and threats presented by VUCA and how we can capitalize on those opportunities to create unprecedented growth opportunities in **Society 5.0** that is shaping new economies. This emerging new society is "**A human-centered society that balances economic advancement with the resolution of social problems by a system that highly integrates cyberspace and physical space**". It is in line with the **O2O** (online to off-line and off-line to online) way that many people live today.

In Society 5.0, organizations need to develop strategies that enable new value creation through innovation to enable the provision of products and services finely tailored to diverse individual needs and latent needs. In this way, it will be possible to achieve a society that can both promote economic development and find solutions to complex social problems (such as the reduction of greenhouse gas emissions, increased production and reduced loss of foodstuffs, mitigation of costs associated with the aging society, support of sustainable industrialization, redistribution of wealth, and correction of regional inequality).

The book elaborates on six new economies that are emerging and should be carefully understood and analyzed by nations, organizations, and individuals to guide their strategy development and implementation. Those future economies include **the Digital Economy, the Experience Economy, the Sharing Economy, the GIG Economy, the Purpose Economy**, and **the Circular Economy**.

The book proposes a new **Strategy Funnel Framework** to help organize and structure the many terms and concepts covered in strategy books today to improve the readers' ability to be more proactive in anticipating the future and in acting today in a manner that ensures sustainable progression.

Finally, to answer the question about what to do to put strategy in action, this book takes a novel approach that integrates the traditional strategy development tools with the concepts of **Design Thinking and Innovation Management as drivers for Balanced Strategy Development (BSD) approach.**

The new proposed BSD approach combines four different types of future-driving strategies for organizations to develop: **The Customer Insights-Driven Strategy, the Culture-Driven Strategy, the Operations-Driven Strategy**, and **the Digital-Driven Strategy**.

But before we dig deeper into all of the presented concepts and tools, we will begin by focusing on the first question: **Why** do we need to have a strategy? This chapter will focus on understanding the VUCA world that drives the need to change our approach to strategy, the value added by adopting strategy as a management way of living, and the risks that organizations face when they fail to update their approach to strategy.

1.2 The VUCA World

The view of the strategy savvy executive can help the company survive a series of challenges and capitalize on opportunities. These roadblocks and challenges are characterized by a fast-paced, continuously evolving business environment. This powerful, continuous change has transformed the fate of several companies: Either turning them into highly successful ones or bringing successful ones from the very top to the ground. In order to avoid a fate similar to the second ones, we need to take into account the environment in which the business is operating before devising a strategy. The reason that this is critically important is that only a few companies have been successful in executing the strategies to thrive in this business environment which is entangled in Volatility, Uncertainty, Complexity, and Ambiguity (VUCA).

VUCA has become a trendy way of saying unpredictable change and has found its way into business lexicons. For the majority of business leaders, this unpredictable nature of the business environment creates a myriad of traps while the rest, more specifically "optimists", see this as an opportunity to master the accompanying challenge and create dominance over its competitors.

For example, if we look only at one element of VUCA—that is Complexity—we see that according to the Boston Consulting Group (BCG) report "Simplifying IT: Six Ways to Reduce Complexity" [2], two types of business complexities are identified: Non-value-creating and value-creating complexities that enable differentiation and lead to major opportunities if properly managed. They identified six levers for reining in complexity. This includes, in the case of information technology management, the following:

1. Intelligent demand management
2. Scenario-based application rationalization

3. Infrastructure technology-pattern reduction
4. Simplified IT organization and an enabled IT workforce
5. Effective governance and simplified processes
6. A shared-services model and optimized sourcing

This list clearly demonstrated that there is no single silver bullet that can help manage the VUCA world. We need to manage the demand, the infrastructure, the organization, the processes, the governance system, and the sourcing. So the question arises as to how to capitalize on this opportunity and create unprecedented growth opportunities.

In order to understand this, we need to understand the meaning of VUCA from the leader's perspective and eliminate significant problems that occur when leaders employ these terms. If you perform a web search of any of the four words comprising VUCA you will realize that all four words are consistently used in consulting blogs, business press, and interviews. Though the words themselves have a related meaning, it is the difference between the terms that is most valuable for the leaders. Hence, it is quite imperative for the business leaders to understand the difference between each of the four terms as each term has a unique meaning that should be instructive to leaders. Second, the business leaders don't have a clear action plan to confront the challenges presented by the VUCA world. Business executives are often seen to mention the challenges of working in a VUCA, but they quickly move on to discussing the simpler topics without discussing how to position themselves in this environment. Those who do discuss it only offer a general solution to four different components concentrating on **innovation**, **creativity**, and **flexibility**.

Considering these two problems it is quite evident that in order to take actionable advice to deal with the VUCA we need to identify the nature of the challenges presented by each of the four components of the VUCA world. This is because volatility, uncertainty, complexity, and ambiguity each require a unique and separate response. Keeping this in view we need to delineate the differences between the term's volatility, uncertainty, complexity, and ambiguity and need to discuss the ways in which leaders need to position themselves to address each individually.

Table 1.1 summarizes the key thoughts regarding Volatility, Uncertainty, Complexity, and Ambiguity [3]. Strategy teams need to use agility to manage volatility, information to manage uncertainty, restructuring to manage complexity, and experimentation to manage ambiguity as follows:

- **Agility**: is the way to manage **Volatility**—resources should be allocated to build flexibility in the company's ability to take advantage of the windows of opportunities presented by the rapidly changing business environment.
- **Information**: is the way to manage **Uncertainty**—companies should learn to integrate and understand relationships and patterns to develop insights to support decision-making. Sales organizations are a great source of valuable information that can support this uncertainty management.
- **Restructuring**: is the way to manage **Complexity**—companies should learn to develop high-performing organization designs that align internal company capabilities with the external complexities in the most efficient and effective manner. Sales organizations represent a big part of the companies' human capital and need to continually evolve and innovate to support complexity management.
- **Experimentation**: is the way to manage **Ambiguity**—learning to put your ideas to the test and leverage the lessons learned is the best way to reduce business ambiguity and engage the teams and reduce anxiety about the changes.

Table 1.1   Distinctions within the VUCA Framework [3]

	What It Is	*An Example*	*How to Effectively Address It*
Volatility	Instability that comes from frequent and unpredictable changes in the business environment	Raw materials prices can be affected by many issues (such as political tensions, transportation costs, regulations, environmental issues, etc.) that cause them to be very volatile	Agility is the best way to handle volatility. Companies should focus on building controlled and well-planned slacks to allow for future flexibility and manage volatility
Uncertainty	Situations are understood, antecedents and consequences can be correlated, but past experiences cannot be used to assess the ramifications and magnitude of the changes	The war on terrorism generally suffers from uncertainty; we understand the root causes of terrorism but not exactly when and how it will hit next	Information based on new sources of data (both online and off-line) coupled with insights is critical to managing uncertainty. Organizations need to embrace a new perspective on information used in business
Complexity	A diverse but interrelated set of information, processes, and procedures that require deep integrated analysis to be usable	International market penetration involves managing a very complex set of relationships, laws, regulations, financing options, and logistics issues	Internal SOPs (Standard Operating Procedures) need to embrace the external environment perspective. Operations need to analyze the market information and integrate it into their practices through effective and efficient restructuring
Ambiguity	Lack of knowledge and inability to link antecedents and consequences of critical issues with limited ability to use lessons learned to make future predictions	The impact of new digital platforms on traditional media channels (TV, radio, and newspapers) has caused many shifts in consumer behavior that is impacting many industries such as Media, Telecomm, and Entertainment	Experimentation is the way to manage ambiguity. Management should develop an effective system for anticipation and deployment of strategies that can handle the unknowns based on the integration of new trends and best practices

The following sections will elaborate on the way to manage in the VUCA world and in situations of extreme uncertainty such as the COVID-19 pandemic that I described earlier as the Super-VUCA world.

Volatility: A volatile situation can be defined as one which is highly unpredictable and unstable; it doesn't necessarily involve complex structure and a critical lack of knowledge. Instead, volatility most commonly refers to the general definition of VUCA commonly used in the business press: Relatively unstable change. In order to overcome the volatile situation, we need to understand both the situation itself and the associated causes and effects. The secret behind managing the volatility is to understand the opportunities and threats presented by the situation.

Many years ago, Southwest Airlines' decision to hedge on fuel prices was highly praised by experts, as a key toward supporting the company's low-cost operating model. Although fuel prices can be quite volatile, they can't be regarded as VUCA. In the case of Southwest Airlines, they were not faced with a significant deficit in knowledge or overwhelming complexity; instead, they figured out that environmental factors beyond their control were the real cause behind the highly volatile fuel market. They were well aware of the change and the reason for bringing that change. All it required was a strategy to deal with that change which allowed them to thrive during this uncertain phase by leveraging its agility, the key to handling volatility.

This hedging strategy from Southwest Airlines could not consider the case we faced during the peak of COVID-19 on April 20, 2020, where oil prices went negative due to demand drying up [4].

Whenever volatility appears to be on the horizon the best way to prepare is to allocate resources toward developing agility. As stated previously Southwest Airlines set a massive fuel hedge plan that stunned its competitors and allowed them to predict the volatility of the future fuel market and leverage its assets to create future agility. When the change is coming but its magnitude and direction are completely unknown, then the definitive way to deal with it lies in agility.

Uncertainty: Uncertainty is the term used to describe a situation which is characterized by a lack of knowledge. There have been varying degrees of misconception between volatility and uncertainty due to the subtle differences between the two. In a volatile situation, the change is likely to happen while on the other hand uncertain situations may be characterized by no change at all. One of the key components of an uncertain environment is the adequate amount of information, so the best way to overcome this is to obtain more information by moving away from existing networks, data sources, and analysis processes to gather information from new partners and different sources.

This principle is well illustrated in the aftermath of the 9/11 attacks, which pushed the world toward uncertainty as to when and where the next attack might take place. To reinforce the distinction between different terms of VUCA, we note that the post-9/11 situation was not volatile: The core issue faced by the world government was not a lack of stability or predictability.

Rather the world governments feared that the success of the attacks would encourage other terrorists to carry out similar measures in the future. In order to address the uncertainty surrounding the potential terrorists' attacks in the future, governments around the world have collected unimaginable amounts of information. New partnerships have been formed, and new information networks have been established, resulting in a relatively successful anti-terror campaign.

Uncertain situations can be made more certain and manageable by collecting large amounts of information by reaching out to partners, customers, researchers, trade groups, and perhaps even competitors to better understand how innovations in products and services might or might not change the marketplace.

Complexity: A complex situation is characterized by interconnected parts which make it distinct from volatile or uncertain situations. In such a situation, we are not faced with a lack of information but the process to digest all the information.

A complex situation calls for a uniquely distinct response that is utterly separated from those necessitated by the other components of VUCA. This highlights the danger of not understanding and defining firm challenges. Although effective in volatile situations, stockpiling resources is useless if the firm doesn't have a clear strategy on where to allocate them in a complex environment. Similarly, establishing new information networks as any firm should do in times of uncertainty results in a greater risk of information overload (also known as **Infobesity**—Figure 1.2), ultimately freezing the firm rendering it impossible to make decisions. Instead, the most effective way to address complexity is to restructure a company's internal operations to match the external environmental complexities. Previous research has shown that companies which adapt themselves to match environmental complexities perform substantially at a higher level as compared to the ones which maintain their past structures and processes in the face of a rapidly evolving business environment. Therefore, organizations need to restructure to align with and take full advantage of the opportunity presented by this complexity.

Figure 1.2 Infobesity as source of complexity

As an example, when a small, informal organization grows, it becomes too difficult for a single person to handle. An organization with a smaller base of operations, smaller group of suppliers, smaller customer base, and few regulations works best within a simple organizational structure, but this structure quickly becomes obsolete as the organization's operating environment becomes more complex. This issue can be addressed by establishing finance, operations, marketing, and human resources functions, with each controlling the part of the organization in which it has expertise. As the organizations grow further so does the complexity and each department is further divided: For instance, the HR department may hire specialists in benefits and compensation administration, talent management, etc. The causes of internal restructuring are not primarily due to the changes within the organization, but it is also due to the changes outside the organization. For example, many organizations in the United States are restructuring their operations in terms of employee benefits due to the ongoing reforms in the healthcare sector. The healthcare law is tremendously complex, and business leaders are finding it increasingly complex to restructure the part of the organization to better align with it.

Ambiguity: Ambiguity is characterized by a situation where there is a doubt about the nature of the cause-and-effect relationship. It revolves around a wholly new product, market, innovation, and opportunity. In an uncertain situation, you might be able to predict what will happen in the future after gathering an adequate amount of information. While an ambiguous situation is much more challenging than that because of the newness as there is little historical information available to determine the outcome of a certain course of action.

Gathering and stockpiling resources which are appropriate for volatile situations will be a huge waste of time and energy for ambiguous situations since you don't know which information is most relevant and useful. Likewise, restructuring the organization will be extremely inefficient because the leaders simply don't know what the restructuring might lead to. All of these scenarios ascertain that the solution that works for one part of VUCA won't work for the other three. Each dimension of VUCA requires a different course of action. So, in case of ambiguity, we believe that the key to success is experimentation and not slack resources, information gathering, and restructuring.

As stated previously the ambiguous situation represents a situation in which the relationship between cause and effect is uncertain. Such could be said of the challenge presented by the digital revolution to the traditional print publishers: How news junkies will want to stay informed and how students want to get their learning material are some of the factors that will require the industry to experiment to come up with the best possible solution. In addition, technology has allowed content providers to entirely circumvent traditional publishers. It is unclear what the revenue model with the highest return will be in the future. Successful publishers have responded to this ambiguity with experimentation and willingness to take risks, and this is exactly what will be best suited to the market environment characterized by ambiguity.

1.2.1 Managing in Extreme Uncertainty

The instances of VUCA that we described above refer to facing uncertainties and complexities in **Normal Times**. In these times, managers deal with challenges by relying on established structures and processes. These are designed to reduce uncertainty and support calculated bets to manage the residual risks. In a serious crisis, however, uncertainty can reach extreme levels, and the normal way of working becomes overstrained. At such times, traditional management operating models rarely prove adequate, and organizations with inadequate processes can quickly find themselves facing existential threats.

Uncertainty can be measured in magnitude and duration. By both measures, the extreme uncertainty accompanying the public health and economic damage created by the COVID-19 pandemic is unprecedented in modern memory. It should not be surprising, therefore, that organizations need a new management model to sustain operations under such conditions.

The COVID-19 pandemic and the resulting economic recession have affected most large organizations around the world. Managers continue to scramble to address rapidly developing changes in the public health environment, public policy, and customer behavior. And then there is the economic uncertainty. The severity and speed of the crisis are reflected in the International Monetary Fund's (IMF) projections for US GDP growth. After an estimated GDP expansion of 2.2% in 2019 (year on year), the US economy, in the IMF's view, was expected to grow at a rate of 2.1% in 2020 (forecast of October 2019). With the onset of the pandemic, the IMF quickly shifted its estimate into contraction, of −5.9% in April 2020 and revised to −8.0% in June. The estimate for October 2020 is less severe at −4.3%, but this would still be the worst result in many decades. The forecasting institution foresees the world economy shrinking at a rate of −4.4% in 2020, after having grown 2.8% in 2019 (estimate) [5].

In a study by London Business School explaining the Economics of a Pandemic [6], it was of course acknowledged that not all sectors are impacted in the same way but everyone is still anxious about the level of impact and the duration of the impact. Figure 1.3 provided a preliminary view of the COVID-19 impact on six sectors—Tourism and Hospitality, Aviation/Airlines, Oil and Gas, Automotive, Consumer Products, and Consumer Electronics/Semiconductors [7]. We all know that COVID-19 has evolved, but it is not over. The lessons learned from this pandemic are here to stay and should always be considered in any strategy discussion. In October 2021, 65% of executives expected improvements in their markets, this down from 73% to 79% that expected improvements in March 2021.

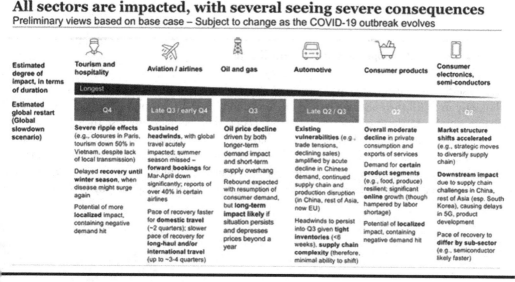

All sectors are impacted, with several seeing severe consequences
Preliminary views based on base case – Subject to change as the COVID-19 outbreak evolves

Figure 1.3   COVID-19 sectoral impact [6]

To better understand the impact of COVID-19 on the economy and businesses, let us see this race between supply and demand. At first, COVID-19 caused supply shock. The disruption happened in global supply chains when China went into lockdown and when many countries decided to limit exporting of its products in fear of extended shortage in global supplies. Quarantine and social distancing policies across the world led to a sharp decline in labor supply.

The supply decline was followed by a decline in demand due to the following four reasons:

- Uncertainty about the progress of the disease
- Uncertainty about government economic policies and the support programs that were introduced
- Loss of income for many employees, especially in hard-hit estruses such as tourism, hospitality, and transportation industries
- Households increase their savings and reduce their nonessential spending
- Firms delay their expansion or investment plans

Figure 1.4 shows the supply-demand curve, and it indicates how Aggregate Supply (AS) declined from AS0 to AS1 and how Aggregate Demand (AD) declined from AD0 to AD1.

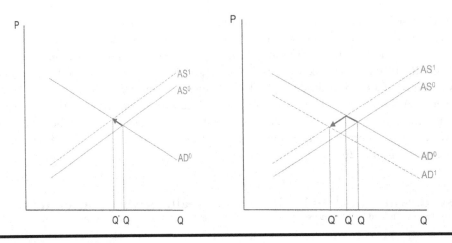

Figure 1.4 Aggregate supply and demand decline [6]

As these supply-demand dynamics continue, firms that are more dependent on cash flows lack the liquidity to fulfill their obligations and are forced to go into bankruptcy. This leads to a further decline in supply, AS declines from AS1 to AS2. People who permanently lose their jobs or small business owners who lose their businesses don't have an income anymore and hence further reduce their consumption, leading to a decline of AD for AD1 to AD2. This cycle is what leads to economic recession/depression (depending on the market) that is different from any other recession/depression experienced before in history. Figure 1.5 shows this supply-demand race ignited by COVID-19.

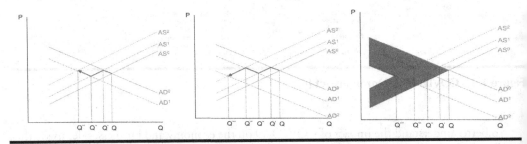

Figure 1.5 COVID-19 supply and demand race toward recession/depression [6]

1.2.2 Operating in Crisis Mode: Discover, Design, and Execute

These rapidly shifting events demand not only speedy decisions but also a wholesale change in the organization's managerial system. The operating cadence in which managers meet, discuss, and take action needs to match the evolution of the crisis. This does not imply a simple speedup of existing processes to accommodate the information needs of managers. Rather, it means creating entirely new procedures.

Extreme uncertainty turns an organization's operating imperatives on its heads. It demands continuous learning and constant review of assumptions. Instead of establishing a plan and ensuring the organization sticks to it, as in more normal times, managers must understand and respond continuously to dynamic and wrenching change. Rather than making periodic reviews of a static plan, they need to meet for iterative decision-making sessions structured around three imperatives: **Discover, Design**, and **Execute**. Managers must work together to diagnose the current situation, consider its practical implications, explore how it might evolve, and establish and execute appropriate actions.

The cycle of learning and redesigning must recur with a frequency sufficient to ensure that responses reflect the evolving situation. Managers must doggedly question established assumptions, especially the ideas adopted under conditions of extreme uncertainty. The organization cannot treat any assumptions as sacred. Organizations should accept that they will be wrong and celebrate learning quickly from experience.

To make informed decisions, managers need specialized knowledge and should actively seek expert advice. Experts can contribute to better decisions by filling gaps in existing management knowledge. For example, managers need external advice—from epidemiologists—to assess the course of the COVID-19 pandemic. Likewise, civil society organizations can have experts who can provide valuable alternative perspectives on such important matters as racial bias, diversity, and the importance of female leaders. Internal expertise is also valuable in crisis times. Managers should reach deep into their own organization for frontline insights—such as those that a customer-service representative could provide on customer experience.

The organization should also systematically challenge proposed solutions. One established way to do this is to create a "**Red Team**" of experts to pressure test managers' decisions, identifying potential weaknesses or overly optimistic assumptions. This type of exercise has been very successful in enabling more robust solutions. Leading companies, including Microsoft and IBM, perform regular exercises in which red teams test cybersecurity infrastructure, for example.

Unprecedented crises frequently require leadership to take unprecedented actions—bold, speedy actions that would feel risky in normal times. A historic case in point is Johnson & Johnson's 1982 decision to recall 31 million bottles of the painkiller Tylenol after some product samples were found to have been laced with cyanide. The swift, decisive action saved this valuable product and enhanced the company's reputation [8].

As they focus intensely on making fast practical decisions, managers must also be prepared to shift course if the situation changes. Actions, furthermore, need to be prioritized. First must come actions to mitigate the "worst-case" scenarios for the organization. Low-cost ("no regrets") actions can also be taken quickly to address issues that could arise in any of several potential scenarios. In an existential crisis, managers must feel comfortable making conscious decisions and taking deliberate action. Otherwise, events will take their course, decisions will be made by default, and organizational control will be lost.

1.3 Does Strategy Matter?

As we will see shortly, strategy has been around us for centuries. It's been used as a tool by the military leadership to conquer territories and create dynasties. Similarly, a lot of work has been done with respect to strategic tools and frameworks to assist business leaders in creating compelling strategies to unlock unprecedented growth opportunities. Such prevalence of strategic tools, frameworks, and future prospects brings us back to the first question of Simon Sinek's model "Why do we need a Strategy"?

According to rigorous management research under the name of "Evergreen Project", financially successful companies have a clear and well-articulated strategy [9]. Figure 1.6 shows the range of advantages that companies with well-articulated strategies can achieve [10].

While many companies might be able to survive without a clearly written strategy, they surely can't thrive without a clearly defined strategy. Still, there will be some companies who will say that we have been in business for many years without a clearly defined strategy and we are doing just fine. Others might claim that although we don't have our strategy in written form, we know it inside and out. Writing down the strategy has several key benefits. A written strategy makes it possible for the entire organization's management to be on the same page when it comes to the organization's strategic planning.

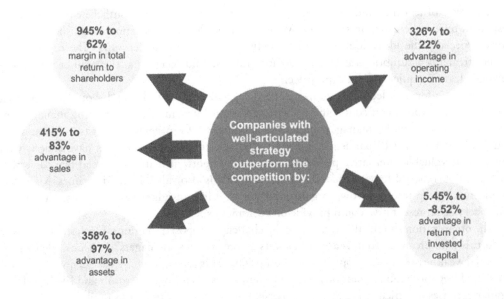

Figure 1.6   Strategy matter

1.4 Strategize or Vanish

For a long time, management experts have encouraged companies to go from good to great. Unfortunately, most of them move in the opposite direction. Recent examples of companies that have gone from good to bad include Nokia and Kodak, to name just a few prominent examples. Microsoft which for so long has been considered a gold standard of corporate excellence was being accused of slipping into mediocrity. Some of the fallen ones such as IBM and Ericson have regained their stride, but others such as NatWest and Anderson have disappeared altogether.

According to the research, good companies go bad because they fall prey to active inertia-responding to the dramatic shifts in the market by accelerating activities that succeeded in the past. When the environment changes, organizations trapped in active inertia repeat the same course of activities, pushing them deeper into the trap. Organizations trapped in active inertia resemble a car with its back wheel stuck in a rut. As managers step on the gas instead of escaping the rut, they only dig themselves deeper.

What locks a firm in the rut? The surprising answer is the same commitment that ensured success in the beginning. Everyone is aware of the success leading to complacency and arrogance. Although clear commitments are required for the initial success of the firm, these commitments become difficult to adhere to as time changes and the environment becomes increasingly competitive. This dynamic leads firms to go bad even when executives try to avoid arrogance and complacency.

In order to win in an extremely competitive market, executives make a set of commitments that will constitute the organization's success formula. A formula that focuses on employees, grants efficiency, attracts resources, and differentiates the company from its competitors. Five different commitments which comprise the success formula are [11]:

- **Strategic frames**: The set of assumptions that determine how managers view the business
- **Processes**: The way things are being done

- **Resources**: Tangible and intangible assets that help us to compete, such as brand, technology, real estate, and expertise
- **Relationships**: Established links with external stakeholders which include investors, technology providers, and distributors
- **Values**: Set of shared beliefs that determine corporate culture

Although these commitments are essential components for success, they tend to harden over time. Initial success strengthens the management belief, and people take these commitments for granted hence failing to consider alternatives. As a result, individual components of success become less flexible: Strategic frames become blinders, processes harden into routines, resources harden into millstones, relationships become shackles, and values turn into dogmas.

The above success formula works as long as the context remains stable. But as soon as the environment starts to shift dramatically, a gap starts to grow between what the market demands and what the firm is able to provide. Managers often see these gaps early on, and they do start to take actions aggressively but their rigid commitment formula channels all their efforts into well-worn ruts. Harder they work, the wider the gap becomes. This causes active inertia.

Figure 1.7 illustrates this phenomenon of active inertia that explains why good companies go bad when they fail to respond to the internal and external opportunities and threats presented by the VUCA World. The five components are:

- Strategic frames become blinders
- Processes harden into routines
- Resources harden into millstones
- Relationships become shackles
- Values turn into dogmas

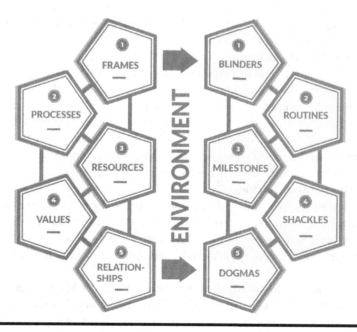

Figure 1.7   Strategic active inertia [11]

■ Strategic Frames Become Blinders

Strategic frames provide organizations with a strategic vision and focus on helping organizations move forward. However, continually focusing on the same aspects of the strategic frames constricts the managers' peripheral vision, preventing them from focusing on new threats and opportunities. As their strategic frameworks grow, managers often cram all the existing information into existing frames or ignore it altogether.

Consider NatWest Bank for example; at its foundation its executives set a clear strategic goal. It was during that time that retail banking was stagnant in the UK, and the country was suffering irreversible decline. They diversified their service portfolio by expanding into new financial services in the US, Europe, the Far East, and the Soviet Union. As the competition heightened, the rivals such as Lloyd TSB refocused on their domestic retail business. In contrast, NatWest responded by accelerating geographic and product diversification. Critics blasted NatWest throughout the 1990s for waiting too long to divest money-losing distractions until RBS acquired NatWest in 2000.

■ Processes harden into routines

Established processes confer efficiency and facilitate coordination across functional and geographic units. Over time, these routines resist change. With repetition, processes become second nature; people stop thinking of them as a means to an end, if they think of them at all. When the environment shifts, managers' commitments to existing processes trigger an actively inert response.

Consider Compaq, which grew to sales of US$3.6 billion in its first 8 years based on processes that consistently produced high-quality products. Manufacturing routines made quality the first priority (and cost a distant fifth) while the product development process sacrificed speed and thrift to get the product specs 100% right every time. Compaq's quality-at-any-price processes served the company well in the early days of the PC industry when customers worried about the product's usability and low-cost alternatives were rare. As PCs became commodities and nimble rivals like Dell rose to the fore, competition shifted to value for money. Compaq relied on its well-honed processes to churn out gold-plated products priced to gather dust on dealers' shelves.

■ Resources harden into millstones

Specialized resources build competitive advantages that rivals cannot easily replicate. Shifts in the competitive environment, however, can devalue established resources. Major airlines historically competed on the strength of their hub-and-spoke systems in which the carriers controlled valuable real estate at hub airports and a fleet optimized for this business model. The rise of low-cost upstarts such as Southwest Airlines and Ryan Air depressed industry pricing and poached customers. Traditional carriers could not easily redeploy their hubs and planes to compete cost-effectively against new entrants.

■ Relationships become shackles

Managers commit to external relationships by investing in specialized facilities to serve a key customer, for example, or writing long-term service contracts. These relationships can make or break a company—think of Microsoft and Intel or Wal-Mart and Procter & Gamble. Over time, however, established relationships can turn into shackles that limit flexibility.

Recall the Daewoo Group, which at its peak approached US$20 billion in revenues and employed 200,000 worldwide before falling into bankruptcy. Daewoo owed much of its growth to cozy relationships with South Korea's General Park, who ruled the country with an iron fist for nearly two decades. Park supported Daewoo and other favored conglomerates with financing and tariffs. In exchange, Daewoo invested in industries targeted for expansion. When subsequent governments ended policies that favored the conglomerates, Daewoo's Chairman Kim tightened links with remaining friendly Korean politicians and forged bonds with politicians in emerging markets such as Vietnam, Sudan, and Uzbekistan to replicate cozy relationships at home.

A new approach that has been developed by Haslam College of Business at the University of Tennessee, Knoxville, tries to address this issue in the very complex supply chain environment most businesses are facing today. This concept is called VESTED.

Vested® is a business model, methodology, mindset, and movement for creating highly collaborative business relationships that enable true win–win relationships in which both parties are equally committed to each other's success. When applied, a vested approach fosters an environment that sparks innovation, resulting in improved service, reduced costs, and value that didn't exist before—for both parties [12]. It includes five main rules, as shown in Figure 1.8.

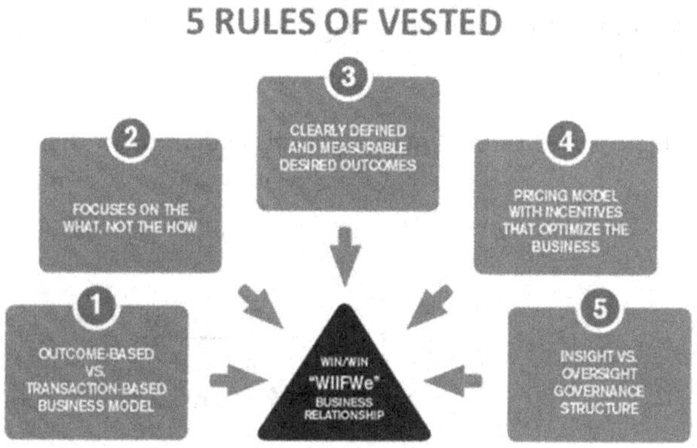

Figure 1.8   Rules of VESTED business relationships [12]

■ **Values turn into dogmas**

Strong values can elicit fierce loyalty from employees, strengthen the bonds between a company and its customers, attract like-minded partners, and hold together a company's far-flung operations. As companies mature, however, their values often harden into outdated dogmas that oppress rather than inspire.

Consider Laura Ashley who founded her company to defend traditional values under siege from miniskirts. Frilly frocks embodying Laura Ashley's commitment to traditional values of modesty initially appealed to many women but lost their attraction as more women entered the workforce. The company, however, continued to pursue outdated designs that embodied an ossified view of its core values.

These reasons highlight the most common business phenomenon, which is also perhaps the most perplexing one: When big companies face challenges in this rapidly changing environment, they often fail to respond effectively. They are unable to defend themselves against their competitors which are armed with new products, technologies, and strategies. As a result, their sales and profits decline, their stocks tumble, and they witness their best people leave.

Those shifts that lead to active inertia and turn *good* companies into *bad* ones make the case for the need to be Strategy Savvy and to reconsider our current approaches to strategy development and implementation. To further support this conclusion, two seminal cases will be briefly reviewed as final reflections for this chapter.

1.4.1 How Nokia Lost the Smartphone Battle?

It is still quite mind-boggling how quickly Nokia fell from being the top player in the phone business and being sold to Microsoft in 2014, and then divested only 2 years later to HMD global. How did this happen? Perhaps the more important question is: Can this happen to other companies as well? These are the questions that researchers tried to figure out by carrying out an extensive study for which they conducted 76 interviews with former Nokia top and middle managers. This study helped to identify several key factors, which included [13]:

- Fear
- Suppression of information
- Overconfidence
- Low technological competence among management
- Competing product lines

Figure 1.9 summarizes factors and the following sections elaborate on them.

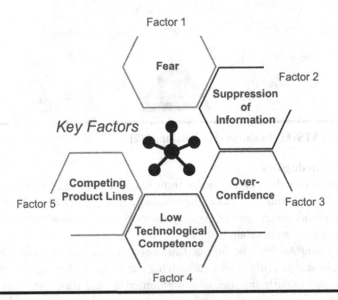

Figure 1.9   Factors which contributed to the fall of Nokia

- **Factor 1: Fear**

    Top management realized as early as 2005 that Apple was working on a smartphone which will run on iOS. This made them realize that they need to come up with a competitive solution. Top management fears were externally focused, and the pressure was put on the middle management to react.

    Middle managers didn't have this amount of external information but had internal focus, including internal fear of losing status. Nokia's tendency to change its organizational structure led to uncertainty among the employees as they need to apply internally and inter-view for new jobs created a high level of uncertainty.

The Nokia culture accounted for aggression from top management that resulted in fear that middle management showed losing status, reputation, or job. Middle managers who would raise objections were subsequently sidelined or demoted.

■ **Factor 2: Suppression of information**

Middle management tends to give wrong information and optimistic reports to the top management that indicate the opposite. This led to top management being blinded by wrong information that confirmed the belief of Nokia's corporate culture, which was based on the principle of "Please Upper Management". In addition, the top management discouraged the middle managers from getting more external information. In the process, these two factors led to the creation of a psychologically unsafe environment, leading to suppression of infor-mation, not being allowed to raise critical issues, punishment of failure, and unable to create trusted relationships.

■ **Factor 3: Overconfidence**

The fact that most middle managers were in Finland and were not exposed to other tech-nology companies led them to believe Nokia employees were the best of the best and the Nokia solutions to be far superior and the best in class. This resulted in them ignoring any advice that contradicted this image. Moreover, they used to assess the competitors' products by comparing Nokia's future development with the competitors' past products. This approach made them view their products significantly better than the competition, and there was noth-ing to learn from it. Moreover, the new and emerging players like Apple and Google were seen as too inexperienced to make any substantial impact in the phone business.

■ **Factor 4: Low technological competence**

Top management at Nokia had a very low competence and couldn't judge the real sta-tus of development. They didn't understand the real status when new product demos were shown to them. In addition, they were ill-prepared for the dramatic shift in hardware and software competence. Nokia's core competence was in the radio technology hardware, but the next generation of smartphones required the hardware and software competence along with the competency in touch screen interface.

■ **Factor 5: Competing product lines**

The fact that Nokia had several dozen product lines launched every year forced the com-pany to update and patch the outdated Symbian operating system to the extent that it became unusable for smartphones.

1.4.2 The Fall of Kodak

The fall of Nokia is a prime example of what other industries can learn from and react to the inno-vation coming from outside. Even a company that was at the top and dominating the market was surprisingly vulnerable and fell from top to bottom in a span of five years. Analyzing these factors and then comparing them with your own company and industry and then reacting to make neces-sary improvements are the first steps for creating a resilient organization.

At one point "**Kodak Moment**" meant something that was worth saving. Today the same term act as an evil spirit for corporations that warn executives that they need to adapt and evolve when disruptive technologies encroach the market [14] (Figure 1.10).

Given that Kodak's core business was selling film, it's not hard to see why the past few decades proved to be challenging for it. Cameras went digital and finally disappeared into cell phones.

Figure 1.10   The fall of Kodak

People's preferences shifted from printing pictures to sharing them online on social networking sites. Although there is still a selective group of people who print nostalgic books and holiday cards, the volume of these is second to none as compared to the Kodak heydays. The company's situation reached a crisis point when it filed for bankruptcy protection in 2012, ultimately exiting the legacy business. The company, which once was one of the most powerful in the world, today has a market capitalization of less than US$11 billion.

1.4.2.1 Why Did This Happen?

An easy explanation for this is the company's lack of vision or what we call myopia. It was so blinded by its success that it completely missed the rise of digital technologies. But at the same time, some people can argue against it since the first prototype of the digital camera was created in 1975 by Steve Sasson who was an engineer at Kodak. That camera had a massive disruptive potential. But spotting something and doing something is a completely different story, so another explanation is that Kodak invented the technology but failed to capitalize on it. In an interview with *New York Times* Sasson stated that the management's response to his digital camera was "That's cute but don't tell anyone about it", a nice response, but not completely accurate. In fact, Kodak invested billions of dollars in developing a range of digital cameras.

Doing something and doing something right are entirely different things. The next explanation revolves around the fact that Kodak mismanaged its investment in digital cameras, overshooting the market by trying to match the performance of traditional film rather than embracing the simplicity of digital. Although Kodak embraced simplicity in the next upcoming years and moved from camera to computer, the real disruption took place when cameras merged with smartphones and Kodak completely missed that!

Another explanation for the demise of Kodak was explored based on the company relationships that became real shackles for it, as explained earlier. The company distribution channel that included thousands of large and small retailers that invested in Kodak film printing machines put tremendous pressure on the company management team to maintain its investments in films for the distribution channel partners not to lose their investments. This ultimately led to a case of lose–lose for all parties. Worries about investments already made in assets—whether physical or intellectual—can become a major threat to our ability to innovate.

But they didn't entirely miss it.

In 2001, Kodak purchased a photo-sharing site called Ofoto. That's where Kodak missed the biggest trick. Imagine if they had truly embraced the opportunity and made themselves the pioneer of a new category of life networking where people can share their pictures and personal information. In reality, unfortunately, Kodak used Ofoto in an attempt to get more people to print digital images and in the process lost the site to Shutterfly in 2012 as part of its bankruptcy plan for less than US$125 million. In the meantime, Facebook acquired Instagram for a whopping US$1 billion.

The demise of Kodak acts as a key lesson for the business executives. Companies often see the disruptive forces affecting their industry. They try to take advantage of it by allocating a sufficient number of resources to participate in emerging markets. However, they sometimes fail to truly embrace the new disruptive business models. As in the case of Kodak, they invested in the technology, created a digital camera, and even understood that in the near future, photos would be shared online. Where they missed the beat was in realizing that online photo sharing was a new business and not just another way of expanding the printing business.

In conclusion, the term "Strategize or Vanish" can provide a good summary of why we need to have a strategy, today more than ever. But we need to open our minds to a new more holistic and inclusive approach to strategy development and implementation to ensure success. I call this approach "Strategy Savvy", and it integrates design thinking and innovation for a Balanced Strategy Development (BSD) approach that helps us Make the Future Happen Today.

References

1. https://www.smartinsights.com/digital-marketing-strategy/online-value-proposition/start-with-why-creating-a-value-proposition-with-the-golden-circle-model/
2. Grebe, M., and Danke, E. (2013). Simply IT: Six Ways to Reduce Complexity – Boston Consulting Group (BCG). http://image-src.bcg.com/Images/BCG_Simplify_IT_Mar_2013_tcm9-96858.pdf
3. Bennett, N., and Lemoine, G. J. (2014). What a Difference a Word Makes: Understanding Threats to Performance in a VUCA World. *Business Horizons*, 57(3), 311–317. https://www.researchgate.net/publication/260313997_What_a_difference_a_word_makes_Understanding_threats_to_performance_in_a_VUCA_world
4. https://globalriskinsights.com/2020/05/making-history-coronavirus-and-negative-oil-prices/
5. Finn, B., Mysore, M., and Usher, O. (2020). When Nothing is Normal: Managing in Extreme Uncertainty. McKinsey and Company. https://www.mckinsey.com/business-functions/risk/our-insights/when-nothing-is-normal-managing-in-extreme-uncertainty
6. Surico, P., and Galiotte, A. (2020). The Economics of a Pandemic – The Case of Covid-19. London Business School. https://sites.google.com/site/paolosurico/covid-19
7. IHS Market Analysis - McKinsey Global Institute Analysis. (2020). McKinney Global Report March 2020.
8. https://www.nytimes.com/2002/03/23/your-money/IHT-tylenol-made-a-hero-of-johnson-johnson-the-recall-that-started.html
9. Nohria, N., Joyce, W., and Roberson, B. (2003). 4+2 = Sustained Business Success. *Harvard Business Review*, July 2003. https://hbswk.hbs.edu/item/42-sustained-business-success
10. Horwath, R. (2006). Does Strategy Matter? Strategic Thinking Institute. https://www.strategyskills.com/Articles/Documents/ST-Does_Strategy_Matter.pdf
11. Sull, D. (2005). Why Good Companies Go Bad. *Harvard Business Review* (1999), 77(4), 42–50. https://pdfs.semanticscholar.org/5d2d/60f3f20a5af063031f6e0882e5fe8d7af4b7.pdf
12. https://www.vestedway.com/what-is-vested/

13. Vuori, T. O., and. Huy, Q. N. (2015). Distributed Attention and Shared Emotions in the Innovation Process: How Nokia Lost the Smartphone Battle. *Administrative Science Quarterly*, 1–43. Johnson – Cornell University. https://knowledge.insead.edu/sites/www.insead.edu/files/images/asq_2015_print _vuori_huy_distributed_attention_and_shared_emotions_in_innovation_process.pdf

14. Anthony, S. D. (2016). Kodak's Downfall Wasn't About Technology. *Harvard Business Review*. https://hbr.org/2016/07/kodaks-downfall-wasnt-about-technology

HOW DOES STRATEGY EMERGE?

Chapter 2

The History and Future of Strategy

2.1 The History of Strategy

Strategy for most of its 2,500-year history has been one-dimensional. Warmongers have largely focused on avoiding wars without initiating them, and businesses were primarily concerned with building **power and monopoly**. However, in the past 50 years, strategy has moved away from this one-way approach and has spawned several ideas and solutions. But as strategies piled up, so did the complexity, and the idea about one strategy fits all seemed to be dead as the environment became highly competitive and intense. However, the main strategic focus areas of the strategy still revolved around (Figure 2.1):

- Power and monopoly
- Productivity and efficiency
- Competitive advantage
- Positioning
- Exclusivity

In ancient China, great strategist and philosopher Sun Tzu's thoughts on strategy are carefully studied by business and military leaders today. One of his best-known works *The Art of War* depicts the creative and deceptive aspects of strategy. The book covers all aspects of waging war and provides plenty of strategic and philosophical advice, which is still being used as a source of information by politicians and business leaders today.

As we move forward toward the 1800s, the business strategy revolved around creating exclusivity and monopolies. In fact, **exclusivity and monopoly** proved to be so effective that numerous wars were fought over them. In his book *The History of Standard Oil Company* [1], Ida Tarbell depicted John D. Rockefeller as a vicious money-grabber who was highly effective in monopolizing the oil trade. Rockefeller further tightened his grasp over the refining business by taking over his competitors and in the process was able to control 90% of the North American refinery industry.

DOI: 10.4324/9781003280941-4

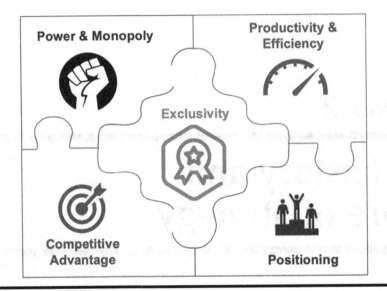

Figure 2.1   Strategic focus areas

Beginning in 1900, the next 60 years or so saw the focus shift from exclusivity and monopolies to pushing the boundaries of industrial operations by looking at different aspects of **productivity and efficiency**. In his monograph *The Principles of Scientific Management*, Frederick Winslow emphasized the importance of making workflow within the organization as efficient as possible. However, his work was criticized for not paying enough attention to industrial operations. Alfred P. Sloan, who helped to make General Motors one of the largest industrial corporations, was accused of the same thing. He further went on to create the Sloan Fellows, the world's first university-based executive education program at MIT. In 1952, the MIT School of Industrial Management was established through the Sloan Foundation grant, later renamed as Alfred P. Sloan School of management, which today is one of the most prestigious business schools in the world.

In addition, this period also saw the emergence of prominent management consultancy firms, which were most commonly referred to as "business engineers". This marked the beginning of true strategic analysis and planning and set the foundation for Strategy heydays for the next 25 years. Strategic management made way for more holistic perspectives that pushed the boundaries of operations by taking into consideration the various aspects of productivity and efficiency.

During these 21 years (1969 to mid-1990s), strategy became a proper discipline being more standalone, analytical, and cerebral. Several ideas and tools emerged during this period such as the "Experience Curve" developed by Bruce Henderson, which formed the basis for strategizing the combination of price setting, production volumes, and production costs against its competitors. Bruce Henderson later went on to publish the Growth-Share BCG matrix made famous by its quadrant names: Cash Cows, Dogs, Stars, and Question Marks. This matrix helped companies with multiple experience curves to manage their ongoing portfolio of services. It was later developed further by GE-McKinsey using Industry Attractiveness and Competitive Strength to propose a nine-box matrix to prioritize investments in different business units.

The concept of **competitiveness** began to expand during this period as more powerful strategy models began to emerge in the form of the Porter five forces model and value chain model developed by Michael Porter. Following Porter's work, two important *Harvard Business Review* articles emerged. The first one was published in 1990 "The Core Competence of Corporation" written by C.K. Prahalad and Gary Hamel, which stressed the importance of creating **competitive advantage** by looking inside the company itself in addition to focusing on the **positioning** in terms of markets and competitors. This ended the debate between inside-out and outside-in strategies when it comes to which holds significant importance over the other.

> The debate between inside-out strategies and outside-in strategies was never a real debate. **Both mattered.**

These concepts shifted the strategy from being one of the daily tasks for senior executives and landed instead in the hands of strategy professionals and planners. This had rather unwanted side effects as it created a distinct handover between strategy formulation and strategy implementation.

In fact, the more sophisticated and complex the strategy became the larger the handover hurdles. With **globalization** things got worse; **change management** and **getting buy-in** were much-discussed topics and strategy implementation gradually became a self-inflicted major issue. The second half of this period saw the emergence of books and articles about organizational change and how to put strategy to work by closing the gap between what an organization needs to do and what it is able to do. One of the examples of such work was the book published in 1996 by John P. Kotter called *Leading Change*.

Performance metrics were another helpful component, with several influential works pushing the envelope for effective strategy execution. The most well-known of those works are those of Robert S. Kaplan and David P. Norton, who wrote articles in 1992 and then published the book *The Balanced Scorecard: Translating Strategy into Action* in 1996.

By the mid-1990s a new strategic age was building, signaling the start of the era of strategic proliferation. Figure 2.2 shows the three shifting forces shaping strategy.

Figure 2.2   Three shifting forces

The fundamental reason for this proliferation was the **Advancement in Technology**, which drastically shifted the developed world from industrial-based to service-based. But this reengineering didn't last long. By the late 1990s, the next strategic revolution had arrived, drawing us all into the big promise of the internet and the notion of the new economy. In 1999, Philip Evans and Thomas S. Wurster of Boston Consulting Group (BCG) made a convincing argument about how the internet changed everything in their work *Blown to Bits: How the New Economics of Information Transform Strategy*. The proliferation of the internet provided a significant boost to the value chain modularity, allowing companies to create networked enterprises and to pursue all sorts of joint ventures, partnering, licensing, and outsourcing deals. Hence, it was never a question about which strategic revolution was the most important, but rather it was more about identifying which offered plenty of opportunities to create or lose the competitive advantage. The internet was proving to be a deal-breaker in this regard as it offered immense opportunities for the next 15 years. This was further augmented by other major strategic shifts such as globalization and Big IT, which were proving to be an increasingly level playing field.

Technology further led to a new way of tapping into resources. Larry Huston and Nabil Sakkab in their 2006 *HBR* article "Connect and Develop: Inside Procter and Gamble's New Model for Innovation" talked about how Procter and Gamble turned the developers inside and outside their company into seamless development capability [2]. Furthermore, in their work, Don Tapscott and Anthony D. Williams showed how distributed capabilities were becoming increasingly mainstream—a community of Apple users solving all kinds of issues, Amazon providing an array of products from a multitude of companies, and Linux being an operating system created by a diverse group of IT professionals.

These distributed capabilities extended into **Social Technologies** that facilitate all sorts of communities with an ever-stronger social fabric and lead toward the creation of new community services such as peer-to-peer lending, hospitality and travel, and products and service recommendations. This range of new service portfolios paved the way for many excellent concepts, recipes, and frameworks for dealing with an individual, strategically disruptive phenomenon, but there was no overriding framework to pull it all together.

All of these strategic shifts and accompanying strategic freedom made the strategy irrelevant. In the rapidly changing business environment, it is quite difficult to predict where things are heading and which players will succeed and when. This dynamic business environment leads to new phenomena every now and then and results in strategy formulation becoming a much more complicated process. Part of this complexity is due to the accommodation of several new factors as part of the strategic plan hence severely undermining the strategy as a competitive guiding force. This situation isn't going unnoticed among the organizations as they are taking several urgent initiatives to remain competitive in this sophisticated business environment. The strategic span has grown excessively to the point that it has become almost unmanageable, and some of the organizations are on the verge of losing internal strategic sense of purpose and directions.

Figure 2.3 was compiled by A.T. Kearny team [1] to demonstrate the key milestones in the history of strategy. They classified it into four stages: The Milestones, The Essence (the late 1960s), The Overload (mid-1990s), and the Ersatz Strategies (from 2011 to 2013).

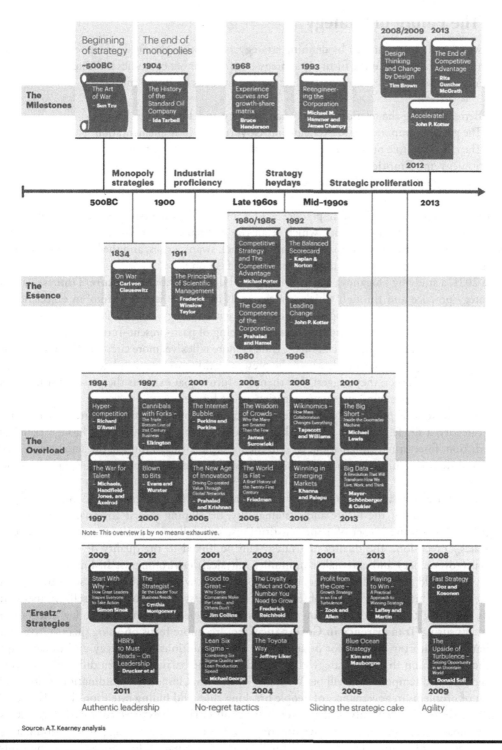

Figure 2.3 The history of strategy [1]

2.2 The Future of Strategy

Since we started our discussion by defining strategy as "Making the Future Happen Today", it is important to briefly look at the future of strategy itself. A number of studies indicate that there are five main streams where strategy work will continue to focus on in the future:

1. Better defining the relationship between Strategy and **Time**
2. The growing importance of Strategy and **Governance** in implementation
3. The changing role of **Resources** in Strategy in uncertain conditions
4. Strategy and **Emotions**
5. Strategy and the **Ambidextrous Organization**

The rise of strategy in theory and in practice is a response to the increasing power the future holds over the present. Disruptive events, which seem the hallmark of our day and age, cut the link between past experiences and future expectations. Black swans, crises, and the like create jolts and jumps that make time appear to move in a nonlinear fashion.

In 2021, a study by Doganova and Cornberger [3] discussed how the **Future/Time** is enacted in strategy practice and through which strategy tools the future is turned into an object of the present. They argue that studying time interaction with strategy is a crucial part of Strategy's future. They argued that assuming the linear sequencing of past–present–future is limiting when we think of strategy. Instead, one can image time as more reflexive, more circular. This means that the future does not exist independently of the present, waiting to be annihilated by the present to become the past. Rather, they suggest that there is a future that exists as the present future: This present future is always our "current anticipation of the future".

In the future, it is proposed to shift the strategic unit of analysis from the future as a monolithic category, a single temporal domain that can be more or less well-known (through exercises of prediction, forecasting, anticipation, etc.) to the multiple forms of futures, the actors who carry them, and the tools through which they are made visible and palpable as part of narratives and calculations.

Another stream that is shaping the future of strategy is its relationship to **Governance** [4]. Since strategy is about the future and sustainability, developing robust governance systems to integrate and coordinate a set of actors, institutions, and collective goals is crucial for successful strategy execution. The quality of strategy can be linked to the quality of observation, of internal (governance) and external (community, physical) environments. In line with systems theory, we would further link the quality of observation with the quality of self-observation or reflexivity. While reflexivity and observation enable the system to observe itself, limits exist: Limits to strategizing, limits to linking futures and strategies, and limits to policy integration coexist. Ensuring **Transparency in Governance**, requires more focus on using quantitative and qualitative monitoring systems for Strategy. The more ambitious the strategy and the attempt at policy integration through strategy, the more delicate the balance between different interests, perspectives, and temporalities will be. We know by now that imperfect coordination is not only a result of problems in governance, of people breaking rules and hiding intentions but also stemming from internal complexity or the match between internal and external complexity. Problems for coordination can arise from positive functions in governance. Increasing participation makes coordination harder, and the same holds for localizing governance, for institutionalizing multilevel governance with more autonomous levels, and for reinforcing checks and balances more generally. Integrative strategy thus balances the powers of steering with risks of undermining differentiation and checks and balances.

The **Resource-Based View** (RBV) makes a significant contribution to strategy by explaining the relationship between resources and firm performance. Particularly in low-uncertainty markets, executives have the foresight and time to build strategically valuable resources in current markets and leverage them into related markets. RBV is also relevant for understanding strategies for market entry, extending the value of technology resources, and broadening the locus of resources within ecosystems. Conversely, in high-uncertainty markets like nascent or disrupted ones, RBV seems less relevant. Resources may not yet exist, or their value (and rarity) may be indeterminate (or changing) [5].

In the future, strategy needs to examine resources from the perspective of industry evolution, extend the value of technology resources, broaden the locus of resources to the organization ecosystem, and view resources as dynamic capabilities. In high-uncertainty markets, information is incomplete, unpredictable, or even unknowable. This creates prediction and interpretation challenges that make it virtually impossible to know which resources will have value (and rarity) and when. This led to the need to propose a new approach known as **Strategy Creation** (SC).

Strategy-Creation approach combines and integrates a number of strategizing approaches:

- Strategizing by Doing: Learning and Related Processes
- Strategizing by Thinking: Managerial Cognition
- Strategizing by Shaping

A hybrid approach can be considered for moderate uncertain markets. Table 2.1 shows the difference between Resource-Based View (RBV), Hybrid, and Strategy-Creation (SC) approaches along the five characteristics [5]:

- Uncertainty
- Setting
- Resources
- Strategic Actions
- Competitive Advantage

Emotion in strategic management has attracted increasing scholarly interest during the past years. Researchers have demonstrated the nature and significance of emotion in strategic management from a broad range of perspectives across different levels of analysis.

Some of the key questions addressed are: How does emotion influence strategic management, and how can the field be further developed?

A 2020 study by Brundin, Liu, and Cyron [6] proposed three areas of future research to inspire the field to develop further: (1) Scope conditions of emotion research in strategic management, (2) capturing emotion in strategic management, and (3) the ethics, power, and politics of emotions in strategic management.

Research has typically focused on understanding the content of strategy and its relationship to organizational performance and the processes of strategy formation and change at an organizational level. However, we have recently witnessed a shift of attention toward the interplay of cognitive, behavioral, and emotional dynamics of significant actors in strategic management.

Table 2.1 Resource-Based View (RBV), Hybrid, and Strategy-Creation Views of Strategy [5]

Characteristic	Resource-Based	Hybrid	Strategy-Creation
Uncertainty	**Low**—predictable and interpretable market. Change slowly occurs. Executives have foresight and time to build renewed resources and leverage them into related markets	**Moderate**— interpretable and somewhat predictable market. Change may accelerate. Executives have some foresight, but firms may suddenly scale	**High**—unpredictable, often uninterpretable market. Change often rapidly occurs. Executives have limited foresight and time
Setting	**Mature** or maturing markets, often established firms	**Growth** markets, often adolescent firms. Reignited markets such as moderately disruptive technologies	**Nascent** markets, often ventures. Disrupted markets by major technology or legal change
Resources	Resources exist with known Value, Rarity, Imitability, and Non-substantiality (VRIN). Resources renewed by acquisitions, alliances, and Do It Yourself (DIY)	VRIN and other resources are identifiable and being built	Resources may not yet exist or may have either indeterminate or changing value
Strategic Actions	**Building**, renewing, and leveraging VRIN and other resources, including dynamic capabilities	**Continuing** to create strategy. Identifying and building VRIN and other resources including dynamic capabilities	**Creating** strategy by doing and thinking. Choosing to shape versus adapt. Beginning to build the scaffolding of resources for scaling
Competitive Advantage	**Long-term** if VRIN resources	**Medium-term** as valuable and rare resources are built and perhaps become inimitable	**Fleeting** and unpredictable duration

Figure 2.4 summarizes the identified themes in the literature and summarizes the identified issues and provides recommendations for future research.

Finally, the highly competitive and highly volatile environment calls for a new kind of flexibility and adaptability. At the same time, standardization, efficiency, and scale must continue. Top executives face the challenge of delivering against both requirements, yet conventional organizational wisdom provides little guidance on how to resolve this trade-off in day-to-day operations. The concept of the **Ambidextrous Organization** offers new, tangible, and balanced answers to this most pressing management dilemma. It helps answer the following three questions:

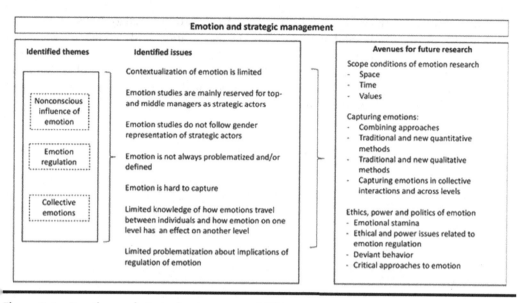

Figure 2.4   Emotion and strategic management [6]

- Where does the organization currently stand in terms of its set of organizational capabilities?
- What organizational capabilities does the business need, considering both the strategic context and business requirements?
- What kind of organizational development path is needed to build a sound balance between scale and productivity and speed and creativity?

In competitive markets businesses need to embrace two sets of capabilities that are often seen as complete opposites—they have to be **Fast and Creative**, while also being **Productive and Scale-driven**. The most obvious and tangible benefit of this organizational canvas is that it enables management teams to discuss organization development issues in a common language and make decisions on development aims and organization transformation priorities [7].

Figure 2.5 shows how combining those concepts in the ambidextrous organization provides the best of both worlds for the organization to apply both an **Exploration Strategy** (taking

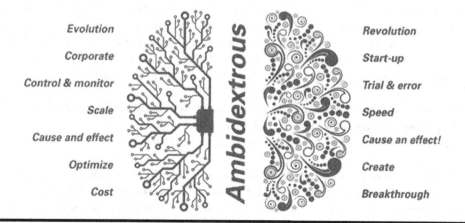

Figure 2.5   The ambidextrous organization—the best of two worlds [7]

advantage of future emerging opportunities) and an **Exploitation Strategy** (taking advantage of current exciting opportunities). For Exploration, the organization needs to embrace a mindset of Revolution, Start-up, Trial & Error, Speed, Cause and Effect!, Create, and Breakthrough. For Exploitation, the organization approach should be Evolution, Corporate, Control & Monitor, Scale, Cause & Effect, Optimize, Cost. Figure 2.6 shows the difference between those two perspectives that need to be balanced to achieve an ambidextrous organization.

Exploitation vs. Exploration

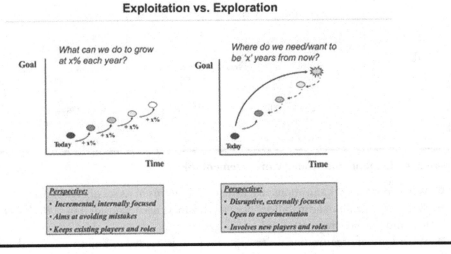

Figure 2.6 Exploitation versus exploration

Amazon is a prime example of the new breed of ambidextrous organizations. Always searching for the most innovative business ideas, it strives to deliver on customers' needs before people realize that they require them. This approach is driven by a well-established culture of invention, curiosity, and bias for action. Complementing its creative side, Amazon has also proven itself to be a champion of productivity. Not only its logistics but also its internal processes for scaling new business models are tailored for pure efficiency and standardization. If a new approach proves to be successful, it is rolled out rapidly, formally established, monitored, and aligned to deliver full productivity. By successfully balancing these two dimensions, Amazon has built a sustainable competitive advantage that has become accepted best practice across multiple industries.

Arthur D. Little has developed an ambidextrous organization development canvas that drills down from six design dimensions into 72 specific capabilities. Its starting point consists of six major design dimensions, which form mutually enhancing pairs. These are:

- **Steering and transformation**—the engine that drives performance and change
- **People and culture**—the glue that holds an organization together
- **Structure and processes**—the hardware of an organization

Each of the dimensions is broken down into design elements, which, in turn, are each made up of a set of capabilities. Figure 2.7 provides an example of a high-level organizational capability canvas of an ambidextrous organization. The canvas breaks down the six design dimensions on the two spectrums of scale and productivity system versus speed and creativity system.

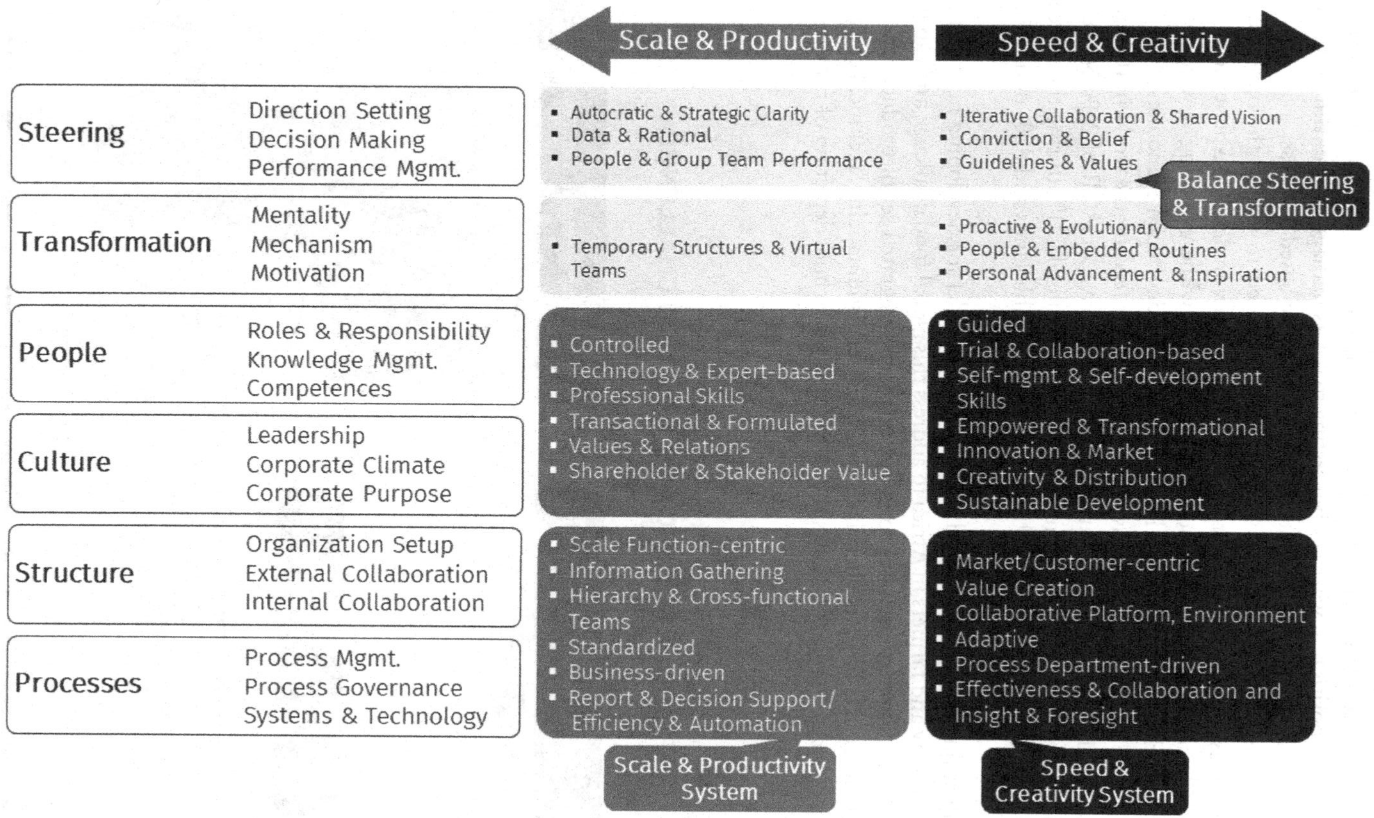

Steering
- Direction Setting
- Decision Making
- Performance Mgmt.

- Autocratic & Strategic Clarity
- Data & Rational
- People & Group Team Performance

- Iterative Collaboration & Shared Vision
- Conviction & Belief
- Guidelines & Values

Transformation
- Mentality
- Mechanism
- Motivation

- Temporary Structures & Virtual Teams

- Proactive & Evolutionary
- People & Embedded Routines
- Personal Advancement & Inspiration

Balance Steering & Transformation

Speed & Creativity

Scale & Productivity

People
- Roles & Responsibility
- Knowledge Mgmt.
- Competences

- Controlled
- Technology & Expert-based
- Professional Skills

- Guided
- Trial & Collaboration-based
- Self-mgmt. & Self-development Skills

Culture
- Leadership
- Corporate Climate
- Corporate Purpose

- Transactional & Formulated
- Values & Relations
- Shareholder & Stakeholder Value

- Empowered & Transformational
- Innovation & Market
- Creativity & Distribution
- Sustainable Development

Structure
- Organization Setup
- External Collaboration
- Internal Collaboration

- Scale Function-centric
- Information Gathering
- Hierarchy & Cross-functional Teams

- Market/Customer-centric
- Value Creation
- Collaborative Platform, Environment

Processes
- Process Mgmt.
- Process Governance
- Systems & Technology

- Standardized
- Business-driven
- Report & Decision Support/ Efficiency & Automation

- Adaptive
- Process Department-driven
- Effectiveness & Collaboration and Insight & Foresight

Scale & Productivity System

Speed & Creativity System

Figure 2.7   High-level organizational capability canvas of an ambidextrous organization [7]

Finally, a good case for combining an ambidextrous organization that used both exploration and exploitation strategies is the case of the OCP Group in Morocco [8]. It is a state-owned phosphate rock miner, phosphoric acid manufacturer, and phosphate fertilizer producer. They are responsible for the world's largest phosphate reserves. For a state-owned enterprise that enjoys a monopolistic market position, it was very interesting to see its management pushing the company to explore new avenues for growth beyond its core commodity-based business.

The management team developed a strategy that continued to exploit the opportunities in their current business, leveraging their strengths (access to raw materials, experience in mining, expertise in fertilizers and phosphoric acid manufacturing) while exploring new opportunities presented by the world shortage of arable lands in most of the developed economies. They saw that Africa represents the last frontier that is available to exploit for feeding the world in the future. As indicated in Figure 18, the world population is expected to have a CAGR of 25% between 2015 and 2050, while arable land per inhabitant will witness a decline of –21% during the same period. The solution is in Africa, where there is 60% of the world's arable lands and 80% of unused arable lands.

OCP exploration strategy introduced a new business model for developing new partnerships between the company and farmers in Africa to address this global food challenge and capitalize on this emerging future opportunity. The company offers an integrated set of products and services to farmers including, of course, its phosphate fertilizers but also financing, technical consultation, and marketing services. Figure 2.8 shows the IMD Business School depiction of the opportunity that OCP management explored.

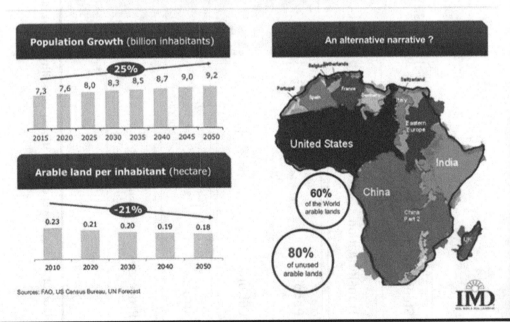

Figure 2.8   OCP company case study opportunity [9]

References

1. Aurik, J., Fable, M., and Jonk, G. (2014). *The History of Strategy and Its Future Prospects*. AT. Kearney.
2. Hustim, L., and Sakkab, N. (2006). Connect and Develop: Inside Procter & Gamble's New Model of Innovation. *Harvard Business Review*. March 2006.
3. Doganova, L., and Kornberger, M. (2021). Strategy's Futures. *Futures*, 125(2021), 102664. https://doi.org/10.1016/j.futures.2020.102664
4. Van Assche, K., Verschraegen, G., and Gruezmacher, M. (2021). Strategy for Collectives and Common Goods: Coordinating Strategy, Long-Term Perspectives and Policy Domains in Governance. *Futures*, 128(2021), 102716. https://doi.org/10.1016/j.futures.2021.102716
5. Furr, N., and Eisenhardt, M. K. (2021). Strategy and Uncertainty: Resource-Based View, Strategy-Creation View, and the Hybrid Between Them. *Journal of Management*, 47(7) September 2021, 1915–1935. https://doi.org/10.1177/01492063211011760
6. Brundin, E., Liu, F., and Cyron, T. (2021). Emotion in Strategic Management: A Review and Future Research Agenda. *Long Range Planning*. https://doi.org/10.1016/j.lrp.2021.102144
7. Lerner, W. et al. (2018). Ambidextrous Organizations- How to Embrace Disruption and Create Organizational Advantage. Arthur D. Little – Prism Magazine.
8. https://www.ocpgroup.ma/
9. Africa: A Solution to the Food Challenge. IMD Business School, Case Study.

Chapter 3

Planning, Practice, Intuition, and Serendipity

3.1 Sustainable to Transient Competitive Advantage

For too long, the business world has been obsessed with the idea of building sustainable competitive advantage. This idea is at the core of most strategy textbooks and forms the basis of Warren Buffet's investment strategy; it's central to the success of companies on the "most admired list". It's quite awesome to compete in this way that others can't imitate. And even today, there are companies that have created a strong position and then defended it for extended periods of time—firms such as GE, IKEA, and Unilever are among the few. But it's now rare for the company to maintain a truly lasting advantage. Competitors and customers have become too unpredictable and industries too amorphous. The forces at work here are quite familiar and characterize the "**VUCA**" world: the digital revolution, fewer barriers to entry, and globalization. And we just saw previously how these disruptive forces can make it extremely difficult even for the giants such as Nokia and Kodak to thrive in and operate efficiently.

In a world where competitive advantage fades away rapidly, companies can't afford to spend months crafting a single long-term strategy. To stay ahead, they need to constantly start new strategic initiatives, building and exploiting many **transient competitive advantages** at once. Though individually temporary, these advantages, as a portfolio, can keep companies in the lead over the long run. Firms that have figured this out—such as Milliken & Company, a US-based textiles and chemicals company; Cognizant, a global IT services company; and Brambles, a logistics company based in Australia—have abandoned the assumption that stability in business is the norm. They don't even think it should be a goal. Instead, they work to spark continuous change, avoiding dangerous rigidity. They view strategy differently—as more **fluid**, more **customer-centric**, and less **industry-bound**. And the ways they formulate it—the lens they use to define the competitive playing field, their methods for evaluating new business opportunities, and their approach to innovation—are different as well.

It's hard to argue how fast-moving competition has completely changed the landscape of strategy to an extent that the field of strategy needs to acknowledge the fact that sustainable competitive advantage is now the exception, not the rule. **Transient advantage is the new normal.**

DOI: 10.4324/9781003280941-5

Any competitive advantage—whether it lasts two seasons or two decades—goes through the same life cycle. But when advantages are fleeting, firms must rotate through the cycle much more quickly and more often, so they need a deeper understanding of the early and late stages than they would if they were able to maintain one strong position for many years.

A competitive advantage begins with a launch process, in which the organization identifies an opportunity and mobilizes resources to capitalize on it. In this phase, a company needs people who are capable of filling in blank sheets of paper with ideas, who are comfortable with experimentation and iteration, and who probably get bored with the kind of structure required to manage a large, complex organization.

In the next phase, ramp up, the business idea is brought to scale. This period calls for people who can assemble the right resources at the right time with the right quality and deliver on the promise of the idea.

Then, if a firm is fortunate, it begins a period of exploitation, in which it captures profits and shares and forces competitors to react. At this point, a company needs people who are good at Megers & Acquisitions (M&A), analytical decision-making, and efficiency. Traditional established companies have plenty of talent with this skill set.

Often, the very success of the initiative spawns competition, weakening the advantage. So, the firm has to reconfigure what it's doing to keep the advantage fresh. For reconfigurations, a firm needs people who aren't afraid of radically rethinking business models or resources.

In some cases, the advantage is completely eroded, compelling the company to begin a disengagement process in which resources are extracted and reallocated to the next-generation advantage. To manage this process, you need people who can be candid and tough-minded and can make emotionally difficult decisions.

For sensible reasons, companies with any degree of maturity tend to be oriented toward the exploitation phase of the life cycle. But as suggested, they need different skills, metrics, and people to manage the tasks inherent in each stage of an advantage's development. And if they're creating a pipeline of competitive advantages, the challenge is even more complex, because they'll need to orchestrate many activities that are inconsistent with one another.

Milliken & Company is a fascinating example of an organization that managed to overcome the competitive forces that annihilated its industry. By 1991, virtually all of Milliken's traditional competitors had vanished, victims of a surge in global competition that moved the entire business of textile manufacturing to Asia. In Milliken, one sees very clearly the pattern of entering new, more promising arenas while disengaging from older, exhausted ones. Ultimately, the company exited most of its textile lines, but it did not do so suddenly. It gradually shut down American plants, starting in the 1980s and continuing through 2009. (Every effort was made, as best I can tell, to reallocate workers who might have suffered as a result.) At the same time, the company was investing in international expansion, new technologies, and new markets, including forays into new arenas to which its capabilities provided access. As a result, a company that had been largely focused on textiles and chemicals through the 1960s, and advanced materials and flameproof products through the 1990s, had become a leader in specialty materials and specialty chemicals by the 2000s.

Hence, in order to create a successful strategy, one should keep in mind the fact that it's not one-size-fits-all, and instead, the strategy approach needs to be modified accordingly based on business requirements and needs. Creating a winning strategy involves a magical mix of art and science that addresses business challenges in a holistic way. The art of strategizing refers to the magic of intuition and serendipity while science is closely associated with the structure and framework. These structures and frameworks refer to what we call formal strategizing. Although formal strategizing has dominated strategic management concepts for a long time, it has recently drawn major criticism from scholars and practitioners as well. Strategy-as-Practice, on the other hand, is an alternative perspective intended to address the shortcomings of formal strategizing and takes a more holistic stance by taking into consideration the wider context of strategy development and implementation.

3.2 Formal Strategizing

Statistical evidence indicates that formal strategizing doesn't make a significant contribution to profits. There are four different factors that support this argument (Figure 3.1).

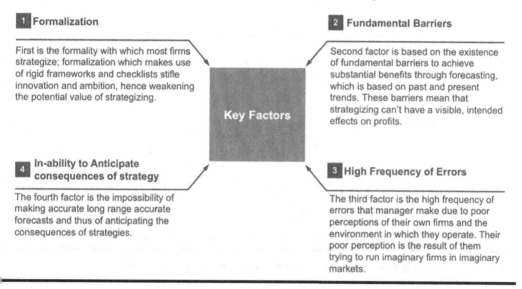

1 Formalization

First is the formality with which most firms strategize; formalization which makes use of rigid frameworks and checklists stifle innovation and ambition, hence weakening the potential value of strategizing.

2 Fundamental Barriers

Second factor is based on the existence of fundamental barriers to achieve substantial benefits through forecasting, which is based on past and present trends. These barriers mean that strategizing can't have a visible, intended effects on profits.

Key Factors

4 In-ability to Anticipate consequences of strategy

The fourth factor is the impossibility of making accurate long range accurate forecasts and thus of anticipating the consequences of strategies.

3 High Frequency of Errors

The third factor is the high frequency of errors that manager make due to poor perceptions of their own firms and the environment in which they operate. Their poor perception is the result of them trying to run imaginary firms in imaginary markets.

Figure 3.1 Key formal strategizing factors negatively affecting profitability

But it is still possible for the firms to operate more effectively through formal strategizing. In order to achieve this, firms must strategize in a way that preserves uncertainties and allow for contingencies. This, in turn, implies that strategists shouldn't take their activities too seriously and instead add more common sense in a world that often ignores them.

Several research activities have been carried out to examine the relationship between formal strategizing and profitability. Some of these studies have found a positive correlation between formal strategizing and profitability. However, these studies were subject to non-reliability due to poor methodology. As a result, researchers improved the methodology and were able to achieve results which suggested that formal strategizing doesn't increase profits to be significant enough to be practically useful.

Grinyer and Norburn conducted one of the best studies about the impact of formal strategizing on profitability. In their work, they extensively studied 21 firms which were selected after careful consideration and after gathering valid information from the executives of these firms. They were able to draw two conclusions which relate profitability and formal planning. Their first key finding suggested that both the **profitable** and **nonprofitable** firms use **formal** as well as **informal methods** of strategizing. The profitability of a firm had a very weak correlation with formal strategizing. Figure 3.2 illustrates such correlation [1].

The second key finding suggested that there is an **inconsistent correlation between a firm's profitability and its objectives.**

It's quite hard to digest the above two key findings, especially for someone who teaches or practices a formal method of strategizing. However, careful analysis suggests that it does make sense and there is no reason that strategizing should result in higher profits. In fact, formal strategizing has two different aspects: beneficial and harmful. The benefits can be achieved when strategies reflect accurate forecasting of future trends and capabilities and everyone works together to achieve results while ignoring the distractions. However, formal strategizing can also produce the worst results when strategies reflect inaccurate forecasting of future trends and capabilities. Research studies suggest that the frequency of positive outcomes is almost equal to the frequency of negative outcomes hence suggesting that formal strategizing has an insignificant effect on the average.

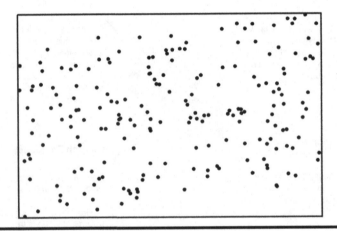

Figure 3.2   Correlation between formal strategizing and firm profitability [1]

Formal strategizing only works under two conditions:

■ When business is subject to a predictable environment
■ When the business possesses several distinctive capabilities

When these two conditions don't hold, it is quite difficult for the formal strategy to be effective. In the previous section, we have already seen that we live in a VUCA world where rapidly shifting environmental and market dynamics are causing disruption at a massive scale. So, the idea of business operating in a predictable environment is almost nonexistent. In addition, there are only a few businesses that possess a level of competencies distinctive enough to create significantly higher profits. In addition, there are four difficulties that firms face when they attempt to increase their profits significantly through formal strategizing.

First, the majority of the firms compete against skilled competitors who possess almost similar amounts of information as them. This allows them to plan their strategic moves brilliantly hence making it very difficult for the competitors to gain a competitive advantage through strategizing.

Second, the strategies that can produce significant profits are illegal, immoral, or impractical; most businesses will not pursue them. High-profit strategies are all variations of monopoly power. Although these strategies have proven themselves very effective, US laws bar nearly all monopolistic strategies, and so American firms risk antitrust actions if they adopt them. Microsoft provides an example. The legal forms of monopoly—such as patents, first moves, and geographic locations—give either small advantages or transient ones. Patents and first moves also tend to be quite expensive; so, the benefit-to-cost ratios are often poor and firms do not use these strategies repeatedly for long periods.

Third, formal strategizing largely emphasizes big issues revolving around large sums and many people. Instead, these issues never turn out to be large or significant enough as anticipated and strategists end up wasting large amounts of resources in the process.

Fourth, most firms use formal strategizing to build strong consensus and to establish strong commitments. However, this use of formal strategizing makes unrealistic assumptions about people's knowledge and about their abilities to forecast accurately. Consensus is dangerous unless the strategies are very likely to produce wanted outcomes. For strategizing to produce wanted outcomes, the strategists need to have realistic perceptions of their firms' capabilities and their market environments. However, the evidence is that most managers do not have realistic perceptions of their firms or their market environments.

3.2.1 So, What Can Formal Strategizing Achieve?

As the ongoing observation clearly indicates that in real life formal strategizing doesn't offer substantial benefits. So, what can a strategist expect to achieve through formal strategizing (see Figure 3.3)?

Benefits of Formal Strategizing

01 — Strategizing can sometimes exploit distinctive competencies, entry barriers, proprietary information and first moves

02 — Strategizing can use forecasts along with anticipation to motivate alertness

03 — Strategizing can inject realism into managers' perceptions

04 — Strategizing can keep strategies flexible

Figure 3.3   Benefits of formal strategizing

■ **Strategizing can sometimes exploit distinctive competencies, entry barriers, proprietary information, and first moves**

Economic theory says that almost the only way to benefit from strategizing involves using resources that other firms lack. Thus, firms should try to identify or develop competencies that make them distinctive and then turn these into competitive advantages. Some firms possess or can create entry barriers that protect them from competitors. Proprietary information can also give a firm an edge; firms can generate proprietary information and try to keep it proprietary long enough to extract benefits from it. Examples include Intel, Google, Facebook, Amazon, and Netflix.

These tactics are much easier to advocate than to execute successfully. Today, it may be very expensive or difficult to create distinctive competencies or entry barriers. When a firm begins to put its strategy into effect, competitors can react to the actual behavior rather than to their theories about it. Proprietary information and proprietary information-processing techniques are rare. For example, even if firms do not know their competitors' costs exactly, they can likely estimate those costs accurately enough. Similarly, all sensible methods of data analysis yield similar inferences. Thus, these tactics can sometimes exploit distinctive competencies, rendering them to be not quite profitable as anticipated.

■ Strategizing can use forecasts along with anticipation to motivate alertness

Forecasts can be partly self-fulfilling prophecies. Because conservative forecasts may lead firms to achieve less than they could, accurate forecasting can be a mistake. Some managers use forecasts to motivate exceptional efforts. But strategists must keep balance. Not only do consistently biased forecasts lose their motivation value but also people learn to distrust them. Accurate forecasts, on the other hand, may help firms to identify important threats and opportunities.

The literature about forecasting proposed several recommendations for making accurate forecasts. Four of these recommendations are to:

1. Allow for seasonality
2. Consider "no change" and "no change in the trend"
3. Average several forecasts
4. Assume that today is not a turning point and wait for that magic moment known as the "tipping moment" when the trends or social behavior will cross a threshold tip and spread like a wildfire.

However, due to rising customer expectations, increasing global complexity, and accelerated technological innovation, forecasting alone proves to be quite ineffective thus making **strategic anticipation** a necessity for large organizations to compete in the future. Strategic anticipation allows the organization to develop the capacity to identify, understand, and respond to future trends and uncertainties, enabling them to assess potential impacts and seize the commercial initiative.

This approach makes people aware of the diversity of what might happen; it motivates alertness for information about how events are actually developing. Firms often overlook important opportunities or threats simply because these were not anticipated; so, firms need to be alert for surprises and not just confirm their expectations.

■ Strategizing can inject realism into managers' perceptions

Because most managers misperceive their firms and their market environments, there is an opportunity for formal strategizing to educate managers about the actual properties of firms and market environments, by gathering and analyzing objective data. However, such education requires persuasion as well as evidence. Objective data becomes more valuable as managers' current perceptions become more unrealistic, yet people grow less willing to accept new information as it deviates more from their expectations.

Formal strategizing also creates diverse opportunities to improve the flow of information upward. Literature shows that top managers do not listen carefully to their subordinates. People in hierarchies talk upward and listen upward: They send more messages upward than downward, and they pay more attention to superiors than to subordinates. They also overestimate how much accurate information they do transmit upward, and they tend to tell the boss what the boss wants to hear. Formal strategizing can expose senior managers to inputs from lower levels.

■ Strategizing can keep strategies flexible

Because managers do misperceive their firms and environments, and because firms tend to exaggerate these errors, explicit strategies often make actions less realistic and less responsive to unexpected events. Thus, formal strategizing should provide for changing strategies in response to new information.

1. Strategists can avoid building strong rationales. Strong rationalizations make behaviors inflexible and make it difficult to evaluate outcomes
2. Strategists can de-emphasize the long term. Long-range forecasts incorporate much larger errors than do short-range forecasts
3. Strategists can avoid generalizations. Generalizations suppress alertness. Managers make better decisions when they focus on particulars
4. Strategists can minimize formalization. Formalized strategies incorporate larger errors than do informal strategies, and managers revise formalized strategies much less often than informal strategies
5. Strategists can emphasize informal communication. Perhaps profitability correlates positively with informal communication because informal communication produces a better understanding
6. Strategists can foster trust and good feelings. Because strategies are so faulty and yield such vague benefits, only foolish managers would stake their careers on strategies or turn formal strategizing meetings into battlefields. Indeed, consensus may itself be a liability, inducing managers to focus too narrowly and to underestimate the actual uncertainty of future events

3.3 Strategy-as-Practice

Strategy-as-Practice (SaP) has been developed as an alternative perspective within the strategic management domain. This perspective recognizes that the traditional approach of the strategy discipline has been to treat strategy as a property of organizations—something an organization has. This has ignored that strategy is also something that executives do [2]. According to Strategy-as-Practice scholars, there is a need to approach holistically "how managers and consultants act and interact in the whole strategy-making sequence" and develop studies that focus more solidly on the practitioners of strategy.

The Strategy-as-Practice perspective views strategizing "**as a socially accomplished, situated activity arising from the actions and interactions of multiple level actors**". Practice researchers try to uncover the detailed actions and interactions that, taken together, over time constitute a strategy process. Hence, the Strategy-as-Practice approach favors managerial agency, situated action, and both strategy stability and strategic change rather than focusing on a set of change events from a firm level of analysis, as most process studies tend to do. According to the activity theory, an organization can be regarded as an activity system comprising three main constituents: **actors, collective social structures**, and the **practical activities** in which they engage.

There have also been a number of other studies focusing on the microlevel aspects of strategizing. A study was conducted on the practices around a new business-planning model in Canadian museums. Maitlis and Lawrence [3] analyzed the failure of members of a UK symphony orchestra to construct an artistic strategy for their organization. These authors argue that failure in organizational strategizing can be understood as resulting from the interplay of certain elements of organizational discourse and specific kinds of political behavior. These empirical research efforts are attributed to the perceived failure of the traditional strategy process to study the microlevel characteristics of how strategists actually think and act strategically in the whole strategy process of the firm. Alongside the growth in attention on this perspective, there have been calls for more critically oriented studies that focus on the fundamental issues of identity and power.

Vaara and Whittington [4] offered a comprehensive review of 57 Strategy-as-Practice empirical studies published since 2003 (24 studies relating to practices, 18 to praxis, and 15 to practitioners) and developed a set of five research directions for the Strategy-as-Practice perspective (placing agency in a web of practices, recognizing the macro-institutional nature of practices, focusing attention on emergence in strategy making, exploring how the material matters, and promoting critical analysis).

Overall, Strategy-as-Practice scholars examine the way in which actors interact with the social and physical features of the context in the everyday activities that constitute practice. They investigate how managerial actors perform the work of strategy, both through their social interactions with other actors and through practices present within a context, as well as habits, tools, events, artifacts, and socially defined modes of acting through which the stream of strategic activity is constructed.

3.3.1 Three Concepts of Strategy-as-Practice

There are three concepts that have been used to encapsulate the Strategy-as-Practice approach: **Practitioners**, **Practices**, and **Praxis**. These three concepts form the 3P framework which helps to reveal the microlevel aspects of strategizing by focusing on "who", "how", "where", and "when" [5]. Figure 3.4 shows the interaction and overlaps of the 3P elements in strategy development.

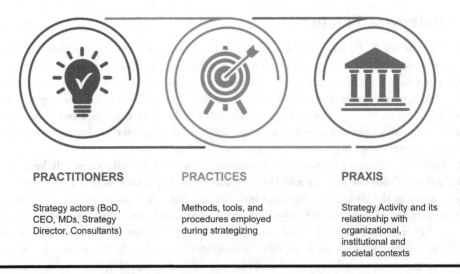

PRACTITIONERS

Strategy actors (BoD, CEO, MDs, Strategy Director, Consultants)

PRACTICES

Methods, tools, and procedures employed during strategizing

PRAXIS

Strategy Activity and its relationship with organizational, institutional and societal contexts

Figure 3.4   The Strategy-as-Practice 3P framework

Practitioners are the actors of strategizing which include managers, consultants, and specialized internal change agents. The concept of practice refers to various methods, tools, and techniques that practitioners utilize when they strategize. In many organizations, these methods tend to become standardized and routinized ways of analyzing strategic issues. In other words, practices are "shared routines of behavior", including traditions, norms, and procedures for thinking, acting, and using things. Praxis refers to the activity comprising the work of strategizing. This work involves all sorts of activities ranging from meeting, consulting, writing, presenting, communicating, and so on in order to make strategy executable.

One thing which is quite important to note when referring to the above framework is that the three concepts overlap with each other. Each area of overlap raises a number of interesting questions about the conduct of strategy. For instance, in the area where the concepts of "Practices" and "Practitioners" meet, we could raise a number of related questions, for instance, "what kind of methods do CEOs use to help them strategize?" or "how are particular planning techniques/tools/ SWOT used in action by consultants?". Similarly, in the "Praxis" and "Practices" area of overlap, we could raise questions such as "what kind of actions do away-days encourage?" and "do particular strategy tools actually help us think in more innovative terms about our strategy?".

3.4 Intuition in Strategy

Intuition is commonly referred to as a decision-making process that relies on rapid, nonconscious recognition of patterns and associations to generate affectively charged judgment [6]. The concept of intuition is directly related to experience. Managers with a great deal of knowledge are able to come up with solutions without being able to show how they achieved the results.

There are some important characteristics that are closely associated with intuition. First of these, it talks about intuition being subconscious. Khatri and Ng [7] highlighted this by stating that people's experiences are stored like a reserve in the subconscious and it is, thanks to intuition, that people can draw and choose among the alternatives which suit them best. This process of intuition builds up in the mind in an unconscious way. Another characteristic of intuition is that it is very quick. Intuition can allow the managers to immediately devise the best course of action to tackle a particular problem. Finally, the last characteristic of intuition is that it's part of all decisions. For instance, when the rational analytic tool is being used, there is a level of unknown that cannot be measured, and this is when intuition is used, for instance, to interpret data.

According to some researchers, intuition is easily recognizable and is viewed as a composite phenomenon involving an interplay between knowing and sensing. Three operational indicators of intuition are stated below:

1. **Reliance on Judgment**

   Decision makers make use of intuition when they need to make quick decisions whilst there is a lack of information and no prior experience. In such cases, judgment is the key factor in the process of creating a solution. Daft and Lengel proposed that if work processes can't be analyzed then executives must employ judgment instead of computational procedures.

2. **Reliance on Experience**

   Intuition comprises experience which is based on deep knowledge of problems, associated with a specific profession or environment. According to Wally and Baum, intuition is described as an ability which can be learned from experience.

3. Use of "Gut Feeling"

Intuition is also characterized as a process of feeling a problem or trusting a person's gut feeling. In case executives make a wrong decision, it makes it extremely difficult for them to defend it since there is no obvious reason on which it is based.

The integrated framework shown in Figure 3.5 helps to examine and analyze the role of intuition in strategic decision-making. According to the framework, strategic decision-making is based on three different and interrelated dimensions: **intuition**, **rationality**, and **political behavior**. These concepts are combined with decision-specific characteristics and company characteristics. The outcome of this process aspires to provide a clear depiction of the role of intuition in a managerial strategic decision-making sense.

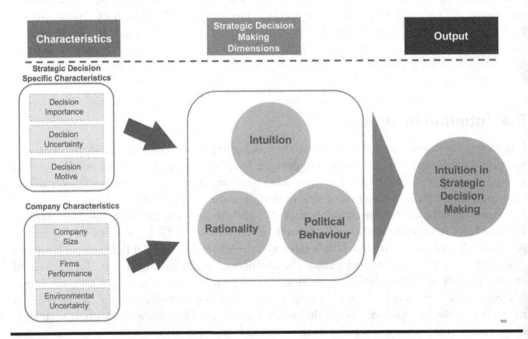

Figure 3.5 Integrated model for intuition, rationality, and political behavior

According to Mintzberg and Westley, companies, to be effective, should embrace both rational analytical tools or models and intuitive or action-oriented forms of decision-making. Mintzberg and Westley describe three main approaches to decision-making, which are "thinking first", "seeing first", and "doing first". According to the authors, the "thinking first" model, which is the classical rational approach (define, diagnose, design, decide) has its limits because most of a decision lay not just in conscious thinking but also in the unconscious. Therefore, according to Mintzberg and Westley, this rational approach needs to be supplemented by two other approaches. According to the "seeing first" model, decisions are driven by what managers see or think. The last approach identified by the two authors is the "doing first" model, and it occurs when managers are required to make decisions without seeing or thinking, in other words when the need to take action is imminent. This theory can be summarized by three steps: enactment, selection, and retention. The meaning of this can be found in the fact that when people are stuck, there is space for experimenting, learning by doing, and therefore the collection of experience. In a summary, Mintzberg and

Westley believe that the rational step-by-step logic is not enough for companies who want to be effective; there is also a need to incorporate a more intuitive or action-oriented decision-making process.

According to Calabretta, Gemser, and Wijnberg [8], rationality and intuition are both valuable for strategic decision-making but, at the same time, they are two different concepts. When these two concepts are utilized together, inevitably it will create tension and contradiction between each other. They claimed that intuitive and rational decision-making are, at the same time, different concepts and both necessary for effective strategic decision-making to create a paradox. This is a new approach that tends to analyze the phenomena of decision-making by considering the concept of intuition and rationality as a whole, putting the focus on the tension rather than putting emphasis only on one of the two elements.

The relation between political behaviors and intuition has been extensively studied. Political behaviors in the context of strategic decision-making can increase decision intuition. The first consideration made is that in the political approach informal discussions are used to address strategic problems ending up in a low exchange of knowledge and information between the executive group members. Therefore, intuitive decision-making becomes more likely. The second consideration concerns the fact that managers' intuition approach tends to increase together with the intensifying of political activities in the strategic decision-making process. The authors state that political behaviors may be an indicator of an intuitive approach of the executives in their strategic decision-making process. It is, therefore, likely that political behaviors have direct implications on intuition.

3.4.1 The Role of Intuition in Managerial Context

One of the main assumptions in decision-making is that rational processes lead to better results than intuitive processes. This assumption has been criticized by various scholars. A number of them indicate that many managers employ intuition as an effective technique for strategic decision-making. In volatile conditions, strategy methods have to be flexible and resourceful.

As Elbanna [9] claims, the use of intuition in the business world is gaining popularity, since only a few strategic decisions have access to sufficient, precise, and timely information. Managers find a number of advantages in the use of intuition in decision-making, which are to speed up decision-making, ameliorate ultimate decisions, accommodate personal development, and promote decisions which are in accordance with the company. It is argued that intuition can be favorable on certain occasions and even the best available alternative. Intuitive processes can deal with more complexity than our conscious minds.

A number of researchers have suggested that top managers utilize intuition in an unstable environment, but few studies examine the relation between intuition and organizational outcomes [9]. One of the research studies [7] found a positive relationship between intuition and organizational performance in an unstable environment, but a negative in a stable one.

However, the use of intuition in decision-making has also been criticized. Sauter states that managers who employ intuition may become impatient with routines or details, reach a decision too fast, disregard important information, or follow a hunch when they should not.

Elbanna and Child [10] identified three decision-specific characteristics, namely decision importance, decision uncertainty, and decision motive.

■ **Decision importance**
As Papadakis, Lioukas, and Chambers [11] state, the perceived importance of a strategic decision is among the strongest characteristics of decision-making behavior. Since not all

strategic decisions have the same level of importance, decision makers can approach them in different ways, for example, executives are expected to utilize more rational processes for the most important decisions. Executives are more prone to rationality when making crucial decisions for achieving the goals of the organization.

■ **Decision uncertainty**

Decision uncertainty forms the essence of decision-making. Elbanna and Child point out that various authors have approached uncertainty as a mystery which cannot be dealt with by rational processes. For instance, Daft and Lengel state high decision uncertainty may result in more intuitive processes, meaning employing judgment and experience rather than computational techniques. Papadakis, Lioukas, and Chambers identify a positive association between decision uncertainty and politicization. They state that in cases when uncertainty is linked to the action needed to be taken or the collection of information, it is possible to anticipate conflicting opinions at the beginning of the problem formulation and the emergence of political activities in the process of solving the problem.

■ **Decision motive**

The way in which executives classify and label a strategic decision as an opportunity or as a crisis greatly affects the decision-making processes that follow. A research study conducted in a chemical company proved that when managers identified the decision as a crisis, they avoided political debate, focusing on facts and ideas. Nonetheless, when the crisis retreated, a number of political activities surfaced. Mintzberg, Raisinghani, and Theoret [12] argue that decision makers are more rational when the decision is perceived as a crisis, while they are prone to respond to opportunities without using rational and analytical processes.

The moderating role of characteristics related to the internal and external environment of a company in the managerial strategic decision-making process are:

■ **Company size**

Company size can affect the strategic decision-making process in a company in such a way that larger firms will utilize a more formal and rational approach. Elbanna and Child claim that in small companies, the formulation of strategy depends on the idiosyncratic capabilities of a single or few individuals. Khatri and Ng argue that company size may interact with intuition so that small organizations are prone to rely more on intuition than large ones. On the same note, it is suggested that managers in small firms tend to rely on their intuition and disregard collected information or conducted the analysis.

■ **Firm performance**

According to Eisenhardt and Bourgeois [13], in high-velocity environments, high-performing companies employ more rational decision-making processes, suggesting that the more rational the strategic decision-making process, the better the performance of the firm. Other authors claim that the success of a decision depends on the availability of both resources, such as money, material, and technology, all of which indicate good performance, and information, which is linked to rationality.

■ **Environmental uncertainty**

In a stable environment, synoptic processes, like rationality, are favorable, whereas in an unstable environment, incremental processes, like intuition, should be used. This is due to the fact that in a stable environment, information is more available and reliable, there is less pressure to collect new information, and the cost of collecting information is sensible. Thus, decisions based on facts and figures may lead to better performance than decisions based on judgment or gut feeling [7].

As we have seen previously, formal strategizing doesn't result in substantial profits and creating a competitive advantage. Hence formal strategizing has been replaced by informal methods of strategizing such as intuition and serendipity to gain competitive advantage. Both of the concepts are discussed in great detail with comprehensive frameworks in order to integrate them into the strategic processes.

3.5 Serendipity as Competitive Advantage

In strategy, I like to consider serendipity as the case when *Opportunities* meet *Capabilities*. It is defined as the ability to recognize and evaluate unexpected information and generate unintended value from it. This unexpected information appears in all spheres of life, especially in professional fields which include science and technology, politics and economics, education administration, library and information science, career choice and development, and entrepreneurship and management [14]. It is quite interesting to note that scientists now openly acknowledge and credit serendipity behind the many inventions and discoveries. In *Serendipity: Accidental Discoveries in Science* [15, 16], Royston Roberts has gathered together dozens of examples of serendipity from just about every conceivable field—from Columbus discovering the New World to Isaac Newton and his famous apple to Edward Jenner and the vaccination for smallpox to the discovery of many of the chemical elements to all manner of materials (such as celluloid, rayon, nylon, polyethylene, artificial ivory, silk, and safety glass) to astronomical serendipities to the vast majority of medications. What do Velcro, Penicillin, X-rays, Teflon, Dynamite, and the Dead Sea Scrolls have in common? Serendipity! These diverse things were discovered by accident, as were hundreds of other things that make everyday living more convenient, pleasant, healthy, or interesting. All have come to us as a result of serendipity—the gift of finding valuable or agreeable things not sought for or "the faculty of making fortunate or unexpected discoveries by accident". Even after all these discoveries and inventions, only a few business managers have so far applied serendipity in any direct fashion to generate value from unexpected information.

The concept of serendipity has been around for years. Most discussions on definitions of "serendipity" start with some version of the story reported by Walpole (1754). Hundreds of years ago, a king named Giaffer educated his three sons to a level that nearly satisfied him but felt they needed a bit more "seasoning" before assuming the duties of the throne. He sent them into the countryside of what was then called Serendip, later Ceylon, now Sri Lanka [14].

In the course of their walks, they noticed and made observations about the information they had not sought or expected, ranging from grass eaten and not, spit wads on one side of the road, bees and flies, and footprints. When they arrived at one town, a farmer asked if they had seen his lost camel. "Is the camel blind in its right eye? Is it missing a tooth on the left side of its mouth? Is it lame in one leg? And is it carrying honey and sugar?" The astounded farmer at once accused the three princes of stealing his camel and demanded that the emperor punish them. But the wise emperor asked first to hear the princes' story. "We noticed along the way that the grass on the left side of the road had been eaten, while the right side was still covered with fresh grass (so we assume the camel is blind in one eye). We saw wads of grass that had dropped onto the ground, through a hole where a tooth should be in the camel's mouth. Bees like honey and flies like sugar, which the camel was carrying in packs on either side of its back and, as it swayed, must have left drops in the road. And finally, we noticed three footprints and a drag where a fourth would be, suggesting the camel was lame in one back leg".

The princes' notoriety came from their ability to notice unexpected information that they were not searching for and, later, turn it into something of value. At the time, their curiosity caused them to notice, but lacking context, they did not connect the various pieces of information. Once they had a context for understanding the unexpected information and a problem (the lost camel), they were able to connect the pieces of a puzzle and offer and explain how they knew about the camel.

The story of Walpole does illustrate the concept of serendipity, but it is not quite useful for people who have tried to define serendipity. In the context of management, several characteristics pertaining to serendipity have emerged. These include:

- Unsought, unexpected, or unintentional event or information
- Extraordinary, surprising, and anomalous findings or theory
- Having a capability which others don't possess allows us to recognize and connect various pieces of information to solve a problem or come up with an opportunity

The above characteristics make it clear that serendipity results from unexpected information, which is anomalous, incongruous, and inconsistent with existing theory or ways of thinking. Scientists, especially, appear to thoroughly seek inconsistent information and that leads to a new direction with major payoffs. In some cases, an individual may be searching for a new idea, problem, solution, or opportunity. For instance, in combinatorial chemistry, which produces new drugs, the idea of blind search is part of the process with serendipity mistakes likely to be part of the research process.

Serendipity is described as the intersection of three "domains" or elements: **search, knowledge/preparation**, and **chance**. An individual needs to be looking for something, such as a solution to a problem or an opportunity. He needs to approach the search with existing knowledge and preparation so that he will be able to recognize an event or information. In addition, the unexpected event or information has to emerge by chance. Thus, serendipity occurs only when all three elements are present and overlap (a search, prior knowledge, and chance event).

Finally, the ability to notice and be aware of unexpected information is critical in order for serendipity to occur. In other words, serendipity is not just the unexpected information or events, instead, it is the ability to recognize and be able to draw some insights out of that information. Specifically, it is the ability of an organization or individual to identify the unexpected information or event and to capitalize on it and in the process adding value to the organization.

For practicing managers and scientists, serendipity appears in several different forms depending upon whether there is a search intent and whether the unexpected information solves some problem and opens the door for other problems or opportunities. Essentially, the researchers have broken down serendipity into two categories:

1. Whether there is a strong intent to find something in order to find a solution to a particular problem
2. Whether unexpected information solves an existing problem and, in the process, offers solutions to unknown problems or opportunities

Figure 3.6 illustrates three different types of serendipity [17]:

- Type 1: Want to solve A, but the solution comes from unexpected B
- Type 2: Looks for a solution to A, but B "falls out" and solves C
- Type 3: Not looking for anything, B appears and ends up as an idea, opportunity, or solution

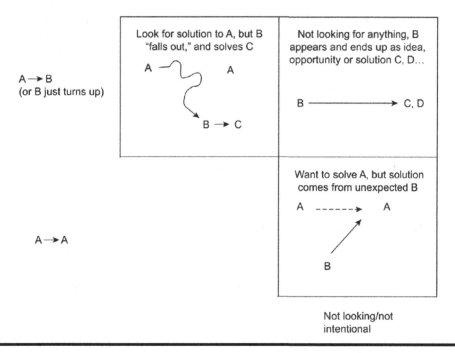

Figure 3.6   Three types of serendipity

Type 1

This is the most common type of serendipity and it occurs when individuals seek a solution to problem A, and it comes from an unexpected piece of information (B). For instance, when researchers tried to find an explanation for obesity, their initial assumption was that psychological and economic reasons were the root cause; individuals had genetic tendencies toward obesity, or they prefer to buy cheaper food which is higher in fat content. But later on, another research presented a completely different explanation which stated that "Your friends can affect your health". People who were overweight tend to associate themselves with those who were overweight, as do smokers with other smokers. Christakis and Fowler further argued that social networks and friendships may influence health, which is a totally different explanation to the initial problem of obesity.

Type 2

Type 2 serendipity occurs when an individual searches for a solution to problem A and instead of finding a solution to A, he uncovers something totally unexpected (B). There are some well-known examples of type 2 serendipity, one of them being penicillin. Fleming was not looking for penicillin but accidentally discovered a mold in his lab that had many uses and implications.

Type 3

The story of the three princes of Serendip reflects a final and, as some might say, the truest form of serendipity. This occurs when a chance or unexpected event or piece of information appears, and an individual then begins to think about what it might mean, and along the way, solves a problem or discovers a new opportunity he or she had not intended or thought of previously. In this case, no intent or overt searching happens, but to gain the benefits of the unexpected event, the individual must still have the knowledge and a prepared mind to notice and then realize its potential value. The legend of the apple falling on Newton's head—combined with his knowledge of science—led to his serendipitous discovery of gravity's properties. Likewise, the also now-famous story of the invention of Velcro: a man who found insistently sticky burrs on his dog was led to wonder whether there might be anything of value that could be made from such an unexpected bit of information.

In Type 3 serendipity, some scholars insist that there must also be a "metaphorical leap" to uncover a possible value or use in the information or event. In Newton's case, a falling apple came to represent gravity's pull on any object; the "burrs on the dog" could be extrapolated to "some sort of material that holds tight".

3.5.1 A Framework for Serendipity

In order to develop a framework for serendipity, we will begin with a definition and its elements and follow with the framework itself. As stated previously, serendipity is defined as the ability to recognize and evaluate unexpected information and generate unintended value from it. There are four critical aspects in the definition [17]:

- The ability
- To recognize and evaluate
- Unexpected information
- Generate unintended value

- **Ability**

    This is an important aspect since it stresses the need to take actions as a result of observing and uncovering information, rather than simply on the discovery or event or piece of information itself.
- **Recognize and Evaluate**

    The ability to recognize and evaluate comprises several pieces. First, recognizing includes two critical acts: noticing and connecting information. The three princes of Serendip observed or noticed bees circling droplets of honey, grass that had been eaten on one side of the road, and three hoof prints and one groove in the sand. Those bits of information, noticed and filed away then, became important only later, within the context of the problem of a lost camel. In a sense, the bits of information were "clues" that they did not realize were "clues". Only within that context of a problem did the princes connect the disparate pieces of unexpected information and put those clues together. After noticing or observing, comes the evaluation of information. The ability to evaluate encompasses both "flash evaluation" and more systematic evaluation in pursuit of creating value. Flash evaluation starts with a "gut feel" that moves toward fuller alertness, which, in turn, can go to a more systematic evaluation that confirms the initial gut feel. The reliance on information—whether from internal (personal or organizational) or external (environmental) sources—may vary, however, and we discuss that in more depth further on.
- **Unexpected Information**

    Serendipity does not necessarily presume any "work" or attempt to solve a problem, other than noticing and having a prepared mind. It can include a search (Type I serendipity that we discussed earlier in this chapter), but it does not require it (Types II and III). Rather, it contains the notion of unexpected information appearing, even when there is no immediate problem to solve. Information could be data, an event, an observation, or a clue. Again, to refer to the three princes, they came across unsought, unexpected, and unplanned information or clues. They made note but did nothing with the information until they encountered a context—problem—which allowed them to connect disparate clues or pieces of information into something of (unintended) value.

■ **Generate Unintended Value**

Finally, the serendipitous experience includes the element of creating unintended value, which refers to the potential outcome of a problem solution, new opportunity, idea, or other direction that was unintended. In other words, serendipity implies the lack of intention to solve a particular problem or find a particular opportunity. Rather it suggests the ability to take unexpected information and create value that, before the information appeared, would not have happened.

The framework for the serendipity process integrates many ideas from existing models. The figure below shows a tentative framework, which offers a process that individuals tend to follow while applying the ability to recognize, evaluate, and create value from unexpected information. The model has four different stages, each consisting of a number of steps. The four stages include:

1. Setting the stage or conditions that will increase the likelihood of unexpected events to occur (A, B, C, and G)
2. Notice unexpected information and connect it to other information (D)
3. Evaluating the information (flash and systematic evaluation) in terms of whether it creates unintended value (E)
4. Taking action upon the information in order to generate the value (F) (Figure 3.7)

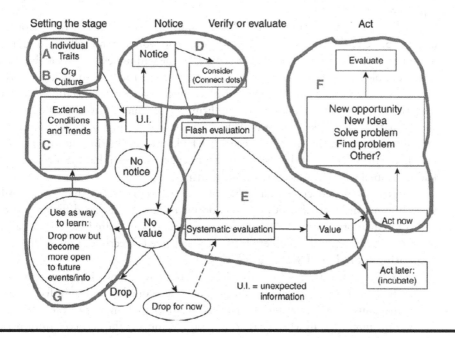

Figure 3.7 Framework for serendipity [17]

- **Setting the Stage (A, B, C, and ... G)**

  The model suggests that conditions at three levels may enhance the likelihood of unexpected information being noticed. First, the characteristics or conditions of an individual (A) that will make her more or less likely to notice anomalous information (e.g., openness, confidence, curiosity, alertness) are ones that many scholars have covered. Organizational culture (B), including an openness to new ideas, a cross-discipline mix of people, and an allowance for "sloppiness", are similar ones that research has addressed.

  Finally, external conditions (C) have been less widely considered and yet could well be more important for different types of settings or industries. For example, in one case, the executives were launching a new product and had market analysis in preparation. In the process, they uncovered unexpected information that suggested their pricing methodology was inaccurate. Because they had been alerted to the notion of unexpected information and were looking for ways to recognize and leverage whatever they might find, they did notice unexpected information about their pricing methodology and evaluated and acted upon it. In the discussion about their experience, they claimed that because they had been alerted to the notion of unexpected information, they were more receptive to noticing and otherwise might have missed it without those "conditions" being favorable to noticing.

  Interestingly, even when information is seen to be of "no value", the simple act of noticing and recognizing possibilities may, in turn, enhance the openness for setting the stage for future noticing (G). Thus, the act of noticing and considering and then doing a flash evaluation may heighten awareness and increase alertness for more unexpected information later.

- **Noticing and Connecting Unexpected Information (D)**

  The process of noticing or being alert to unexpected information and then beginning to connect unexpected bits of information is one of the most critical steps in the serendipity process and framework.

  Gaglio and Katz [18] call this the "What's going on?" step, which involves noticing an unusual piece of information and then beginning to wonder (and follow through) what it might mean. Critical in this phase, of course, is the willingness to pursue the anomaly. One example involved a former employee who had left the firm to gain expertise in a very different area than his previous job. He joined another organization and realized he missed working at the manufacturing firm; so, he contacted the head of operations saying that he would like to return to the firm and was willing to go back to his former job. Simultaneously, the operations executive had been considering the question of how to help the firm develop and move into the very expertise arena that the former employee had developed while he was away from the firm.

  The executive had decided that he had no option but to develop an internal candidate since finding an external candidate was deemed likely to be too difficult and costly. Unexpected information (the former employee with the desired expertise) calls. His reemergence thus solved a problem from an unexpected direction (Type 1 serendipity).

- **Evaluating—Flash and Systematic (E)**
  - *Flash Evaluation.* Initially and coupled with the early connecting of information bits is a flash evaluation, in which an individual does a quick, almost gut feel assessment of the unusual information. That initial gut feel then may lead the individual to become more alert to whether there are ways to connect the observed information to other already known information, both internal and external.

- *More Systematic Evaluation.* A more systematic evaluation would include an analytical assessment that leads toward a clearer confirmation of the information's possible value. That process of assessing unexpected information for potential value is affected by factors such as risk tolerance, level of uncertainty surrounding the information and evaluation, timing, and finding additional information that will help confirm or dispute the initial unexpected information. Depending upon how evaluators/decision makers take those factors into account when assessing unexpected information may lead to better or worse outcomes.

– **Creating Unintended Value (F)**

The ability to recognize and evaluate unexpected information is not valuable in itself. To be a competitive advantage, the assessment must yield value and action: the unintended value is thus a critical part of the process. Whether it results in solving an existing or not-yet-tackled problem, finding an opportunity, or generating new ideas for future use, the use of serendipity (as an ability) must be that individuals and the organization as a whole can leverage it to create value.

Although the four approaches discussed above are helpful in tackling the most pressing strategic challenges, they fell short in resolving the root cause of all strategic problems: how to turn an incomplete strategic game plan into comprehensive organizational energy. Or in other words "**How to make Future happen Today**". Fortunately, there are three different ways of thinking which when combined together can lead to the formulation of a compelling strategy which can help us solve the root cause of these strategic issues. These three lines of thinking are (Figure 3.8):

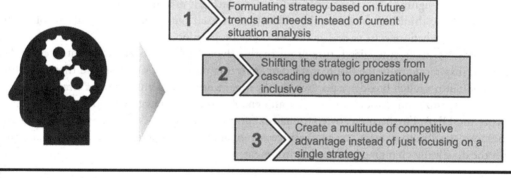

Figure 3.8 The three lines of strategic thinking

- **Formulating strategy based on future trends and needs instead of current situation analysis:** While developing the strategies, we need to shift our focus from what we know based on our current situation analysis to what we can anticipate about the future. This will allow us to thrive in a faster-changing environment.
- **Shifting the strategic process from cascading down to organizationally inclusive:** Although it may sound simple enough to adopt the design thinking future-in approach, in reality, it requires a lot more strategic capacity, which goes well beyond user inspiration to include strategic inspiration. In his book *The Innovators' Dilemma*, Clayton Christensen argued that larger organizations with a strong interest in ongoing business are ill-equipped and less prepared to capitalize on the disruption. This

makes them quite vulnerable to failure as disruptions are a way of life in today's world.

Hence, it is imperative for the organization to capitalize on the opportunities provided by disruptive technologies. Arming with the latest collaborative and social technologies allows people to contribute ever more increasingly toward the company's success. There are many practical benefits of organizational inclusiveness and the resulting outcomes including the capacity to create and activate strategy. The handovers that take place during the strategy formulation and implementation are eliminated, and the resulting strategies are more easily implemented because they are crafted with a strong stamp of organizational DNA.

- **Create a multitude of competitive advantages instead of just focusing on a single strategy:** Devising a strategy based on future aspirations is a good way to identify a coherent set of competitive advantages. But it is also necessary and useful to think about strategy in terms of an ongoing portfolio of strengths rather than a single winning formula. Rita Gunther McGrath in her book *The End of Competitive Advantage: How to Keep Your Strategy Moving as Fast as Your Business* argued that competitive advantage is no longer sustainable, and it requires learning to initiate, grow, and adapt to the circumstances. There is one crucial conclusion that can be drawn from the Gunther McGrath findings: If competitive advantages are transient, we need more of them in parallel, and we need to manage them as an ongoing portfolio of competitive advantages with interdependencies, so when one of the competitive advantages has run its course, there is another one to take its place.

  Maintaining an ongoing portfolio of competitive advantage brings more to the table and makes strategy easily manageable rather than the sequential approach of designing a grand strategy and then executing it in a multilayer cycle.

Each one of the thinking above is quite interesting in itself but when we combine all of them together that's when we start to realize the real value proposition.

In order to make strategies future-proof in this dynamic business environment, we should draw our inspiration from the future instead of analyzing the current situation and then take this inspiration into a much broader aspect within the organization. This enhances the strategy capacity of the organization through motivation and enables to align strategy with the organizational culture and DNA. Furthermore, by continually capturing the outcome of a portfolio of strategies, it becomes possible to manage the competitive advantage on an ongoing basis and keep it aligned with the drastically changing business environment.

References

1. Starbuck, W. (2006). Strategizing Realistically in Competitive Environments. Stern School of Management, NY University. http://pages.stern.nyu.edu/~wstarbuc/mob/strategizg.pdf
2. Paroutis, S., Heracleous, L., and Angwin, D. (2013). Practicing Strategy: Text and Cases. SAGE Publishing. https://uk.sagepub.com/en-gb/eur/practicing-strategy/book244734; https://warwick.ac.uk/fac/soc/wbs/subjects/sib/people/sotirios_profile/01_Paroutis_Ch-01.pdf
3. Maitlis, S., and Lawrence, T. B. (2003). Orchestral Maneuvers in the Dark: Understanding Failure in Organizational Strategizing. *Journal of Management Studies*, 40(1) January 2003, 0022-2380.
4. Vaara, E., and Whittington, R. (2012). Strategy-as-Practice: Taking Social Practices Seriously. *The Academy of Management Annals*, 6(1), 285–336.
5. Whittington, R. (2006). Completing the Practice Turn in Strategy Research. *Organization Studies*, 27(5), 613–634.

6. Marinos, G., and Rosni, N. (2017). The Role of Intuition in Executive Strategic Decision Making. Master's Program in Management Thesis, Lund University, School of Economics and Management. https://pdfs.semanticscholar.org/d669/4da0360ff9587fecfc20ddc28c00527f3904.pdf
7. Khatri, N., and Ng, H. A. (2000). The Role of Intuition in Strategic Decision Making. *Human Relations*, 53(1), 57–86.
8. Calabretta, G., Gemser, G., and Wijnberg, N. M. (2017).The Interplay between Intuition and Rationality in Strategic Decision Making: A Paradox Perspective. *Organization Studies*, 38(3–4), 365–401.
9. El Banna, S. (2006). Strategic Decision-Making: Process Perspective. *International Journal of Management Reviews*, 8(1), 1–20.
10. El Banna, S., and Child, J. (2007). The Influence of Decision, Environmental and Firm Characteristics on the Rationality of Strategic Decision-Making. *Journal of Management Studies*, 44. https://doi.org/10.1111/j.1467-6486.2006.00670.x
11. Papadakis, V., Lioukas, S., and Champers, D. (1998). Strategic Decision-Making Processes: The Role of Management and Context. *Strategic Management Journal*, 19, 115–147.
12. Mintzberg, H., Raisinghani, D., and Théorêt, A. (1976). The Structure of "Unstructured" Decision Processes. *Administrative Science Quarterly*, 21(2), 246–275. https://www.jstor.org/stable/2392045
13. Eisenhardt, K. M., and Bourgeois III, L. J. (1998). Politics of Strategic Decision Making in High-Velocity Environments: Toward a Midrange Theory. *The Academy of Management Journal*, 31(4), 737–770. https://www.jstor.org/stable/256337
14. Napier, N. K., and Voung, Q. H. (2013). Serendipity as a Strategic Advantage? In T. Wilkinson (Ed.), *Strategic Management in the 21st Century (Volume 1: The Operational Environment)* (pp. 175–199). Chapter: 8. Praeger. https://www.researchgate.net/publication/265207078_Serendipity_as_a_strategic_advantage
15. Roberts, R. M. (1991). *Serendipity: Accidental Discoveries in Science*. Wiley Science Editions.
16. Lawley, J., and Tompkins, P. (2011). Maximizing Serendipity: The Art of Recognizing and Fostering Unexpected Potential – A Systemic Approach to Change. Conference Proceedings: NLPtCA Annual Conference 2013. https://www.researchgate.net/publication/280624819_Maximising_Serendipity_The_art_of_recognising_and_fostering_unexpected_potential_-_A_Systemic_Approach_to_Change
17. https://ebrary.net/3639/management/tentative_framework
18. Gaglio, C. M., and Katz, J. A. (2001). The Psychological Basis of Opportunity Identification: Entrepreneurial Alertness. *Small Business Economics*, 16, 95–111.

WHAT DOES THE FUTURE HOLD?

3

Chapter 4

Society 5.0 and the Future Economies

4.1 The D.A.R.Q. Age

Organizations need to be more alert and agile when responding to future trends and uncertainties. This can be attained by establishing a robust system for **Strategic Anticipation**. Here we are not talking about traditional forecasting techniques or traditional market research studies that try to predict the future. What businesses need in the VUCA world is a dynamic capability that allows them to listen to fade signals of market shifts and systemic changes that will reshape our world, and then reflect this on their business operating model. One of the most important systemic shifts that will affect our world is the evolution of Society 5.0 driven by the digital economy.

Even though Information Society (known as Society 4.0) still appears to be novel in many parts of the world, there is already a new society on the horizon with the aim of creating a society where we can resolve various social challenges by incorporating the innovations of the Fourth Industrial Revolution (e.g., IoT, big data, artificial intelligence (AI), robotics, etc.) into every industry and social life. This coming era has been called the **D.A.R.Q.** age of:

- **D**istributed ledger (blockchain)
- **A**rtificial intelligence
- **R**eality that is virtual and augmented
- **Q**uantum computing

By doing so, the society of the future will be one in which new values and services are created continuously, making people's lives more conformable and sustainable. This new society is referred to as Society 5.0. The following section will provide an overview of this future-shaping evolution.

4.2 The Evolution of Society 5.0

We as a society have come a long way from being a hunter-gatherer society to an information society. The new society naturally builds on previous ones. First, there was the hunter-gatherer society (Society 1.0), where most or all the food was obtained by foraging. Then people learned to master

DOI: 10.4324/9781003280941-7

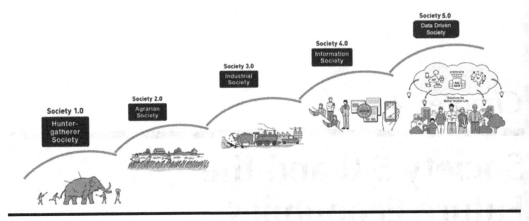

Figure 4.1   The evolution from Society 1.0 to Society 5.0

agriculture, and this led to settling down instead of wandering around in search of food (**Society 2.0**). The development of the steam machine meant the beginning of the Industrial Revolution (**Society 3.0**). Mass production provided many people with a higher quality of life. With the development of personal computers and the internet, the information society was entered (**Society 4.0**). Figure 4.1 shows this evolution.

Society 5.0 is defined as "**A human-centered society that balances economic advancement with the resolution of social problems by a system that highly integrates cyberspace and physical space**".

The "**cyber-physical system**", in which cyberspace and the physical space are tightly integrated, becomes a pervasive technological mode supporting Society 5.0. This is in line with the **O2O** (online to offline and offline to online) way that many people live today.

Social problems that must be solved in opposition (as a trade-off) to such economic development have become increasingly complex. Here, a variety of measures have become necessary such as the reduction of greenhouse gas (GHG) emissions, increased production and reduced loss of foodstuffs, mitigation of costs associated with the aging society, support of sustainable industrialization, redistribution of wealth, and correction of regional inequality, but achieving both economic development and solutions to social problems at the same time has proven to be difficult in the present social system.

In Society 5.0, the new value created through innovation will eliminate regional, age, gender, and language gaps and enable the provision of products and services finely tailored to diverse individual needs and latent needs. In this way, it will be possible to achieve a society that can both promote economic development and find solutions to social problems.

For many countries, Science, Technology, and Innovation (STI) policy has become a mainstream political agenda. For example, in Japan, the Ministry of Education, Culture, Sports, Science, and Technology (MEXT) and the Ministry of Economy, Trade, and Industry (METI) are leading the Society 5.0 progression agenda. They use their Society 5.0 plans to support the achievement of the United Nations 17 Sustainable Development Goals (SDGs) and have made it the theme for EXPO 2025, which will be held in Osaka.

Japan's transformation into Society 5.0 has been made possible by two factors:

- **Abundant accumulation of real data**: Based on health and medical data from a universal healthcare system and a wealth of operating data from numerous manufacturing facilities, Japan has an environment rich in real and usable raw data ready for use in the current market economy and industry.

■ **Technology cultivated from "monozukuri":** Japan's advanced technology cultivated from "monpzukuri" (Japan's excellence in the manufacturing of things) and years of basic research will work as advantages toward creating products using information technologies like big data and AI, which can be released into society.

Compared with Society 4.0, Society 5.0 is characterized by problem-solving and value creation, diversity, decentralization, resilience and sustainability, and environmental harmony [1].

■ **A society where value is created.** Societies 3.0 and 4.0 pursued scale and efficiency via mass production and consumption in order to guarantee material wealth to growing populations. In such societies, it was considered important to comply with traditional rules and plans and to follow a plan-do-check-act cycle. Goods and services were uniform and standardized processes were applied.

■ **A society in which everyone can exercise diverse abilities.** In Societies 3.0 and 4.0, people were required to accept uniform goods and services and live uniform lives in conformity with standardized processes. Society 5.0 will require people to have the imagination to identify diverse needs and challenges in society and turn them into real businesses. Diverse people will exercise diverse abilities to pursue diverse values in society. People will be able to live, learn, and work free from the suppression of individuality, such as discrimination by gender, race, nationality, etc., and alienation by ways of thinking and sense of values.

■ **A society in which anyone can get opportunities anytime, anywhere.** In Society 4.0, the concentration of wealth and information in limited hands increased disparity. In Society 5.0, wealth and information will be distributed and decentralized throughout society, and socioeconomic players will share roles horizontally. In spite of growing anxiety about disparity increased by digitalization, we will not leave disparity as it is in Society 5.0. We will make sure that wealth and information will not be concentrated so that people will be liberated from disparity, and anyone will be able to get opportunities to play a part anytime, anywhere. Data and benefits derived from them will be shared by diversified players, not concentrated on specific companies. Opportunities to study and work will also be guaranteed to children born in poverty or remote areas.

■ **A society in which everyone can live and pursue challenges with peace of mind.** In Society 4.0, vulnerabilities became apparent such as deterioration of infrastructure developed rapidly and in large quantities, serious damage caused by earthquakes and floods, deterioration of public security associated with increasing disparity, growing social anxiety about terrorism and other crises, and a major surge in damage caused by cyber-attacks. In Society 5.0, new, diversified, and decentralized social infrastructure will enhance resilience 10 and enable sustainable development. People will be liberated from anxiety and live in security. Specifically, resilience against terrorism and disasters in physical spaces and attacks in cyberspace will be enhanced, and safety nets for unemployment and poverty will be strengthened. A high level of medical care will be accessible regardless of location.

■ **A society where people can live in harmony with nature.** In Societies 3.0 and 4.0, humans depended on models with high environmental impact and mass consumption of resources. In Society 5.0, as data utilization increases energy efficiency and decentralization, there is the option of moving off-grid and not depending upon traditional energy networks. At the same time, water supply and waste management will also advance in both technological and systemic terms, enabling people to live sustainable lives in any region. This will create alternatives for living not only in big cities but also in a diversity of regions in harmony with nature. As the sharing economy develops and interest in traceability grows, food that is better for the environment and health will command a large premium, and food wastage will drop sharply.

This new Society 5.0 will have a drastic impact on the future of many sectors including **Healthcare**, **Mobility**, **Infrastructure**, and **Financial Sectors**. Below, we have outlined its impact on these areas as examples.

■ **Healthcare**. By connecting and sharing medical data that is now dispersed in various hospitals, effective medical treatment based on data would be provided. Remote medical care makes it possible that elderly people no longer have to visit hospitals frequently. In addition, people will also be able to monitor their health on the go, thus making it possible for people to extend their life expectancy.

■ **Mobility**. People in rural areas often find it difficult to visit markets and hospitals due to a lack of public transportation. However, autonomous vehicles will enable them to travel more easily and delivery drones will make it possible for them to receive whatever they need.

■ **Infrastructure**. By employing new technologies including information and communication technology (ICT), robots, and sensors for inspection and maintenance systems that require specialized skills, detection of places that need repair can be made at an early stage. By doing so, unexpected accidents will be minimized, and the time spent on construction work will be reduced, while at the same time safety and productivity will increase.

■ **Fintech**. Overseas remittance is burdensome because you have to spend time and pay bank fees. Blockchain technology will reduce time and cost while assuring safety in global business transactions.

Both government and businesses believe that Society 5.0 will continue to evolve as a result of undergoing a dramatic transition due to the emergence of four fundamental disruptive forces:

1) The age of urbanization
2) Accelerating technological changes
3) Aging population
4) Greater global connections

As compared to the Industrial Revolution (see Figure 4.2), the dramatic shift caused by these forces is happening 10 times faster and 300 times the scale or roughly 3,000 times the impact [2].

Figure 4.2   The impact of the four disruptive forces compared with the Industrial Revolution

Although we are aware of these disruptions taking place around us, most of us fail to comprehend and leverage the opportunities provided by these disruptive forces. Just as waves amplify each other by interacting with one another, so too these trends are gaining strength, magnitude, and influence as they interact with one another and feed upon one another. Together these four fundamental trends are producing monumental change on a massive scale.

1. The Age of Urbanization

The first trend is the shifting of the locus of economic activity and dynamism to emerging markets like China. These emerging markets are going through simultaneous industrial and urban revolutions that have been shifting the center of the world economy east and south at a speed never witnessed before. Recently, **95%** of the fortune global 500 companies such as Airbus, IBM, Nestle, Shell, and The Coca Cola Company, to name a few, were headquartered in developed economies. By 2025 when China will be home to more large companies than the United States or Europe, it will be not surprising to see nearly **50%** of the world's large companies defined as those with revenues of US$1 billion or more to be headquartered in emerging markets. Perhaps equally important is the locus of economic activity shifting within these markets. The global urban population has been rising at an astronomical rate of 65 million people during the past three decades. Nearly **50%** of the global GDP growth will come from small- and medium-sized cities that many western executives may not even have heard of before. As a matter of fact, these trends are already taking place. According to the Euromonitor International report, as of 2018, twenty megalopolises, a set of roughly adjacent city agglomerations forming a continuous urban region, have been identified across the world. Nine of these are in North America, seven in the Asia Pacific, three in Europe, and one in Latin America. These megalopolises are known for their sheer economic size and their massive contribution to the global economy. To put into perspective, they generate roughly US$30 trillion in GDP, which is equivalent to **35%** of the world's economic output, and house **9%** of the world's population. Due to their major influence on the direction of the global economy, the United States and China are quite rampant in their efforts to advance the role of megalopolises in national and regional growth policies. While the "America 2050" initiative gained attention back in 2005, China's megalopolis vision, part of China's 13th-year development plan, involves identifying 19 regional megapolises that will be responsible for driving national, regional, and provincial growth. The success of these megalopolises offers several key benefits including thick labor markets, scale economies, economic spillovers, and smaller cities (as illustrated in Figure 4.3) and hence act as investment pools.

THICK LABOR MARKETS	SCALE ECONOMIES	ECONOMIC SPILL-OVERS	SMALLER CITIES
A large and abundant labor force that is equipped with the relevant skills to seek employment in various industries. Governments can use this as a tool to diversify and reduce overreliance on a single industry	The sharing of facilities, infrastructure and other non-tradable inputs can provide lower costs and improve profitability. With transport infrastructure in consumer and freight mobility.	The provision of high-level transport infrastructure can provide spill-overs to drive other industries. For example, the opening of cargo rail can also help to improve commuter links and tourism	Fast and efficient transport, allows Megalopolises to help proliferate income and economic growth to inhabitants of smaller cities. This can reduce regional income inequalities

Figure 4.3   The benefits of megalopolis success

2. **Accelerating Technological Change**

The second trend is the rapid expansion in scope, scale, and the economic impact of technology. Technology from the very beginning has been a major force in overturning the status quo, from printing presses to steam engines and the internet. However, the only difference now is the pervasiveness of technology in our lives and the progression speed. As shown in Figure 4.4, it took almost four decades for the radio to attract 50 million listeners, but Facebook managed to attract 50 million users in 2 years, and it took 1.5 years for Instagram to attract 50 million users [3].

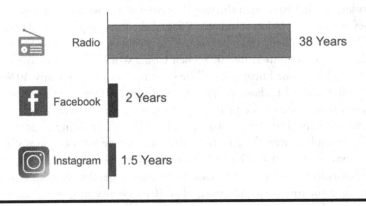

Figure 4.4   Accelerating technological change

China's mobile text- and voice-messaging service WeChat has 1.25 monthly billion users [4], almost three times the entire population of the United States. Accelerated adoption invites accelerated innovation. In 2009, two years after the iPhone's launch, developers had created around 150,000 applications. By 2021, this number had hit 3.74 million [5], and users had downloaded more than 130 billion total apps on the apple app store [6], almost 20 for every person on the planet. As fast as innovation has multiplied and spread in recent years, it is poised to change and grow at an exponential speed beyond the power of human intuition to anticipate.

Speaking of computing power, the continual cramming of more silicon transistors onto a chip, known as Moore's Law, has been the feedstock of exuberant innovation in computing for decades. Moore's prediction of doubling the number of transistors on a chip every two years has been kept alive so far, with Intel leading the charge. The impact of processing power made by Moore's law and connectivity is multiplied by the concomitant data revolution, which places unprecedented amounts of information in the hands of consumers and businesses alike, and the proliferation of technology-enabled business models from online retail platforms like Alibaba to car-hailing apps like Uber. Thanks to these mutually amplifying forces, more and more people are enjoying a golden age of gadgetry, instant communication, and apparently boundless information. Technology offers the promise of economic progress for billions in emerging economies at a speed that would have been unimaginable without the mobile internet. Technology allows businesses such as WhatsApp to start and gain scale with stunning speed while using little capital. Entrepreneurs and startups now frequently enjoy advantages over large, established businesses. The furious pace of technological adoption and innovation is shortening the life cycle of companies and forcing executives to make decisions and commit resources much more quickly.

3. **Aging Population**

The human population is getting older. Fertility is falling, and the world's population is graying dramatically. While aging has been evident in developed economies for some time—Russia and Japan have seen their populations decline over the past few years—the demographic deficit is now spreading to China and soon will reach Latin America [7], as shown in Figure 4.5.

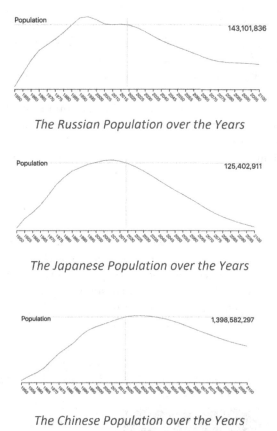

The Russian Population over the Years

The Japanese Population over the Years

The Chinese Population over the Years

Figure 4.5   The Russian, Japanese, and Chinese population change from 1950 to 2100

For the first time in human history, aging could mean that the planet's population will plateau in most of the world. Thirty years ago, only a small share of the global population lived in the few countries with fertility rates substantially below those needed to replace each generation—2.1 children per woman; but by 2013, about 60% of the world's population lived in countries with fertility rates below the replacement rate. This is a sea change. The European Commission expects that by 2060, Germany's population will shrink by one-fifth, and the number of people of working age will fall from 54 million in 2010 to 36 million in 2060, a level that is forecast to be less than France's.

China's labor force peaked in 2012 due to income-driven demographic trends. In Thailand, the fertility rate has fallen from 5 in the 1970s to 1.4 today. A smaller workforce will place a greater onus on productivity for driving growth and may cause us to rethink the economy's potential. Caring for large numbers of elderly people will put severe pressure on government finances.

4. **Greater Global Connections: Trade, People, Finance, and Data**

The final disruptive force is the degree to which the world is much more connected through trade and through movements in the capital, people, and information (data and communication)—what we call "**flows**". Trade and finance have long been part of the globalization story but, in recent decades, there's been a significant shift. Instead of a series of lines connecting major trading hubs in Europe and North America, the global trading system has expanded into a complex, intricate, sprawling web. Asia is becoming the world's largest trading region. "South–South" flows between emerging markets have doubled their share of global trade over the past decade. The volume of trade between China and Africa rose from US$9 billion in 2000 to US$211 billion in 2012. Global capital flows expanded 25 times between 1980 and 2007. More than 1 billion people crossed borders in 2009, over five times the number in 1980. These three types of connections all paused during the global recession of 2008 and have recovered only slowly since. But the links forged by technology have marched on uninterrupted and with increasing speed, ushering in a dynamic new phase of globalization, creating unmatched opportunities, and fomenting unexpected volatility.

In summary, transitioning from Society 4.0 to Society 5.0 will create a new paradigm that will change societies in five dimensions (see Figure 4.6) [8]:

1. Move from Economies of scale to liberation from focus on efficiency only to achieve problem-solving and value creation
2. Move from Uniformity to liberation from suppression of individuality to reach diversity
3. Move from concentration to liberation from disparity to reach decentralization
4. Move from vulnerability to liberation from anxiety to achieve resilience
5. Move from high environmental impact mass consumption of resources to liberation from resources and environmental constraints to achieve sustainability

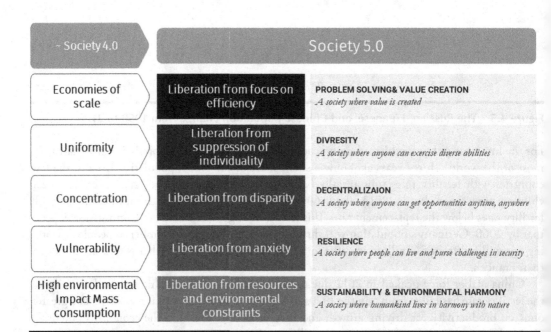

Figure 4.6 The impact of transitioning from Society 4.0 to Society 5.0 [8]

4.3 The Digital Economy

The foundation for Society 5.0 is the rapid evolution of the digital economy. Almost all organizations are developing **Digital Transformation Strategies,** but most of them fail to realize the expected benefits because those strategies are developed without the proper integration into the bigger picture of Society 5.0 developments and mega forces outlined in the previous section. Hence, they suffer from a myopic perspective that can be addressed only when we understand the broader perspective of the digital economy and its implication for the development of five other future economies (experience, sharing, GIG, circular, and purpose).

The digital economy is changing the world view on value creation. It will not only transform the way we convert our resources into economic value-added outcomes but also redefine our views on the available resources and how to utilize them to address existing economic and social challenges. Digital transformation has vast effects on society at many levels. It allows the automation of business operations resulting in operational efficiencies, such as reduction of transaction costs, which ultimately impacts productivity. Furthermore, it offers new business opportunities, thus affecting employment and entrepreneurship. It also enhances the provision of public services, such as health and education, and improves the interaction between citizens and their governments. In addition, digital transformation affects human relationships and individual behavior, through facilitating communication and social inclusion [9]. Thus, enhancing digitization and creating digital markets can result in considerable economic and social benefits to societies and communities, through its potential to increase productivity, accelerate growth, facilitate job creation, and enhance the quality of life for society in general.

Information technologies have been a significant contributor to the growth of developed economies over the past decade. For example, in 2011, regardless of the poor global economic situation, digitization provided increased world economic output by about US$193 billion and created 6 million jobs worldwide [10]. Digitization is 4.7 times more powerful than the average impact of broadband rollout in boosting economic growth, which is an average of 0.16% of per capita GDP. The economic effect of digitization is also accelerating as the degree of countries' digitization progresses.

For instance, the digital economy in the Asia Pacific reached US$1.16 trillion in 2021, accounting for 60% of the GDP, up from about 6% from 2017, an IDC study has found (see Figure 4.7).

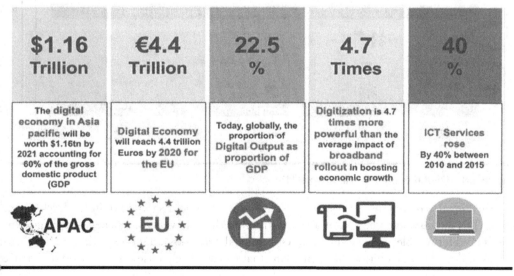

Figure 4.7   The EU and APAC digital economy

Commissioned by software giant Microsoft, the study, which polled 1,560 business decision makers across 15 Asia Pacific Accreditation Cooperation (APAC) economies, also found that digital products and services enabled by mobility, cloud, the Internet of Things (IoT), and AI would grow the region's GDP by 0.8% each year [11]. Similarly, Europe Digital Single Market creates opportunities for new startups and allows existing companies to reach a market of over 500 million people. Completing a Digital Single Market will contribute **US$465 billion** (EUR 415 billion) per year to Europe's economy, create jobs, and transform its public services [12].

4.3.1 Digital Economy Framework

I developed the "Digital Economy Framework" as part of a study for the League of Arab Nations on the potential and impact of the digital economy on the future of the Arab World. It is divided into four main components: First, foundations and pillars that are required to activate the process of digital transformation and ensure its effectiveness; second, catalysts/technologies that support the success of the digitization process; third, the sectoral applications of the developed digital tools/models. Their sustainability helps in reaching the required social and economic impact, which is the fourth component of this framework [13].

Figure 4.8 shows the components of the framework and how they enable and influence each other to achieve the vision of **transforming the Arab world into a digitally enabled economy and advancing the region toward a sustainable, inclusive, and secure digital future to enable an innovative, empowered, and integrated Arab community.**

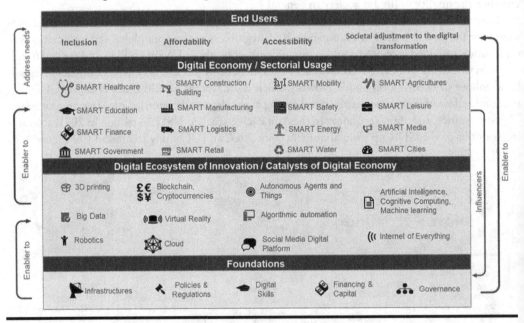

Figure 4.8   Digital economy framework [13]

The digital economy requires a suitable environment to flourish and attain its development goals. This environment consists of an infrastructure that individuals, businesses, and governments need for reliable and widespread access to digital networks and services. The aim is to benefit from digital opportunities and regulations that create a lively business climate and enhance firms' competence and innovation in digital technologies and the hyper-connected world. Skills are also created that allow workers, entrepreneurs, and public servants to effectively benefit from digital opportunities, in addition to institutions that are accountable to citizens who are empowered through the efficient use of technology.

Digital technologies add two further dimensions to the foundations of economic development. First, they raise the opportunity cost of not undertaking the necessary reforms. Second, they are perceived as an enabler, and perhaps an accelerator, toward development by raising the quality of services.

4.3.1.1 Foundations

- **Digital infrastructure**: This includes efficient, reliable, and widely accessible broadband communication networks and services, data, software, and hardware. Individuals, businesses, and governments need reliable and widespread access to digital networks and services to benefit from digital opportunities. This requires adequate investment in digital infrastructures and competition in the provision of high-speed networks and services. There is also the need for organizational change, including investments in data and other knowledge-based capital, to realize the full potential of the digital transformation.
- **Policies and regulations**: This is a mandatory pillar that supports the development of the digital economy. It includes updates and creates new policy frameworks to promote investment, competition, and innovation. It also protects consumer interests and expectations by using new digital solutions.
- **Digital skills**: Access to digital networks provides the technical foundation for the digital transformation of the economy and society but does not by itself necessarily guarantee effective use. This effective use of digital technologies requires a wide range of skills, including ICT specialist skills, generic ICT skills, **STEM** (Science, Technology, Engineering, and Math) + **IE** (Innovation and Entrepreneurship), as well as complementary skills, such as information processing, self-direction, problem-solving, and communications These skills interact with the available technology allowing routine tasks to be automated. Workers with the right abilities leverage technology to become more productive. Education systems should have a role in shaping these skills in the early stages. Notably, the pace of change is quick, and the types of skills in demand change rapidly. Thus, workers need to upgrade their skills frequently throughout their careers. On the other hand, technology can play a role in shaping three types of skills needed in the modern economy, which include (a) cognitive and foundational skills (e.g., literacy, numeracy, and higher-order cognitive skills), (b) social and behavioral skills, and (c) technical and technological skills developed through postsecondary schooling or training or acquired on the job, as well as skills related to specific occupations (for example, engineer, IT specialist).
- **Financing and capital**: For digital transformation to occur, budgets need to be assigned based on outcome measurement, performance-based budgeting, or results-based budgeting. Thus, governments and businesses need to work on assigning the appropriate budgets to apply digital technologies and reap their gains.

■ **Governance**: There are two types of necessary institutions in the process of digital transformation:
  – **Formal institutions**, which include laws, rules, and regulations, that facilitate technology penetration and the development of business activities. This is through regulations that ensure easy entry and exit of firms and facilitate competition to lower prices and increase coverage and quality, besides an open trade regime that exposes companies to foreign competition and investment. Digitization-ready legislations, similar to the Danish approach, further facilitate and do not hinder innovation and use of technology but rather protect rights, privacy, etc. Technology interacts with such rules to create new ideas, such as new methods of producing goods and services. Technology is traded across markets and borders, while most rules are established locally. When it encounters rules that do not match, technology fails to deliver the expected benefits. Barriers to competition, for example, lessen the need of firms to reach for the technological frontier and sometimes prevent new businesses with new technologies and lower prices from entering the market and competing with existing firms.
  – **Informal Institutions**, which are socially shared rules, usually unwritten, that are created, communicated, and enforced outside the official channels. In this context, they may include the level of innovation and conditions that allow the digital transformation level of trust in the digital economy, as well as digital security and awareness to flourish

4.3.1.2 Technologies and Digital Concepts as Catalysts of Digital Economy

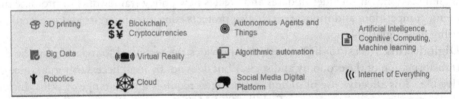

The digital economy is based on a set of emerging technologies that disrupt the traditional business model and introduce new innovative alternatives. These emerging innovations and digital concepts include distributed ledger technologies/blockchain, big data analytics, Internet of Things, cloud computing, artificial intelligence, biometric technologies, and augmented/virtual reality. These digital technologies act as a catalyst and impact the value creation in the delivery of experience, sharing, GIG, circular, and purpose economies.

4.3.1.3 End Users

Inclusion	Affordability	Accessibility	Societal adjustment to the digital transformation

■ **Inclusion**: By reducing the cost of acquiring information, making more information transparently available, providing secure systems, and encouraging legal frameworks, digital technologies can make new transactions possible and people could easily access services that previously were out of reach. Digital and financial inclusion can be promoted by improving digital literacy.

■ **Affordability**: Governments and businesses need to provide digital goods and services at affordable prices to citizens.

■ **Accessibility**: Making digital technologies universally accessible should be a global priority. Individuals, businesses (including small- and medium-sized enterprises (SMEs)), and governments need reliable and widespread access to digital networks and services to benefit from digital opportunities. Through inclusion, efficiency, and innovation, access provides opportunities that were previously unreachable by the poor and disadvantaged.

■ **Societal adjustment to the digital transformation**: Society is quite affected by the digital transformation in several ways. On the one hand, automation may reduce employment in some occupations while job platforms may increase nonstandard jobs i.e., short-term, part-time, or low-paid jobs, and widen the gender wage gap. On the other hand, e-services, particularly e-health, may help society to address the challenges of the aging population and increasing social expenditures.

4.4 Future Economies

The evolution of the digital economy created a set of new five economies that uses digital as its backbone and are creating new types of value for companies, individuals, and societies at large. This does not mean that digital is the only enabler for those future economies, but it sure accelerates the development of those new ways of living. The following section will review the following five future economies that must be reviewed and assessed for their implications on the strategy of any firm in the future. They include:

1. The experience economy
2. The sharing economy
3. The GIG economy
4. The circular economy
5. The purpose economy

Of course, those economies are not mutually exclusive. An organization can incorporate in their strategy more than one of those economies to build their future Target Operating Model (TOM).

4.4.1 The Experience Economy

In recent years, faced with the choice of buying a trendy designer jacket or a shiny new appliance or attending a show, consumers are increasingly opting for the show, or, in a broad sense, they prefer experiences with their friends and family. As a matter of fact, in the past few years, personal consumption expenditure on experience-related services—such as attending spectator events, visiting amusement parks, dining at the restaurant, and traveling—have achieved monumental growth 1.5 times (6.3% versus 3.7%) faster than the overall personal consumption spending and nearly 4 times (6.3% versus 1.6%) faster than expenditure on goods [14] (Figure 4.9) ... *Welcome to the emerging experience economy!!*

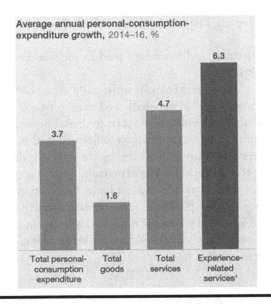

Figure 4.9   Expenditure growth of experience-related services [15]

Some of the companies were quick to identify this monumental expenditure growth in experience-related services. This led to them creating superior customer experiences and lasting impressions in the minds of the consumers. Some of the examples include preexistence leading sectors and companies as shown in Figure 4.10.

Figure 4.10   Examples of customer experience leading companies

Traditionally, economists have typically associated experiences with services, but experiences are a distinct economic offering different from services, as services are different from goods. Today's economic offering based on experience is easily identifiable because consumers unquestionably desire experiences, and businesses are responding by explicitly designing and promoting them. As services like goods become increasingly commoditized, experiences have emerged as the next step in what we call the *progression of economic value*. This has resulted in leading companies as to whether they sell their products or services to consumers or businesses to create unprecedented competitive advantage by offering superior customer experiences.

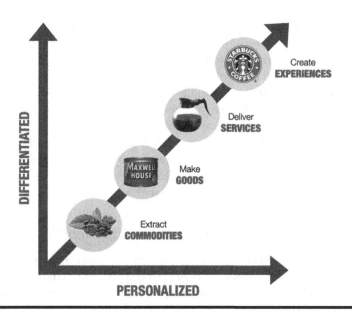

Figure 4.11   Progression of economic value from commodities to experiences

In fact, the experience economy has fundamentally changed how companies go to market, influence their buyers and engage people throughout the customer journey. Experience is the king; consumers' loyalty and dollars go to experiences and not products. Figure 4.11 demonstrates how value is maximized when we create experiences based on personalization and differentiation. This is known as the progression of economic value from commodities to experiences.

4.4.1.1 Experience Is King

Consumers of all ages are opting for experiences, with millennials leading the charge. A McKinsey consumer survey found that the average millennial outspends the average Gen Xer and baby boomer on entertainment- and fitness-related memberships. The fact that millennials are now the largest spending cohort, and that the cohort of higher-income consumers is growing as well, creates greater confidence in the sustainability of the trend. To understand the underlying drivers of this shift in consumer spending behavior, we see three key factors, which are particularly applicable to millennials but hold true among older consumer cohorts too: a more holistic perspective on what leads to happiness, the growing importance of social media, and an increasing fear of missing out. They are unlikely to dissipate, which suggests that this shift in spending behavior will stick.

A stronger link to happiness. Shared experiences with friends and family have a deeper psychological link to long-term intrinsic happiness than buying products does. A recent study conducted at Cornell University found that consumers' evaluations of their material goods went down from the time of the initial purchase to the present, but their evaluations of their experiences tended to go up, indicative of hedonic adaptation to the possessions but something quite different for their experiences.

The research suggested three potential drivers of this behavior: experiences are more open to positive reinterpretation, they tend to become more meaningful parts of one's identity, and they do more to foster social relationships.

A quest for "likes". Social media also appears to have helped accelerate the growing demand for experiences. Facebook and Instagram, like and creative snaps, are now the ultimate social currency for millions of Americans, especially millennials, and the quest for likes requires a constant stream of new shareable content in the form of stories and pictures. Experiences play into this thirst for content because they are more likely to lead to such stories and pictures than the purchase of a new product would be. Even experiences that don't turn out as expected—say, a long flight delay or a rainy football game—eventually turn into shareable stories

Fear of missing out (FOMO). Keeping up with the Joneses used to be about wanting to own the same expensive products your friends or neighbors did. But with more consumers opting for experiences—whether that means seeing the musical Hamilton or visiting Hanoi—and sharing their stories and pictures online, people feel peer pressure to join in or keep up. This anxiety is so deeply embedded in the social fiber of millennials that they have given it a nickname: FOMO. The term was even added to the Oxford English Dictionary back in 2013

4.4.1.2 How to Deliver Exceptional Customer Experience?

The customer experiences are made up of many touchpoints, interactions, and exposures that consumer has with a brand—its product, service, employees, and market message across multiple channels—over the duration of the relationship. However, in order to improve and deliver a memorable customer experience for optimal business outcomes, companies need to move from touchpoints to journeys. Figure 4.12 shows a three-step approach to improve customer experience by moving from touchpoints to journeys.

OBSERVE
Customer journeys consist of a progression of **touchpoints** that together add up to the experience customers get when they interact with companies. **Seeing the world as their customers** do helps leading companies better organize and mobilize their employees around customer needs.

SHAPE
Designing the customer experience requires re-shaping interactions into different sequences and, though the effort may start small, soon entails **digitizing processes, reorienting company cultures**, and nimbly refining new approaches in the field.

PERFORM
Rewiring a company to provide leading customer experiences is a journey, often taking **two to four years** and requiring high engagement from company leaders and frontline workers alike.

Figure 4.12   Steps to deliver exceptional customer experience

1. **Observe: Understand the interaction through the customers' eyes**

    Technology has handed customers unprecedented power to dictate the rules in purchasing goods and services. Three-quarters of them, research finds, expect "now" service within five minutes of making contact online. A similar share want a simple experience, use comparison apps when they shop, and put as much trust in online reviews as in personal recommendations. Increasingly, customers expect from all players the same kind of **immediacy, personalization**, and **convenience** that they receive from leading practitioners such as Google and Amazon.

2. **Shape: Redesign the business from the customer back**

    Customer-experience leaders start with a differentiating purpose and focus on improving the most important customer journey first—whether it be opening a bank account, returning a pair of shoes, installing cable television, or even updating address and account information. Then they improve the steps that make up that journey. To manage expectations, they design supporting processes with customer psychology in mind. They transform their digital profile to remove pain points in interactions and to set in motion the culture of continuous innovation needed to make more fundamental organizational transformations.

3. **Perform: Align the organization to deliver against tangible outcomes**

    As the customer experience becomes a bigger focus of the corporate strategy, more and more executives will face the decision to commit their organizations to a broad customer experience transformation. The immediate challenge will be how to structure the organization and rollout, as well as figuring out where and how to get started. Applying sophisticated measurement to what your customers are saying, empowering frontline employees to deliver against your customer vision, and a customer-centric governance structure form the foundation. Securing early economic wins will deliver value and momentum for continuous innovation.

4.4.2 The Sharing Economy

Around the world, a new wave of peer-to-peer access-driven businesses is shaking up established businesses. Whether borrowing goods, renting homes, or using entertainment content in exchange for money, consumers are showing greater interest and appetite for sharing-based economies. According to the survey, 44% of US consumers are familiar with the sharing economy [15]. Sharing economies has allowed individuals and groups to make money from underused assets. For instance, a car owner may allow someone to rent his vehicle while he is not using it; similarly, an apartment owner may rent out his apartment while he is on vacation. Some examples of sharing-economy companies are given in Figure 4.13.

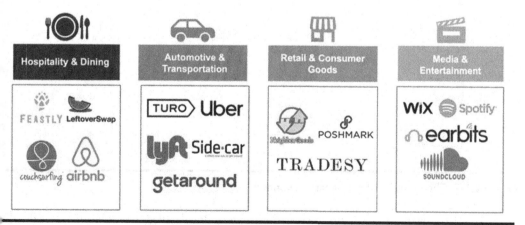

Figure 4.13 Examples of the sharing-economy companies

Figure 4.14 shows a snapshot of the sharing economy.

Figure 4.14   Snapshot of the sharing economy

Trust, convenience, and sense of community are the three main factors influencing the adoption of the sharing economy. Courtesy of consumers who are willing to try mobile apps have not only lowered the barriers to entry but also made it easier to build and scale brands. In addition, US adults familiar with the sharing economy associate several benefits with it: **affordability, convenience, efficiency,** and **being environment-friendly,** to name a few. Figure 4.15 provides the results of a survey that indicates the consensus (63% to 89% agreement) among consumers about the sharing-economy benefits.

Figure 4.15   The benefits of the sharing economy

An inspiring example is a platform created in 2014 in Brazil called *Tem Açúcar?* It was developed to facilitate the sharing of consumer needs and stimulate collaboration between people. The platform wants to make it easy to share things between neighbors. They seek to encourage collaboration, camaraderie, and a sense of community. After the pandemic, the uptime in the app has more than doubled.

On the business front, the impact created by this emergent ecosystem of sharing economy is upending mature business models across the globe, which business executives need to take into consideration while making future strategic moves. To put into perspective the scale of disruption caused by the sharing economy, Airbnb averages 425,000 guests per night, which is 22% more than Hilton worldwide. Uber, hailed as an archetypal disruptive business, has certainly played havoc with the taxi industry in 600 cities worldwide by tearing up the rule book [16]. Recent projections show that travel, car sharing, finance, staffing, music, and video streaming are key sharing sectors, generating global revenues of US$334 billion by 2025. These figures have made investors increasingly intrigued by the potential of the sharing economy as it continues to upend how we consume goods and how we work to afford them.

At the heart of this disruptive change lies the internet and, with it, the rise of social media, analytics, and cloud computing. Our access to information has never been greater or more tailored to specific needs. Transactions are shifting more and more to real time by way of mobile and the cloud, and social is playing a huge role in driving increased trust in commerce. Tech pioneers like Amazon, eBay, Google, Apple, and PayPal laid the foundation. For sellers with goods to unload, Amazon and eBay conjure up buyers. GPS-enabled smartphones point us toward the nearest provider, and online payment systems like PayPal cement the transaction.

As these companies softened the risks of peer-to-peer transactions, the economic downturn left many consumers rethinking the necessity of possessions. A survey by BAV Consulting showed that 66% of consumers (and 77% of millennials) preferred a pared-down lifestyle with fewer possessions. And while the economy has rebounded, many recession-fueled values have stuck. Today, only one in two consumers agree with the statement that "owning things is a good way to show my status in society". Four in five consumers agree that there are sometimes real advantages to renting over owning, and adults ages 18 to 24 are nearly twice as likely as those ages 25 and older to say that access is the new ownership. Happiness studies show that experiences increase contentment far more than purchases do, and young people's intrinsic understanding of this is fueling an experience economy.

4.4.2.1 Putting the Sharing Economy in Action

The sharing economy is too big an opportunity to miss while being too big a risk not to mitigate. Therefore, it is increasingly important for businesses to recognize these opportunities and disruption risks in order to prevail and be effective in the sharing economy. It may sound scary, but if the business can't figure out how to disrupt itself, then someone else will do it. Below we have stated some key recommendations for the business to thrive in this increasingly unpredictable sharing-economy business environment (see Figure 4.16).

Create marketplace: Organizations need to assess the potential for consumers to band together in a peer network that can undermine their value proposition. These networks are most likely to emerge in categories where products and services are widely distributed, involve high fixed costs but low marginal costs, and are often underutilized. The automotive and hospitality sectors were among the first to see peer networks, but this network effect is equally viable in industries that hold similar characteristics. High-end retail and utilities are susceptible to this model—in the communications sector, Fon already enables Wi-Fi customers to share their connection with others in return for free access to other Fon hotspots around the world.

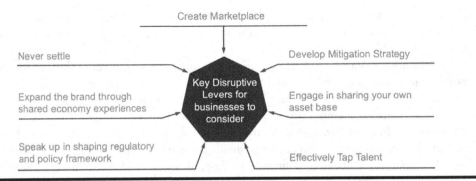

Figure 4.16   Key levers for success in the sharing economy

Develop mitigation strategy: Whether acquiring a new entrant, partnering, or investing in them, companies can mitigate the risk of a sharing-economy insurgency and even capitalize on sharing-economy revenue to bolster their business. For instance, a manufacturer of high-end hardware goods could partner with a sharing-economy network to circulate its wares, capitalizing on the growing appetite for higher quality, more durable goods that offer greater resale or longevity to buyers. This builds on the current practice of providing a network of contractors, extending it to include shared economy providers who can supply their tools or labor.

Engage in sharing your own asset base: The sharing economy demands a sharing organization, one that monetizes spare capacity and improves business outcomes through sharing underutilized assets (tangible and intangible), which can be more effectively shared across entities, both inside and outside the organization. Today on average manufacturing facilities operate at 20% below capacity, and half of the desks in an average office go unused. All of these are instances where a sharing economy can lead toward maximum efficiency. Marriott, for instance, has partnered with the online platform LiquidSpace to convert empty conference rooms into rentable workspaces. The result is not just a new revenue stream but also a way to increase exposure to Marriott properties. Pharmaceutical giant Merck recently signed an agreement to share Medimmune's manufacturing facility, providing long-term utilization of excess capacity for Medimmune while giving Merck flexible access to manufacturing facilities as needed. Another opportunity is to facilitate the sharing of intangible assets. That means intellectual property, brainpower, and brand—which collectively make up around 80% of a global corporation's value. In the United States, the top five patent filers—IBM, Samsung, Canon, Sony, and Microsoft—collectively filed more than 21,000 in 2013 alone, but because of high investment costs, only a fraction of these resulted in products brought to market. By contrast, General Electric spearheaded a partnership with Quirky, an online inventor community. The US$30 million deal gave Quirky's inventors open access to GE's patents and technology, resulting in joint-venture products such as a smartphone-controlled window air conditioner, a propane tank gauge with fuel sensors, and a home monitor that can be set to track motion, sound, and light.

Effectively tap talent: One of the more controversial aspects of the sharing economy is the impact it has on the labor force and the perceived shift toward contract-based employment that trumpets agency over regulation. For some, this is regarded as a benefit, enabling workers to earn wages on their own time and terms. For others, it heralds an era of depressed earnings and greater reliance on welfare and other government subsidies; 78% of adults said they expected that in 30 years, working multiple jobs would be the new normal for wage earners. Companies need to be mindful of this tension and adapt their employment strategy accordingly. For starters, that means offering wages and benefits that attract good, reliable talent and project the values that today's consumers seek.

Speak up in shaping regulatory and policy frameworks: Regulatory flashpoints are everywhere, and they are the most immediate impediment to sharing-economy growth—a situation that's relevant to both disruptors and more mature players. In order for sharing-economy businesses to thrive, regulations need to be solidified that will make sharing-economy business models to be fully legitimized both by law and in the minds and hearts of the consumers. This will motivate the companies across all the sectors to get ahead in carving out a place in the conversation with policymakers. In this setting, companies can credibly measure the economic, fiscal, social, and environmental impact of the sharing model in the communities in which they operate. There is no question that the regulatory and tax framework needs to be fit for the new age. The right balance of solutions needs to be built from the bottom-up, where local authorities can quickly trial and experiment with new models. Not surprisingly, this is more easily done when both sides work together. For instance, Airbnb worked with Amsterdam's local council to pass an "Airbnb-friendly law" in February 2014, which permits residents to rent out their homes for up to 60 days a year, provided that the owner pays the relevant taxes.

Expand the brand through shared economy experiences: By design, the sharing economy disrupts the balance of the marketing mix for nearly every industry it touches. Price points are upended. Product has a new set of metrics—of which quality gets a new premium, and standardization and consistency can matter more or less, depending on the market. The place is reconsidered as new points of access emerge. And the very nature of promotion has shifted, with "sharing" engendering new means of trial and exposure.

Brand is still very relevant today—but companies need to reassess their brand pillars in light of these new marketplaces, new business models, and new consumer values. Today's fast-paced lifestyles leave little time to maintain expensive assets. One in two consumers agrees that owning things is a good way to reflect status in society. As a result, forward-looking companies must reexamine what creates brand value and position themselves accordingly in the marketplace.

Never settle: The sharing economy has proved that business models should not be taken for granted in this fast-changing world and should therefore be subject to continuous evolution. Today's disruptors can easily be disrupted tomorrow. The ride-sharing model could be obsolete when self-driving cars materialize—or these companies could adapt by purchasing their own fleet of self-driving cars, removing the cost center of today's drivers.

To stay nimble, companies need to continuously examine ways to bundle and unbundle the value exchange for maximum consumer benefit and maximum competitive advantage. They will need to capitalize on opportunities for expansion, assessing ways in which new models can be leveraged to reach untapped consumers. They will need to explore gaps in revenue management, finding cost efficiencies and opportunities to free up capital that can be more effectively applied in other capacities.

4.4.3 *The GIG Economy*

While the idea of pooled resources is by no means a peculiar concept, the onset of digital networks as means to connect freelancers with customers is a rapidly evolving phenomenon. "GIG economy", often used synonymously or in relation to "sharing economy" or "freelance economy", refers to the digital platforms that allow independent freelancers to connect with individuals or businesses for short-term services or asset sharing. The key component behind the understanding between freelancers and the business is the involvement of online or digital platforms. SIA

(Staffing Industry Analysts)—a consulting firm specialized in staffing solutions—propose that the GIG economy is fueled by the new Human Cloud (online GIG economy platforms). They define both B2B and B2C Human Clouds. They forecast the total value of the GIG economy (both online and offline components) to reach US$3.7 trillion. This includes independent contractors, temporary agency workers, temporary workers sourced directly by companies, SOW consultants, and human cloud workers [17].

According to Mastercard & Kaiser Associates, the size of the online-driven GIG economy platforms was approximately US$204 billion in annual gross volume in 2018. Of these US$204 billion, two-thirds of it is distributed among the millions of freelancers, while the remaining is collected as a commission by digital platforms or distributed to third parties involved in the GIG ecosystem [18].

Since the majority of the gross volume is generated from platforms that are relatively new to the market, the outlook for continued industry expansion is positive. GIG platforms are projected to continue extending their operations regionally and offer a greater diversity of services to customers, thus enabling the industry to expand and mature. The GIG platforms can be segmented into one of four sectors based on the type of services they provide their customers. Figure 4.17 shows the four sectors' description, their subsectors, and example platforms.

Sector	Description	Sub-Sectors Included	Example Platforms
Asset-Sharing Services	Digital platforms that facilitate short-term P2P rentals of one owner's (or "freelancer") property to another individual	Home-sharing, car-sharing, boat-sharing, parking space-sharing, P2P equipment sharing	HomeAway, airbnb, TURO
Transportation-Based Services	Digital platforms that require a freelance driver to complete the requested transport service	Ride-sharing, carpooling, restaurant delivery, and goods delivery	BlaBlaCar, Careem, DOORDASH, Uber
Professional Services	Digital platforms that connect freelancers directly with businesses to complete projects	Business work, microwork, design, tech/coding, writing/translation, administrative	Upwork, CATALANT, guru
Handmade Goods, Household & Miscellaneous Services (HGHM)	Digital platforms for freelancers to sell homemade crafts or offer on-demand services for household-related tasks	Home-services, babysitting, handmade crafts, tutoring, pet services, and misc. (DJ, events, etc.)	Care.com, Airtasker, Etsy

Figure 4.17   GIG economy sectors [18]

4.4.3.1 GIG Economy Growth Drivers

With the online GIG economy, gross volume is projected to grow to US$455 billion by the year 2023, a figure that represents a 17% CAGR from 2018 to 2023. With a projected gross volume growth of approximately 123% over five years, there are virtually a number of societal, environmental, and technological trends that are a major driving force behind the expansion of the GIG economy and will continue to spur industry development in the future. Figure 4.18 shows the projected gross volume of the GIG economy between 2018 and 2023 in billion US$ [18].

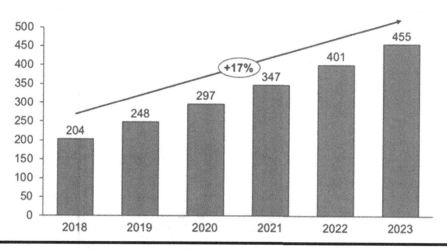

Figure 4.18 Projected gross volume growth of the GIG economy (billions US$)

The increasing supply of GIG economy freelancers offering their services to GIG platforms is motivated by the following factors:

- **Evolving social attitudes about P2P (peer-to-peer) sharing** of personal items are now more accepting and even encouraging of sharing underutilized assets for profit
- **Increasing digitization rates** through rapid smartphone adoption and increasing internet access in underserved regions is expanding the number of eligible GIG freelancers
- **A cultural shift toward embracing a "flexible" work–life environment** is altering the working population's expectations of a typical 9-to-5 workday
- **The rising costs of living** paired with a **shrinking middle class** is compelling the employed lower-to-middle class to seek additional part-time income through GIG work

On the demand side, consumers and businesses demonstrate an accelerated uptake in requesting GIG services, in part driven by the following elements:

- With the **boom of "on-demand" services**, millennials have become accustomed to fulfilling their needs instantaneously through a variety of platforms, an expectation new GIG entrants are required to meet to remain competitive
- **Significant levels of venture capital funding**—especially in industries such as ride-sharing—have enabled even earlier-stage platforms to launch direct-to-consumer marketing campaigns to rapidly attract consumers
- In the face of rising overhead costs to corporations and SMEs alike, **businesses are outsourcing short-term tasks and/or noncentral functions** to contracted GIG workers instead of full-time employees (FTEs)

The demand for GIG workers is not limited to a specific industry. In a study conducted by BCG about the future of work [19], 10 different industries showed growing demand for freelance workers, with 4% of respondents indicating that GIG work is the primary source of income and 19% as a secondary source of income (see Figure 4.19).

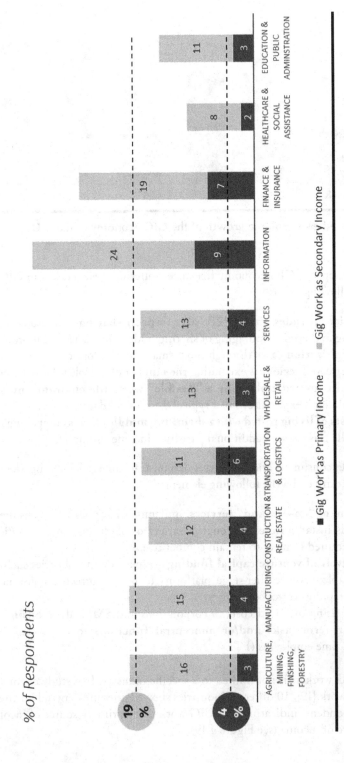

Figure 4.19 GIG work as primary and secondary income [19]

4.4.3.2 *Disrupting the Traditional Talent Model*

The evolving work model enabled by the GIG economy is producing a ripple of talent and structural implications for many organizations. On the one hand, some may feel the need to combat the growing popularity of the GIG economy with a talent campaign that extenuates the full-time career benefits their organization can provide. Alternatively, some organizations have strategically embraced the GIG economy as the new normal focusing efforts on how to effectively integrate GIG workers into their talent ecosystem. Either way, having a greater understanding of the specific talent implication brought on by the GIG economy will help organizations make better talent decisions. Organizations taking the following actions will more effectively embrace and exploit this disruption [20]:

1. **Reexamine the workforce composition**. Reexamine the makeup of the workforce and the impact on the business as a whole. If there is a stronger desire for current and future employees to participate in GIG work, organizations should ensure their number of full-time positions reflects business needs. If the need for specific roles is likely to reduce due to automation, for example, now may be a good time to revisit strategic workforce planning efforts.
2. **Infuse a "GIG" culture into the work environment**. Given the emphasis younger generations are placing on entrepreneurial spirit, incorporating more entrepreneurial aspects to existing roles in the organization and how they incorporate this to enhance the employee experience could reap major benefits for the growing Generation Z workforce. Where possible, offer more virtual flexibility and create new career paths where employees will develop skills such as autonomy, analytical thinking, and problem-solving to name a few, which can be leveraged throughout various parts of the business.
3. **Redefine the employee value proposition**. Since GIG employees do not have the same legal protections or benefits as full-time salaried employees, organizations may consider revamping their employee value proposition to shine a light on this advantage, particularly for those talented employees they want to retain. Currently, many of the GIG economy jobs require a lower skill set to support transactional work, not requiring a degree or specialization. This not only puts some GIG work at risk of being eliminated to automation but also may limit those workers' career development for a short-term paycheck. If organizations are able to articulate the value and opportunities to develop strategic capabilities and skills for the future, they may be more successful in retaining talent.
4. **Evaluate HR policies**. Revisit HR policies and align them to their strategic talent efforts as it relates to the GIG economy. Policies such as noncompete and the benefit packages between full- and part-time employment may need to be modified to account for GIG employment.

4.4.4 *Circular Economy*

The circular economy is a massive US$4.5 trillion [21] business opportunity with the potential to transform the production and consumption processes since the First Industrial Revolution 250 years ago. Untapping circular innovation will not only lead to monumental global economic growth but support people and communities around the world to fulfill the Paris Agreement and tackle the sustainable development goals. Often defined as a "New way of looking at relationships between markets, customers and natural resources", the concept of circular economy is widely misunderstood by businesses, and capitalizing on its opportunity will remain a challenge until or unless more business leaders adopt the **"Circular Mindset"**. Below we have listed four companies in different industries (food, chemicals, flavors/fragrances, and FMCG) that have adopted this **"Circular Mindset"** approach (Figure 4.20).

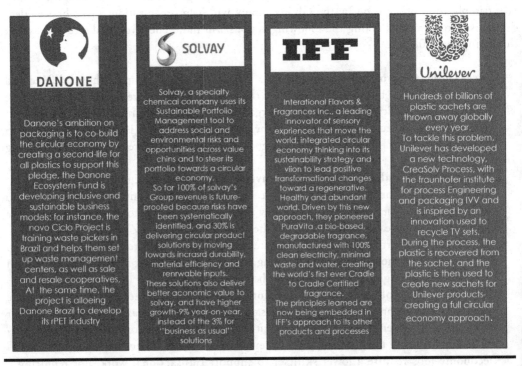

Figure 4.20   Companies leading the way with a circular mindset

Other examples include smaller but inspiring cases for the circular economy. The following cases highlight some of the success stories to learn from.

- Patagonia: Patagonia is a clothing company that designs for durability and repair. They also design for attachment and trust and have their own support on how to repair products on the website which encourages buyers to repair or reuse products. They have launched an e-commerce Worn-Wear platform where the company sells used Patagonia clothing and gear online, sourced directly from its customers. The retailer launched Worn Wear in 2013 as a way to encourage consumers to take care of their gear, washing and repairing as needed, and eventually recycling once the garment can no longer be used. This website also contains a section with stories of customers and their Patagonia clothing. This expresses the success of Patagonia in designing for attachment and trust. Patagonia's Worn-Wear repair facility repairs over 45,000 items per year, and the company operates retail repair stations around the world, in addition to providing its customers with free tools for repairing their own clothing.

■ Gerard Street: Gerrard Street is a start-up in Amsterdam that produces high-quality modular headphones. The headphones are offered through a subscription model, where customers pay either a monthly or annual fee (respectively €7.50 or €70 for the standard headphone and €10and €100, respectively, for the wireless headphone). There is also a completely refurbished model, which costs €6 per month or €60 per year. The headphones are of high quality and designed to break down less quickly. The headphone is being delivered in separate components and can be easily (dis)assembled. The modular design has the benefit that if any part or component of the headphones is broken, customers can return that part to Gerrard Street for repair or recycling—which is included in the fee. Through this service model, they can reassure that their clients can always enjoy a perfect sound.

■ Eosta: By rethinking the reason for plastic packaging, Eosta has created an alternative for stickers and packaging on vegetables in supermarkets. They have created a laser for providing information on biologically produced food. A high-definition laser removes part of the pigment from the outer layer of the peel of the fruit or vegetable, leaving a permanent mark. As this mark is clearly visible, it is no longer necessary to pack the products in harmful plastic foil. The method is completely safe, and no additional substances are used. Furthermore, the method is so superficial that it has no effect on taste, quality, or shelf life. The energy needed for a marking is less than 1% of the energy needed for a sticker. Through Natural Branding Eosta is saving large amounts of plastic. Just for one product line for one retailer, they are saving over 750,000 packaging units.

■ Peeze: Peeze has created coffee capsules that are a sustainable solution to the wasteful standard coffee capsules. The new capsules and sealing foil are made of polylactic acid, PLA, a bio-based and compostable material. The packaging complies with the European standard for compostable packaging EN-13432. This allows the cups to carry the Vegetable logo and to be disposed of at the biodegradable GFT (vegetable, fruit, and garden) waste.

4.4.4.1 The Restart Project

The Restart Project is a social enterprise located in the UK that organizes events where people teach each other how to repair their broken and slow devices. It was born in 2013 out of frustration with the throwaway, consumerist model of electronics that companies have been promoting and the growing mountain of e-waste that it's leaving behind. By bringing people together to share skills and gain the confidence to open up their stuff, they give people a hands-on way of making a difference, as well as a way to talk about the wider issue of what kind of products we want. During the COVID-19 pandemic, laptops were donated, fixed, and upgraded to be distributed to locals in need to stay connected remotely during the lockdown.

As seen from the above examples, the circular economy moves away from the orthodox "**Take-Make-Dispose**" economic model to the one that is regenerative by design. The key objective is to retain as much economic value as possible from resources, products, parts, and materials to create a system that allows for long life, optimum use, remanufacturing, and recycling. Furthermore, a great example people talk about is vegetable-based packaging. Think about it this way: you go buy a burger, then you throw away the box. What happens if you can eat the box? What happens if you can heat up the box and put it into your soup? What if it's algae-based or protein-based? Then you can reuse it but not reuse it as a package—but in a different application. You can end up eating it. Or your dog can end up eating it. Those are the kinds of innovation you're going to see in the next 5, 10, and 15 years. Accenture [22] presented an outline of the circular economy that was adopted from the Ellen Macarthur Foundation (EMF). Figure 4.21 provides the details of this integration of the Technical Materials and the Biological Materials sides with the manufacturing, retailing, consumption, and collection for energy recovery and landfill use process.

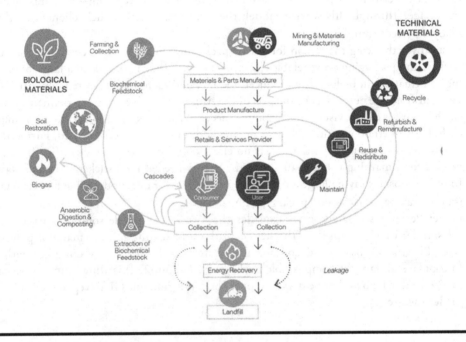

Figure 4.21   Outline of the circular economy [22]

Companies are moving toward a circular economy in order to mitigate risks due to the depletion of natural resources in addition to offering tremendous amounts of growth opportunities.

- ■ **Risk Mitigation**
  - – **Resource scarcity and fluctuating commodity prices**. Resource demand and consumption are driven by population and economic growth. The extraction of materials has more than tripled in the past 40 years. As the population grows, the total demand for resources is expected to reach a staggering 130 billion tons by 2050. That's an overuse of Earth's total capacity by more than 400%.
  - – **Resource price volatility**. The accelerated demand for resources coupled with the frequent price fluctuations will lead to a long-term increase in prices and supply insecurity.

■ **Opportunities Capitalization**
- **GDP growth**. A transition toward a circular economy will contribute approximately US$4.5 trillion toward the global GDP.
- **Policy readiness**. Moving toward a circular economy can help companies get ahead of upcoming policy, regulation, pricing of externalities, and potential shifts in taxation models. Companies delivering economic and sustainability benefits through successful circular transformations serve as proof points for policymakers and encourage them to make new policies that level the playing field. Circular economy measures can help achieve the Paris Climate Agreement and the UN Sustainable Development Goals.

■ **Business and Societal Benefits**
- **Job creation**. The circular economy has created 500,000 additional jobs in France.
- **Reduced energy consumption**. Circular economy solutions could offer a 37% reduction in energy consumption in the EU.
- **Reduced greenhouse gas emissions**. In India, implementing circular solutions presents the opportunity to reduce emissions by about 40%.
- **Increased resource scarcity**. Sustainably managed forests ensure the long-term availability of renewable resources for producing bio-based materials; applying circular economy principles to water management can greatly reduce the issues related to the management of water resources.
- **Innovation driver**. The potential revenue that can be generated by circular economy business models for automotive companies could grow to US$400–600 billion in 2030.

Five business models are proposed for companies to consider: the use of circular supplies, the recovery of useful resources, the product life extension, connecting users on sharing platforms, and moving from product ownership to Products-as-Service. Figure 4.22 provides an overview of those models.

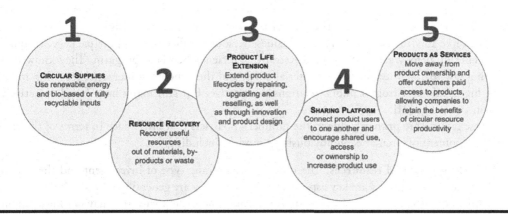

Figure 4.22   Five business models for circular economy

Three disruptive technologies have also been identified in order to implement a circular economy and leverage the growth opportunities provided by it. This includes digital technologies, physical technologies, and biological technologies. Figure 4.23 provides an overview and examples of those technologies.

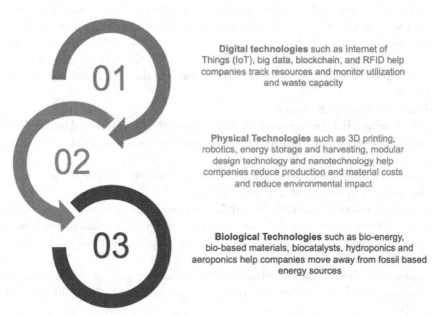

Digital technologies such as Internet of Things (IoT), big data, blockchain, and RFID help companies track resources and monitor utilization and waste capacity

Physical Technologies such as 3D printing, robotics, energy storage and harvesting, modular design technology and nanotechnology help companies reduce production and material costs and reduce environmental impact

Biological Technologies such as bio-energy, bio-based materials, biocatalysts, hydroponics and aeroponics help companies move away from fossil based energy sources

Figure 4.23   Technologies to implement circular economy

4.4.4.2 *Circular Economy for SMEs*

Small- and medium-sized enterprises (SMEs) are the economic backbone of most countries. They generate a significant number of employment opportunities. As well as being economically important, SMEs are also environmentally important: Although their individual impact is small, their cumulative impact on the environment is significant.

SMEs are increasingly aware of the benefits of improving resource efficiency, a message that has been actively promoted across the UK for the past 20 years or so through active government programs like Envirowise and WRAP's Business Resource Efficiency support package, through to the current Zero Waste Scotland led Resource Efficiency Scotland program. They know that reducing raw material usage, saving material costs, and the benefits of increased recycling make sense financially and from a public relations perspective. But still many have failed to actively implement change [21].

These failures are primarily due to the number of barriers that SMEs face in terms of the current development of circular economy business models, including:

■ **Lack of financial resources**: The upfront costs of any type of investment and the anticipated payback period are key aspects for SMEs, as they are generally more sensitive to additional financial costs, particularly in the recent economic climate, and may not know about possible funding sources
■ **Time and resource constraints**: SMEs often don't have sufficient staff or time to research and investigate alternative business models

■ **Lack of awareness/knowledge of the potential benefits**: Because they are "flat out" delivering on a daily basis, they may not have researched or appreciated the opportunities that are out there

There are three critical areas that are vital to drive the adoption of circular thinking among SMEs. These are:

■ Provision of technical support to SMEs to assist them with initial thinking and action
■ Clear drivers and signals from the government that leads the direction of travel
■ The inclusion of circular economy principles within public sector procurement processes

There a number of programs of support being delivered in parts of the UK to support SMEs to identify opportunities that the circular economy can provide to their business, including national programs such as the Zero Waste Scotland Resource Efficiency Advisory Service, and their grant funding support is available via the Circular Economy Investment Fund, WRAP's REBus project, as well as regional examples such as that provided in London by LWARB.

4.4.4.3 Six Business Benefits of Circular Economy for SMEs

The concept of a circular economy provides inspiration for businesses to increase their resource efficiency. By adopting circular economy strategies and practices, entrepreneurs can realize all sorts of different business benefits. These benefits depend on the adopted strategy, the degree to which the business processes are circular, the environment in which the company is active, and the role of the company in the value chain. Nevertheless, we have identified six general business benefits for SMEs of adopting circular economy strategies which help to explain why adopting circular economy strategies and practices is beneficial for SMEs [21].

1. **Reduced exposure to rising and the volatility of resource prices**: The increasing scarcity of nonrenewable natural resources (e.g., fossil fuels, metals, and minerals) results in increasing resource prices and price volatility, which in turn results in higher material costs for businesses. By adopting circular economy strategies and practices, businesses can reduce the amount of materials they require for their production and for meeting their clients' needs. Thereby they reduce their exposure to the risk of rising and more volatile resource prices.
2. **Thinking circular stimulates innovation**: The concept of the circular economy provides inspiration for businesses to increase their resource efficiency. It provides a new lens to look at a company's business model and operations. Looking through this lens may provide new insights and thereby stimulate innovation. For example, in search of ways to reduce the amount of materials used in construction, the Dutch construction company BAM invented new building materials made from plastic waste.
3. **Creates a green image**: Consumers, businesses, and governments are more aware of the environmental impact of the products which they use. They, therefore, are more tuned in to sustainability when making their buying decisions. By adopting circular economy strategies and practices, businesses can reduce the environmental footprint of their products and thereby differentiate themselves from their competitors.
4. **Opens new markets and opportunities for growth**: Circular solutions may also create new markets/niches. For example, in the textiles industry, there are various businesses which produce yarns from discarded clothing or from textiles waste. Since consumers are looking

for sustainable clothing, this has grown into a separate market which exists next to the market for regular textiles.

5. **Increased customer loyalty and more stable revenue streams**: Transitioning to circular may be facilitated by adopting a different business model. For example, remaining the owner of manufactured products instead of selling them (e.g., getting paid per wash cycle instead of per sold washing machines) helps to be able to retrieve the parts and materials in the product at the end of the use period. Adopting such business models have the benefit that they increase customer loyalty and provide more stable revenue streams.

6. **Environmental benefits:** Adopting circular economy strategies and practices is beneficial to not only business but also the environment. Becoming more circular requires companies to reduce their environmental impact by reducing their:
   - Use of raw materials
   - Energy consumption and using solely green energy
   - Freshwater consumption.

4.4.4.4 How to Transform Your Vision into Results in Circular Economy

1. **Set a circular vision**: Leadership can create the business imperatives, cultural changes, and governance to promote the circular mindset, objectives, and integrated goals/metrics.

2. **Choose your circular model**: Move beyond waste and recycling to leverage the full suite of circular business models. Use disruptive technologies to make the most of your circular transformation.

3. **Work in teams**: Achieving a circular transformation requires teamwork across functional areas (i.e., R&D, procurement, supply chain, manufacturing, and marketing).

4. **Start small and scale**: To get started, start small and pilot innovative programs that could lead to long-term strategies. Celebrate successes, re-evaluate failures and work on scaling up.

5. **Collaborate**: Engage with other companies and stakeholders to remove barriers and work on solutions that will create growth while reducing the impact.

6. **Track progress**: Use financial, environmental, and social metrics to measure and track the impact circular innovation has on business.

4.4.5 The Purpose Economy

Based on PwC's data in their 24th Global CEO Survey [23], it appears the majority of CEOs now share the vision that purpose is the new driving force of the economy. They see that understanding the importance of purpose—for employees, clients, and customers—will soon mark the difference between competitive companies from others that fall off the map.

The purpose-driven economy is concerned with what we do with our professional lives. This purpose-driven economy has its roots in both the corporate purpose statements and the nonprofit sector. But it is not about fighting for a certain cause but more about finding a way of living and working where the purpose of what you are doing is an important driver shaping your decisions, actions, and ways of working. It is evident that an increasing number of people and organizations are following this path, developing new business models that reflect the shift in mindset from pure profit to profit and purpose, or even the 3Ps (People, Profit, Planet). Examples include the rise of B-Corporations, hybrid nonprofit and for-profit organizations, social entrepreneurship, and crowd-driven philanthropy. Collaboration and innovation are at the heart of many of these business models, allowing ordinary people to do "Big Things" while also making money.

Driven by trends including increasing globalization, the advent of new technologies, geopolitical events, cross-industry competitions, and the new millennials mindset, we can expect more individuals' businesses and organizations to embrace the purpose-driven economy.

To understand the purpose economy, it is critical to understand the purpose and how it is created for people. The definition and nature of purpose are often misunderstood. There are three well-researched, core categories that consistently echo through the words of the professionals who applied to the Taproot Foundation: **Personal Purpose**, **Social Purpose**, and **Societal Purpose** [24]. Together, they represent the needs that the new purpose economy addresses.

4.4.5.1 Personal Purpose

Warren Brown was one of over a million lawyers in the United States. As he describes,

> My moment of truth came very late on a Friday night when I was still practicing law. On this night, I was making a cake for one of the senior managers in my office, and I was trying to make it look extra nice.

He was good at his job, but it was only a job—what he really loved was baking and what started as a hobby became a bakery, CakeLove, and later a café, the LoveCafe. Both the bakery and café became wildly successful, and he eventually left his job as an attorney. And yet, just a few years in, Warren wasn't happy. Despite doing what he loved, he was in fact spending all of his time running the bakery. What he loved most was talking to his customers about cake and creating the kinds of amazing cakes that wowed them. As it turned out, his passion had been making cakes, not managing a bakery.

After recognizing the gap between what he was doing and what he wanted to be doing, Warren hired a manager to run his business and refocused his energy on baking and looking for new ways to create cakes. He talked to his customers about what they loved and found that while his customers clearly loved cake, they had trouble eating it neatly. After a little trial and error, a solution emerged: Cake Bites, small cakes baked and served in tiny jars. The Cake Bites were an instant hit, and Warren was soon selling them to Whole Foods. His business boomed. By following his passion, Warren had not only found a profound sense of purpose but built a great business in the process. "In living my passion, when I wake up, I'm all go. I'm spiritually amped—ready and willing to dive into the satisfaction I get every day from baking". Passion is a crucial element of purpose.

For Warren, the pursuit of purpose was deeply personal. It began with him recognizing a problem, cultivating the self-awareness to understand what needed to change, and pushing himself to make the necessary changes so that he could grow. It's no different for our generation. We find purpose when we do things we love, attempt new challenges, and express our voice to the world

4.4.5.2 Social Purpose

Kristine Ashe's family was fractured and living all over the country. She longed to share her life with them but knew it was unlikely unless she created the opportunity for it to happen. Though she knew very little about farming or winemaking, Kristine decided to buy a vineyard.

Unlike Warren Brown and his connection to the craft of baking, Kristine's dream was not to make wine but rather to create a business that would bring her family together and build a community. The wine business had a relatively low barrier to entry and a strong community of mentorship in winemaking—you looked to your neighbors for help. Her hope was that it would be a way to finally bring her family together in one place, all working on the vineyard. It could be a business that was focused on community and relationships.

Remarkably, her field of dreams worked. Kristine built the vineyard around her family, creating a ranch that allowed her to work with her kids by her side. Her extended family also got involved in ways she never imagined. Her sister moved to the farm, and her brother-in-law now leads the vineyard's operations. Her father even built their website.

Kristine decided to call the vineyard *Entre Nous*, French for "between us". Kristine explained her motivation to create the vineyard: "The connections between us bring the greatest joy, the highest passion, and the most authentic satisfaction in our frequently impassive, impersonal, and impatient world". The work of winemaking was rewarding and pushed her to her limits, but it was the ability to share that work with the people she loved that made it truly meaningful and gave her such a strong sense of purpose.

Research shows that purpose is not a solo act. Michael Steger at Colorado State University has created a Laboratory for the Study of Meaning and Quality of Life. In his study of over 250,000 people, he found evidence that what Kristine had felt applies on a much broader level. When it comes to meaning in life, relationships matter to humans more than anything else. They reinforce our sense of value, require us to engage, and ultimately help us grow.

4.4.5.3 Societal Purpose

When NASCAR's Kate Atwood was asked to speak at a camp for kids who had lost a parent, she wasn't expecting her life and career trajectory to change. But when she found herself in front of hundreds of kids telling the story of losing her own mother to cancer when she was 12 years old, something shifted. It was the first time she had ever shared her story. "Until that day, the death of my mom had been about me", Kate shared with me. "After that day, I knew it was much bigger than myself".

Later that evening, a little girl about 10 years old tapped Kate on her shoulder and asked, "Are you Kate?" "Yes", she replied. The girl then continued to tell her the story of losing her own mom and dad in a car accident. "To this day, that moment stands as the time I first brushed up with the power of purpose", she explains.

> Two years later, at the tender age of 22, this thirst (to find purpose in my life) led me to my boss's office, to let her know I was leaving the company to start a nonprofit for kids who had lost a parent or sibling.

Kate left NASCAR to start Kate's Club. For the next 10 years, she expanded it, and it became a well-established community for children and teens in Atlanta navigating life after the death of a parent or sibling. It was with Kate's Club that her personality manifested, both as a survivor of loss and as a kid who just wanted to know that grief changed her life but did not end it. She learned that your darkest moment could become your biggest gift if you are able to make it about something beyond yourself.

Today people want to make profits but at the same time also want to make a difference with businesses and individuals by addressing global and local challenges. In organizations around the globe, purpose plays a key role in shaping agendas. In addition, there is a new breed of organizations emerging which combine purpose with profit, from nonprofit undertaking some business activities to generate more predictable cash flows to fund longer-term projects to business organizations pursuing societal as well as economic value. And the public support for such businesses and organizations is on board as well. According to a report, in 2012, 76% of the consumers believe that it is OK for brands to support good causes and make money at the same time [25].

4.4.5.4 The Rise of Social Entrepreneurship

Social entrepreneurs are popping up everywhere, demonstrating through innovative approaches that profit-making and social good can go hand-in-hand. Examples include:

Okhtein: The Egyptian brand Okhtein which means "two sisters" is one of the country's hottest exports. The high-end brand, started by two sisters, is known for its quirky, cute, and ultrafeminine bags and scarves, with all designs approached with philanthropy in mind. To manufacture their products, the sisters take a philanthropic approach to their work based on their desire to incorporate more handmade embroidery and straw into their leatherwork. The pair set up a collaboration with several local NGOs that provide assistance to skilled female workers from economically unstable backgrounds in the country.

Vava Coffee: Launched by one of the natives in Kenya. Viva coffee buys and exports some of the finest Kenyan coffee from smallholder farmers who have traditionally lacked access to fair markets. These vulnerable people have been victims of the market as much as participants in it. Vava works with them to assure them a fair price for their coffee and proudly exports it.

ThinkImpact: An educational travel company that does not have volunteer, intern, or study abroad programs and does not perform traditional international development work. Rather, it seeks to bring together students and local community members to spark ideas and create businesses in rural Africa and Latin America by sending students around the world to explore different cultures, tackle tough challenges, and form relationships with people they would not otherwise meet. It started as a nonprofit but is now reincarnated as a for-profit.

Doodle Factory: A design-centric Egyptian brand that inclusively empowers children in need by enabling them to take part in bettering their own lives. Through utilizing the children's creativity, Doodle Factory designs products which fund the medical, educational, and shelter needs of the children.

VEJA: Since 2005, VEJA has been making sneakers differently, infusing each stage of production with a positive impact: Environmentally friendly sneakers, made with raw materials sourced from organic farming and ecological agriculture, without chemicals or polluting processes; sneakers that treat humans with respect are produced in dignified conditions, in direct consultation with producer associations and manufacturers; and sneakers with greater economic justice, without any advertising or marketing expenses.

Warby Parker: Around the world, 2.5 billion people need glasses but don't have access to them; of these, 624 million cannot effectively learn or work due to the severity of their visual impairment. To help address this problem, Warby Parker works with a handful of partners worldwide to ensure that for every pair of glasses purchased, a pair of glasses is distributed to someone in need. Alleviating the problem of impaired vision is at the heart of what they do, and with the help of their customers, over eight million pairs of glasses have been distributed through their Buy a Pair, Give a Pair program.

Government funding and private donations have slowed down as a consequence of the financial crisis and nonprofits, as well as individuals and businesses have had to find new ways to finance their projects. Crowdfunding is an increasing source of funds, for example:

Watsi—Crowdfunded medical treatment for the developing world: Watsi is utilizing crowdfunding to provide medical care in the developing world. It enables donations as small as US$5 to directly fund medical care and resources and, unlike many other nonprofits, donates 100% of its proceeds. Modeled after for-profit companies, the organization was able to raise US$1.2 million while spending only US$135,000, meaning that every dollar spent produced US$9 for low-cost, high-impact medical treatment in another country. The company's day-to-day running costs are funded separately through private donors, foundations, and corporations. To date, the organization has funded medical treatments for more than 1,110 patients in 16 countries.

My Ideal City—crowdfunding Bogotá, Columbia: Just like many other cities around the world Bogotá in Columbia has experienced rapid population growth in recent years. This has triggered infrastructure issues such as problems with transportation, security, and housing, while widespread corruption and lack of political consensus have delayed progress in the city. To redevelop Bogotá a team of partners has launched the global conversation site "My Ideal City". The site is open to everyone and discusses trends in urban living across the world. Its ultimate goal is to prepare Bogotá for the future by presenting an urban redevelopment plan to city planners. Bogotá is also home to the world's first-ever crowdfunded skyscraper. The world's largest crowdfunding initiative has generated over US$200 million from more than 3,500 supporters to build the highest skyscraper in Colombia, not to mention the first new one in 40 years

4.4.5.5 Why Purpose-Driven Organization Matters

Tapping into a rising consciousness among customers, employees, and other stakeholders, many organizations and businesses are stepping up to a new role to enable positive innovation and change to tackle societal and economic challenges and at the same time promote business growth. In many areas, they are seeking to build legitimacy—and the license to operate—in the eyes of demanding and discerning consumers, who care about the impact and motivations of companies from whom they buy. In many cases, this is also to the benefit of the organizations that are seeking to develop long-term visions and ambitions in which purpose is a priority.

From a consumer point of view, purpose has become personal and the new generation empowered by technology, high connectivity, and social media has more power than ever to influence and make a difference in the world's economic and societal challenges. While from a business point of view, there is a strong correlation between purpose and building business confidence, both short term and long term. According to Deloitte's "Core belief and culture survey", 82% of the respondents who work for an organization with a strong sense of purpose say that they are confident that their organization will grow this year. Examples of corporations that are working toward making purpose a priority include:

PepsiCo is focusing on "Performance with a purpose", building on three pillars: (1) Human sustainability, which means providing a wide range of foods and beverages, from treats to healthy eats; (2) environmental sustainability, which means finding innovative ways to cut costs and minimize the impact on the environment through energy and water conservation as well as reduced use of packaging materials; (3) talent sustainability, which means providing a safe and inclusive workplace globally and respecting, supporting, and investing in the local communities where PepsiCo operates

Deloitte has made it a priority to embrace a culture of purpose, realizing that successful companies must be "keenly aware of the purpose they fulfill for clients, employees, community, and other groups". They have integrated these goals into their business's core activity

Google has invested in creating an exceptional work environment that reflects its vision, with themed workspaces, slides between floors, free gourmet food, and radical amounts of employee autonomy

Zappos is innovating around ways to "deliver happiness"—their mission—through untraditional benefits like surprising 80% of customers with free overnight shipping

IDEO has created IDEO.org to solve poverty-related challenges by offering its talented designers to communities that need them the most

Tapping into a rising consciousness among customers, employees, and other stakeholders, many organizations and businesses are stepping up to a new role to enable positive innovation and change to tackle societal and economic challenges and at the same time promote business growth. From a consumer point of view, purpose has become personal, and the new generation empowered by technology, high connectivity, and social media has more power than ever to influence and make a difference in the world's economic and societal challenges.

4.5 The Five Walls

Moving toward Society 5.0 and the evolution of the digital economy and the continuous development of the other future economies is not optional; hence societies need to work hard to create the environment that allows for this evolution to happen. This will require the demolition of five walls that exist in most societies today.

- **The wall of the ministries and agencies**
  This necessitates the "formulation of national strategies and integration of the government promotion system". This includes the architecting of a national "IoET (Internet of Everything) system" and a "think-tank function".
- **The wall of the legal system**
  Whereby laws need to be developed to implement new economic models. In practice, this would also mean innovative regulatory reforms and a push for administrative digitization. For example, Japan is promoting the idea of expanding World Trade Organization rules beyond goods and services to encompass trade in data as well.
- **The wall of technologies**
  The quest for the formation of the "knowledge foundation". It's clear that actionable data plays a foundational role here as do all technologies/areas to protect and leverage it, from cybersecurity to robotics, nano, bio, and systems technology. This means a serious R&D commitment on various levels.
- **The wall of human resources**
  Educational reform, IT literacy, and broadening the available human resources with specializations in advanced digital skills are crucial. This should also include the promotion of women's participation to discover potential talents.

■ **The wall of social acceptance**
Educate the public, address privacy concerns, and continuously examine the ethical, legal, and social implications (ELSI) for all stakeholders. The examination must cover everything from the relationship between humans and machines (AI and robots) to philosophical issues such as the definition of individual happiness and humanity.

References

1. Dinana, H. (2020). Society 5.0 and the Future Economies. The Cairo Review of Global Affairs, Spring 2020, American University in Cairo (AUC), School of Global Affairs and Public Policy (GAPP). https://www.thecairoreview.com/main-home-page/society-5-0-and-the-future-economies/
2. Dobbs, R., Manyika, J., and Woetzel, J. (2015). The Four Global Forces Breaking All the Trends. McKinsey Global Institute. https://www.mckinsey.com/business-functions/strategy-and-corporate -finance/our-insights/the-four-global-forces-breaking-all-the-trends
3. https://blog.interactiveschools.com/blog/50-million-users-how-long-does-it-take-tech-to-reach-this -milestone
4. https://www.statista.com/statistics/255778/number-of-active-wechat-messenger-accounts/
5. https://www.statista.com/statistics/268251/number-of-apps-in-the-itunes-app-store-since-2008/
6. https://techcrunch.com/2016/06/13/apples-app-store-hits-2m-apps-130b-downloads-50b-paid-to -developers/
7. https://www.populationpyramid.net/world/2021/
8. Keidanren (Japan Business Federation). (2018). Society 5.0 Co-creating the Future. https://www .keidanren.or.jp/en/policy/2018/095_booklet.pdf
9. https://www.itu.int/en/Pages/default.aspx
10. Sabbagh, K. et al. (2013). Digitization for Economic Growth and Job Creation: Regional and Industry Perspectives. The Global Information Technology Report (2013). World Economic Forum. http:// www3.weforum.org/docs/GITR/2013/GITR_Chapter1.2_2013.pdf
11. https://www.computerweekly.com/news/252435429/Digital-economy-to-make-up-60-of-APACs -GDP-by-2021
12. https://ec.europa.eu/digital-single-market/en/policies/shaping-digital-single-market
13. Arab Federation for Digital Economy. (2019). Arab Digital Economy Strategy: Towards a Sustainable, Inclusive and Secure Digital Future. https://www.arab-digital-economy.org/wp-content/uploads /2019/12/Integrated-summary-report-V18-.pdf
14. Goldman, D., Marchessou, S., and Teichn, W. (2017). Cashing in on the US Experience Economy. McKinsey and Company. https://www.mckinsey.com/industries/private-equity-and-principal-inves tors/our-insights/cashing-in-on-the-us-experience-economy
15. Puthiyamadam, T., and Reyes, J. (2018). Experience is Everything: Here's How to get it right. Price Waterhouse Coopers. https://www.pwc.com/us/en/zz-test/assets/pwc-consumer-intelligence-series -customer-experience.pdf
16. https://www.businessofapps.com/data/uber-statistics/
17. Staffing Industry Analysts (SIA) Report. (2018). The Human Cloud: The GIG Economy and the Transformation of Work.
18. Mastercard, and Kaiser Associates. (2019). The Global Gig Economy: Capitalizing on a $500B Opportunity. https://newsroom.mastercard.com/wp-content/uploads/2019/05/GIG-Economy -White-Paper-May-2019.pdf
19. Wallenstein, J. et al. (2019). The New Freelancers: Tapping Talent in the Gig Economy. BCG – Henderson Institute - Future of Work Gig Economy Report.
20. KPMG. (2019). Plugging into the Gig Economy: The Truth about the Gig Economy and How it is Influencing the Future of Talent Management.
21. European Commission—Flash Eurobarometer Report. (2017). SMEs Resource Efficiency and Green Markets. http://ec.europa.eu/commfrontoffice/publicopinion

22. World Business Council for Sustainable Development - WBCSD. (2017). CEO Guide to the Circular Economy. https://docs.wbcsd.org/2017/06/CEO_Guide_to_CE.pdf
23. PWC 24th Annual Global CEO Survey. (2021). A Leadership Agenda to Take on Tomorrow. https://www.pwc.com/gx/en/ceo-agenda/ceosurvey/2021.html
24. https://taprootfoundation.org/
25. http://www.globaltrends.com/2014/06/02/gt-briefing-june-2014-the-purpose-driven-economy/

WHAT TO DO TO PUT STRATEGY IN ACTION

Chapter 5

Strategy Savvy: Define the *Future* and Understand *Today*

5.1 Strategy Savvy

To effectively contribute to Society 5.0 and engage in the new economies, we need a Strategy Savvy mindset and way of acting. Being strategically savvy is mostly concerned with thinking like a strategic leader which revolves around creating a vision, engaging others, and developing a plan and implementing it to achieve the vision. Simply stated Strategy Savvy is [1]:

> The ability to insightfully identify root causes to entrenched problems and develop clear, simple, targeted approaches that both explain circumstances and pave the path toward a solution.

> *DiversityBestPractices.com*

While this may have been relevant in the past for high-level executives and strategic planners only, traditional wisdom assumes that it is not highly useful for professionals and operational managers within organizations. Middle managers need a different model because they are rarely responsible for developing the vision or strategic plan but are often required to contribute to it, comment on initiatives and policies being developed by others, implement strategies they have not been involved in creating, or devise policies or processes that have strategic fit. Most of these involve some level of interaction or relationship with strategic thinkers and planners. In this book, we tend to differ with traditional wisdom and believe that in order to thrive in the VUCA world and capitalize on the opportunities presented by the new economies, organizations need to develop Strategy Savvy professionals at all levels of the organization.

This chapter will introduce a Strategy Savvy model, will propose a framework—The Strategy Funnel—to help you organize your thoughts on how to go from Vision to Results, and will review some of the widely used tools to define the Future and understand Today. This will help the organization to build the needed bridge between Today and Tomorrow.

DOI: 10.4324/9781003280941-9

To get a feel for how strategists view the world, imagine you had a magic carpet, like in the story of Aladdin, and you sat on the carpet, zoomed up into the sky, and hovered high above your organization. Now envisage that your organization and everything else impacting it is transparent. Now you see your organization across all its parts and from top to bottom. You also see all the other players impacting you—like competitors, customers, government, shareholders, employees, and so forth. You can see how things interact and connect, and how shifting one element of this picture creates consequences for other elements. You can look out further and see into the future of your organization and its industry, markets, technology, and operating environment. You see how you want your organization to look and to be, and you predict how changes now might impact that future. This is the view of the strategist.

So, a Strategy Savvy professional thinks from a high perspective about their organization and issues confronting it. They consider impacts widely across the organization and across its industry and markets. They also view ideas through time—being able to envisage the concept into the future and seeing impacts and consequences as they relate to the organization and its vision of itself. They tend to use a variety of models or tools, subconsciously or consciously, to view an idea. They also draw on a range of knowledge and information. They view an idea from a variety of viewpoints, not from one area of expertise. Strategic thinkers also treat ideas as just that and generally do not consider implementation issues early on. This does not mean that implementation should not be considered, but strategic thinkers recognize that implementation issues come further down the track and are comfortable looking at a concept in terms of how it links to vision, values, and high-level priorities. They are able to discern how the idea or concept fits with these now and into the future.

When strategic issues are being discussed it is easy for operational or professional experts to quickly judge ideas from an implementation perspective. Often these people can quickly and accurately judge the operational impacts of strategic ideas, but their questions and comments frustrate the strategists who can perceive them as negative and too low level. "Strategic Savvy" is about asking the right questions at the right time in order to understand where strategic ideas are coming from and to indicate to others that you have heard and understood the strategic implications before considering the operational impacts. Handling these conversations effectively can avoid others from perceiving you as "not strategic". The following five-step model [2] can help you become Strategy Savvy (Figure 5.1).

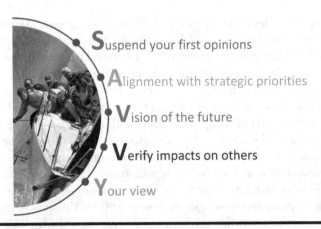

Figure 5.1   The five-step Savvy model

5.1.1 The Five-Step Savvy Model

■ **S**uspend your first opinions

First, to *suspend* your initial thoughts, knowledge, or problem-solving reaction. Suspend the things you initially want to say. This is the first thing that you must do in any conversation or when giving feedback if someone has suggested an idea or raised an issue.

You must suspend your initial reaction. That doesn't mean you are going to sit there and say nothing—steps 2–5 give you plenty to say—it does mean that you need to take that initial reaction or thought and put it on a pretend shelf in your mind and save it for a bit later. You're going to bring it back down and look at it again in a while. For now, you suspend it and do not voice it.

■ **A**lignment with strategic priorities

The second step of the *Savvy* model is to check out this idea, concept, or issue in terms of *alignment* with the organization's strategies. So, this is where understanding the organization's vision, values, and strategic priorities is really important. You need to be able to make the linkages. Now if this idea, issue, or concept (no matter what you initially might think of it, because you've suspended that thought) has some alignment, it's really good to be able to voice that.

You might also find that there is some misalignment either with other strategies or with values or vision. In order to raise that you ask questions. So, you can ask a question about how this issue or idea aligns with particular strategies or values that you can see there is a misalignment.

■ **V**ision of the future

The third step in the model—so far, you've suspended your initial reaction, holding it aside for later, then you've explored the strategic alignment of this idea, issue, or concept—the third step is to take a look at how this fits with the future. So, you're going to *vision* the future of the organization and explore what this might mean. The next chapter will elaborate on Society 5.0 and the Future Economies and can be of great help for you to develop your vision of the future to be a Strategy Savvy professional.

Now, some questions you might ask at this stage include, "How might we look in 2–5 years (or whatever timeframe your organization usually talks about in terms of the future) if we do this?" Or perhaps even more importantly, "How might we look in 2–5 years' time if we *don't* do this?" Another question might be, "If we do this, what impact might it have for us, if things change in the future (e.g., if the economy strengthens, or if technology overtakes your current services?)". So, this is now drawing on your general knowledge of what's happening in the world, what's happening in your industry, and predictions people are making about the future of your industry and your operating environment. Hopefully, you can see now that without those first three steps, you'll struggle to participate fully and appropriately in these critical conversations. So based on that knowledge you've developed, you are going to ask some questions that indicate your good knowledge of your operating environment and future predictions.

■ **V**erify impacts on others

The fourth area to explore is how this idea, concept, or suggestion impacts others. Now, this reflects your understanding of systems thinking across your organization and perhaps a little bit wider to suppliers or your distribution chain. So, *verify* the impacts. Having explored the strategic alignment and the fit for your organization in the future, you now want to explore the impacts within your organization. What existing strengths might this idea build on, where might it throw up some issues that might need to be addressed down the track—they don't have to be addressed then and there—for good implementation?

A good tool to do this is to perform a **Population Impact Analysis (PIA)**. It is a tool to identify the change readiness of the populations and guide them through an engagement process which allows them to buy in the change and makes it happen. Driving the Population Impact Analysis is the idea that without identifying, engaging, and monitoring the populations which would be highly impacted by a transformation no transformation would occur and be sustainable. PIA helps the Strategy Savvy leaders and organizations to:

- Analyze the nature and the size of the change
- Detect the populations' levels of knowledge of the change
- See the populations' possible resistance
- Track the existing leadership and communication practices
- Define the key impact moments to integrate with the hard milestone roadmap

In business organizations, populations are groups of people with similar objectives, roles, backgrounds, experiences, competences, satisfaction criteria, and/or challenges. The first step in PIA is the clustering (grouping) of the Organization Populations using different dimensions such as:

- **Organizational**: Current or future organization, job family, hierarchical level, etc.
- **Environmental**: Work environment (shop-floor, office, field force, etc.)
- **Work-related**: Type of work (physical, intellectual, etc.)
- **Change-related**: Impact of change, competency and willingness to change, attitudes, subjective norm, and perceived personal control
- **Other**: Age, nationality, statute, and criticality

In this step, you can also be exploring impacts on other divisions or roles, not only your own. If you are working with an external client, you can help them explore how it might impact others (including other stakeholders) in their organization or their supply/distribution chain.

Strategy is a process of change that requires a complex number of steps for people to Adopt Change. Figure 5.2 indicates the seven levels of adoption of the change, from understanding the why to adoption and commitment to apply the needed change.

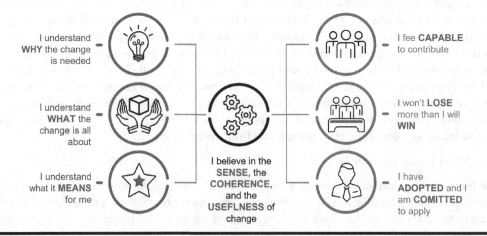

Figure 5.2 Levels of adoption of the change

Following Figure 5.3 is a demonstration of how different population attitudes toward change (move) can be graphically presented and monitored during the strategy/change process. The "Change Impact" can also be presented for each function and/or unit during the different strategy/change/transformation phases, as shown in Figure 5.4, based on two dimensions:

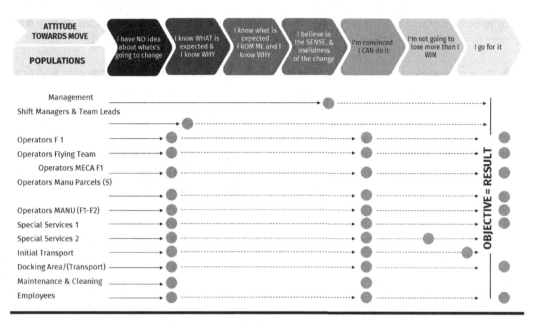

Figure 5.3   Different population attitudes toward change

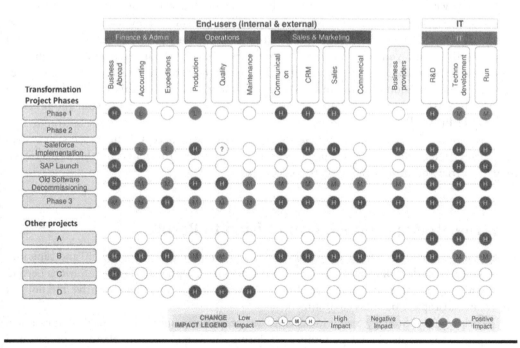

Figure 5.4   Change impact for each function/unit at each stage

- Its impact type from positive to negative (four grades)
- Its impact degree from low to high (four grades)

Your view

Having gone through this process so far and asked some exploratory questions, you're now at a point to be able to take off that mental shelf your initial thoughts that you suspended. It may now be time to voice *Your* view. By this stage, one of three things could have happened:

- As you've worked through this, your initial thought or view has been confirmed and others have also reached that conclusion. So, whether you were for or against the idea initially, everyone involved in this conversation is now thinking alike. If this is the case, it is unlikely you need to comment at all, but if you do, it's just confirming your agreement with the group view and any aspects of importance to note from your area of expertise.
- You still hold your initial view, but others have a different view, or alternatively, you have changed your initial view and others have a different view. In this case, you may now want to point out some issues and challenges as you see them, from your own area of expertise.
- You have changed your initial view and hold the same view now as others. So, having worked through this model, the new perspectives that have arisen have caused you to reach a different conclusion.

Whichever of those three it is, it is wise that you have not yet voiced your opinion. You've had time to explore, to think about how you now might voice your view. So now you're going to talk about the key impacts as you see them from your professional position or from your perspective of experience and expertise. You'll now explain how in your view this idea could work or not work. By this time, you've made it obvious that you're prepared to explore this issue from a strategic perspective; you've been willing to look at how it impacts others and on the organization as a whole. At the end of the day, you don't have to agree with every idea put forward, so now you are simply going to observe some of the impacts and consequences of going ahead (or not) with this idea. Of course, if you have reached a stage where you agree with the group decision over the matter, you may choose not to use this step. It depends on how the discussion has unfolded up until now. You may never need to voice your thoughts, or you may feel it's still wise to do so.

This five-step Savvy model is a way to think about an idea, concept, issue, process, or system that relates strategically to what's happening in an organization. This model can be used successfully in a variety of settings and a variety of forums.

5.2 The Strategy Funnel: From Vision to Results

Using your Strategy Savvy approach to move your organization toward Society 5.0 and capitalize on the continuous development of the future economies is not optional; the organizations need to work hard to ensure their arrival into the future in a way which allows them to thrive and not just survive in a disruptive business environment.

To help you put Strategy Savvy in action, I am proposing a simple framework that can help you organize the jungle of strategy terms used during the formal strategic planning process and to link the **Future** (the vision) with **Today** (the Results). This framework is called the **Strategy**

Funnel. It does not only help organize the different strategy-related terms but also show their inter-relationships and connections.

I noticed during my work with many executives during strategy development workshops and strategy training sessions that they get lost in what I call the "Jungle of Strategy Terms". They use those terms interchangeably, they don't understand their order, and they don't comprehend their inter-relationships.

I do an exercise where I ask them to **order/arrange** the following set of terms: **Vision, Strategies, Goals, Mission, Initiatives, Strategic Direction, Targets, Projects, Objectives, Programs, Measures, Results, KPIs, Strategic Plan, Values**, and **Tactics**.

The discussions help the managers in two ways. First, develop a common definition for those terms to help the management team communicate in a more efficient and effective way to be truly Strategy Savvy. Second, develop an initial understanding of the roles played by different stakeholders (such as the Board of Directors, the Executive Management Team, and Management and Staff) in the strategy development process.

Using the Funnel metaphor is meant to highlight the fact that we move from very broad/general terms such as Vision and Mission to very specific terms such as KPIs and Results. The funnel organizes the terms in a manner that makes them actionable. Figure 5.5 shows the Strategy Funnel order and relationship of terms and its layers and the stakeholders engaged in each part.

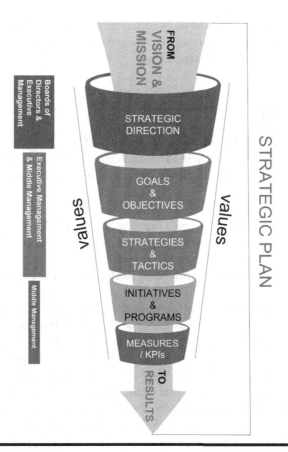

Figure 5.5   The strategy funnel

At the top of the funnel, we have the **Vision & Mission (V&M)** statements that act as a "Reference Point" for strategy development. Contrary to common understanding V&M is not part of the strategy they are communication statements and are only used to reflect the alignment of the strategy with the stated statements of where we see ourselves in the future (Vision) and why we exist (Mission). Strategy Development starts with the Board of Directors' engagement with the Executive Management Team to develop and agree on a clear **Strategic Direction** for the organization (in some organizations it is also referred to as the mandate). This step is a very crucial step for the Executive Management team to effectively start the Strategic Planning process by translating the Strategic Direction into a more defined set of **Goals and Objectives**. Those Objectives provide a very precise definition of the organization's future to be achieved during the agreed-on strategy time frame (nowadays it revolves around two to three years max.). We will further elaborate in the next section on the characteristics of those Objectives.

The next step involves a broader set of the management team to develop **Strategies** and **Tactics** to achieve the agreed-on Strategic Objectives. The strategies get executed using a number of **Initiatives** that could include a number of **Programs** and **Projects**. Once again, the funnel clearly indicates the order of those terms from the higher level to the lower level of precision.

The execution of the projects requires monitoring and control using a set of **Measures and Key Performance Indicators (KPIs)** that are linked to the Measurable Strategic Objectives we set earlier and against agreed-on **Targets**. At the end of the funnel, we get **Results** that accumulate to help the organization realize its Vision and Mission.

I define organization **Values** and the walls of the funnel since they should guide the whole process and define the boundaries of what we can and can't do in a particular organization. Finally, the whole funnel is considered the **Strategic Plan**.

5.3 Define the Future

Since this book is about **Making the Future Happen Today**, it is very crucial for us to have an actionable definition of the future. My research and experience indicate that management teams can effectively engage in acting on the future when it is precisely defined based on three pillars. Objectives need to be:

1. **ALIGNED** with the Goals, Strategic Direction, and Vision/Mission
2. **BALANCED** (includes the four perspectives of the Balanced Scorecard—Financial, Market/Customer, Operational, and Organizational)
3. **SMART** (Specific, Measurable, Achievable, Realistic, and Time-bound)

Satisfying those three characteristics when defining the Objectives as shown in Figure 5.6 provides a clear answer to the team about where we want to be. So we are all moving in tandem and pulling in the same direction. It is recommended that we limit the number of objectives to only three to four per perspective. This gives a total number of 12 to 16 objectives to manage and communicate.

Developing a balanced set of objectives implies the importance of the linking/inter-relationships between the four types proposed. This is not a very easy task, and applying the Strategy Savvy five-step model presented earlier becomes a very valuable approach during those difficult and critical discussions. For example, improving our financial results can be achieved by reducing the training and development cost. While this can help the organization today, it sure will lead to serious problems with the ability to achieve the Operational and Customer objectives that will

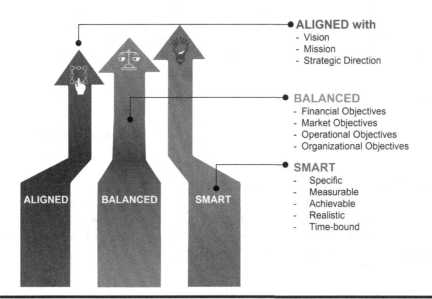

Figure 5.6 Aligned, balanced, and SMART objectives

ultimately lead to greater financial losses than those achieved by the savings realized from cutting the training and development budget.

Another example that can demonstrate the need for achieving a true balance between the objectives is the case of improvements that can be realized by reducing the Down-Time and Mean-Time-To-Repair (MTTR) for the production lines by increasing the level of Spare Parts inventory. This, of course, will come at the cost of our ability to maintain a healthy level of our Cash flow. Discussions around the issues of parts availability, delivery time, costs, break-down frequency, etc. need to take place to achieve the needed balance for the objectives that will guide our Strategy Journey moving forward. Figure 5.7 shows those interconnections and how they balance the perspectives for defining the future.

Figure 5.7 The balanced perspectives of the strategic objectives

One of the questions I get asked frequently is about examples of the areas where those objectives can be defined for. The following sections will provide examples of the objectives and KPIs that can be considered during the management team discussion about the future.

5.3.1 *Financial Objectives*

Figure 5.8 outlines the key financial objectives that are usually developed around five main areas [3]:

- **Profitability**: Gross, EBITDA, Net, ROI, ROE, etc.
- **Liquidity**: Quick Ratio, Cash Ratio, Inventory to Networking Capital, etc.
- **Leverage/Solvency**: Debt to Asset, Debt to Equity, Times Interest Earned, etc.
- **Efficiency/Activity**: Inventory Turnover, Asset Turnover, Average Collection Period, etc.
- **Market Valuation**: Price/Earnings, Dividend Payout, etc.

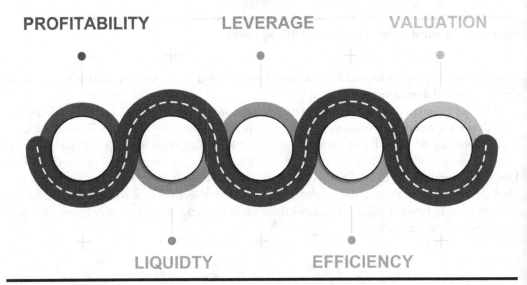

Figure 5.8 Financial objectives

Figure 5.9 provides a listing of different financial ratios related to those five areas with an explanation of how to calculate them and how they are expressed and their meaning. This can be a very valuable tool for nonfinancial managers to understand the basic financial objectives and indicators that can drive the strategy.

	Formula	How Expressed	Meaning
1. Liquidity Ratios			
Current ratio	$\dfrac{\text{Current assets}}{\text{Current liabilities}}$	Decimal	A short-term indicator of the company's ability to pay its short-term liabilities from short-term assets; how much of current assets are available to cover each dollar of current liabilities.
Quick (acid test) ratio	$\dfrac{\text{Current assets} - \text{Inventory}}{\text{Current liabilities}}$	Decimal	Measures the company's ability to pay off its short-term obligations from current assets, excluding inventories.
Inventory to net working capital	$\dfrac{\text{Inventory}}{\text{Current assets} - \text{Current liabilities}}$	Decimal	A measure of inventory balance; measures the extent to which the cushion of excess current assets over current liabilities may be threatened by unfavorable changes in inventory.
Cash ratio	$\dfrac{\text{Cash} + \text{Cash equivalents}}{\text{Current liabilities}}$	Decimal	Measures the extent to which the company's capital is in cash or cash equivalents; shows how much of the current obligations can be paid from cash or near-cash assets.
2. Profitability Ratios			
Net profit margin	$\dfrac{\text{Net profit after taxes}}{\text{Net sales}}$	Percentage	Shows how much after-tax profits are generated by each dollar of sales.
Gross profit margin	$\dfrac{\text{Sales} - \text{Cost of goods sold}}{\text{Net sales}}$	Percentage	Indicates the total margin available to cover other expenses beyond cost of goods sold and still yield a profit.
Return on investment (ROI)	$\dfrac{\text{Net profit after taxes}}{\text{Total assets}}$	Percentage	Measures the rate of return on the total assets utilized in the company; a measure of management's efficiency, it shows the return on all the assets under its control, regardless of source of financing.
Return on equity (ROE)	$\dfrac{\text{Net profit after taxes}}{\text{Shareholders' equity}}$	Percentage	Measures the rate of return on the book value of shareholders' total investment in the company.
Earnings per share (EPS)	$\dfrac{\text{Net profit after taxes} - \text{Preferred stock dividends}}{\text{Average number of common shares}}$	Dollars per share	Shows the after-tax earnings generated for each share of common stock.
3. Activity Ratios			
Inventory turnover	$\dfrac{\text{Net sales}}{\text{Inventory}}$	Decimal	Measures the number of times that average inventory of finished goods was turned over or sold during a period of time, usually a year.
Days of inventory	$\dfrac{\text{Inventory}}{\text{Cost of goods sold} \div 365}$	Days	Measures the number of one day's worth of inventory that a company has on hand at any given time.
Net working capital turnover	$\dfrac{\text{Net sales}}{\text{Net working capital}}$	Decimal	Measures how effectively the net working capital is used to generate sales.
Asset turnover	$\dfrac{\text{Sales}}{\text{Total assets}}$	Decimal	Measures the utilization of all the company's assets; measures how many sales are generated by each dollar of assets.
Fixed asset turnover	$\dfrac{\text{Sales}}{\text{Fixed assets}}$	Decimal	Measures the utilization of the company's fixed assets (i.e., plant and equipment); measures how many sales are generated by each dollar of fixed assets.

Figure 5.9   Financial ratios (Continued)

Formula		How Expressed	Meaning
Average collection period	$\dfrac{\text{Accounts receivable}}{\text{Sales for year} \div 365}$	Days	Indicates the average length of time in days that a company must wait to collect a sale after making it; may be compared to the credit terms offered by the company to its customers.
Accounts receivable turnover	$\dfrac{\text{Annual credit sales}}{\text{Accounts receivable}}$	Decimal	Indicates the number of times that accounts receivable are cycled during the period (usually a year).
Accounts payable period	$\dfrac{\text{Accounts payable}}{\text{Purchases for year} \div 365}$	Days	Indicates the average length of time in days that the company takes to pay its credit purchases.
Days of cash	$\dfrac{\text{Cash}}{\text{Net sales for year} \div 365}$	Days	Indicates the number of days of cash on hand, at present sales levels.
4. Leverage Ratios			
Debt to asset ratio	$\dfrac{\text{Total debt}}{\text{Total assets}}$	Percentage	Measures the extent to which borrowed funds have been used to finance the company's assets.
Debt to equity ratio	$\dfrac{\text{Total debt}}{\text{Shareholders' equity}}$	Percentage	Measures the funds provided by creditors versus the funds provided by owners.
Long-term debt to capital structure	$\dfrac{\text{Long-term debt}}{\text{Shareholders' equity}}$	Percentage	Measures the long-term component of capital structure.
Times interest earned	$\dfrac{\text{Profit before taxes} + \text{Interest charges}}{\text{Interest charges}}$	Decimal	Indicates the ability of the company to meet its annual interest costs.
Coverage of fixed charges	$\dfrac{\text{Profit before taxes} + \text{Interest charges} + \text{Lease charges}}{\text{Interest charges} + \text{Lease obligations}}$	Decimal	A measure of the company's ability to meet all of its fixed-charge obligations.
Current liabilities to equity	$\dfrac{\text{Current liabilities}}{\text{Shareholders' equity}}$	Percentage	Measures the short-term financing portion versus that provided by owners.
5. Other Ratios			
Price/earnings ratio	$\dfrac{\text{Market price per share}}{\text{Earnings per share}}$	Decimal	Shows the current market's evaluation of a stock, based on its earnings; shows how much the investor is willing to pay for each dollar of earnings.
Divided payout ratio	$\dfrac{\text{Annual dividends per share}}{\text{Annual earnings per share}}$	Percentage	Indicates the percentage of profit that is paid out as dividends.
Dividend yield on common stock	$\dfrac{\text{Annual dividends per share}}{\text{Current market price per share}}$	Percentage	Indicates the dividend rate of return to common shareholders at the current market price.

Figure 5.9   (Continued) Financial ratios

5.3.2 Market Objectives

Market Objectives can be developed around five main areas known as the 5-Cs, with a focus on the market-related elements (see Figure 5.10) as follows:

- ■ Customers: Satisfaction, Loyalty, Base, Value, etc.
- ■ Competitors: Share, Stance, etc.
- ■ Company: Marketing Mix, Depth and Breadth of Product Range, Brand Equity, Distribution Network Coverage, Dealer Loyalty, Sales Force, etc.
- ■ Climate: Adoption of MarTech, Big Data, Analytics, AI in Marketing, etc.
- ■ Collaborators: Distributors, Business Partners, Strategic Alliances, etc.

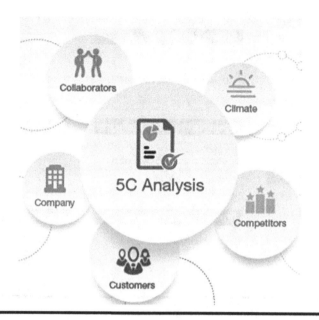

Figure 5.10   5Cs market objectives

5.3.3 *Operational Objectives*

Operational objectives cover both manufacturing and service delivery issues. They can be developed around the following areas:

- Agility
- Responsiveness
- Reliability
- Productivity
- Sustainability
- Innovation
- Losses Eradication

Some of the well-known models that can be used to define the Operational Objectives are the WCOM (World Class Operations Management) Model [4], the SERVQUAL (Service Quality) model, and the SERVPERF (Service Performance) model [5].

The WCOM Model shown in Figure 5.11 provides the components of Operational Excellence used by world-class companies around the globe. It includes the pillars for improvement in many of the domains of the organization's operations. This includes seven domains: manufacturing, supply chain, sales and marketing (growth functions), business processes, procurement, innovation, and sustainable development.

Another model that drives operational excellence in service-oriented organizations is the SERVQUAL model. Figure 5.12 provides the dimensions of this model and their definitions. This includes five dimensions: Radiality, Responsiveness, Assurance, Empathy, and Tangibles.

Finally, another model that is used by service organizations is the SERVPERF (Service Performance) model. Figure 5.13 provides the four dimensions of this model. This includes Responsiveness and Caring, Tangibles and Adequacy, Safety and Convenience, and Dependability. Some studies argue that the SERVPERF model provides more accurate measurement of customer experience with the provided services.

Manufacturing Excellence

> Focused Improvement
> Autonomous Management
> Planned Maintenance
> Progressive Quality
> Education & Training
> Safety & Environment
> Lean Flow
> Early Equipment Management
> Early Product Management

Supply Chain Excellence

> Value Chain Leadership
> Customer Value
> Plan to Serve
> Logistics Focused Improvement
> Reverse Flow & Sustainability
> Lean Flow
> Autonomous Management
> Safety
> Education & Training

Growth Excellence

> Customer Management
> Offering Management
> Marketing and Sales execution

Business Process Excellence

> Lean Process
> Office Focused Improvement
> Service Quality
> World Class Office Management

Procurement Excellence

> Procurement Cost
> Supplier Development
> Sustainable Procurement
> Education & Training

Innovation Excellence

> Innovation Management
> Lean Development
> Lean Design
> Early Equipment Management

Sustainable Development

> Governance
> Environment Protection
> Social Progress and Wealth
> Economic Value Development

WCOM™

Figure 5.11   World-class operations management model (WCOM)

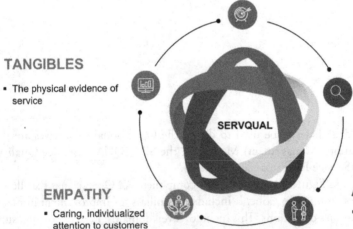

RELIABILITY

- The Ability to perform the service right the first time

TANGIBLES

- The physical evidence of service

RESPONSIVNESS

- The Ability to provide prompt service

SERVQUAL

EMPATHY

- Caring, individualized attention to customers

ASSURANCE

- The knowledge and courtesy of employees

Figure 5.12   SERVQUAL (Service Quality) dimensions

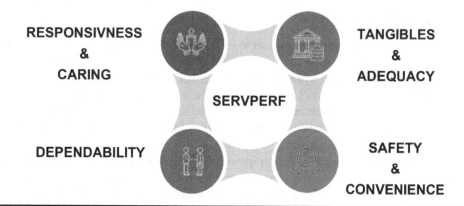

Figure 5.13   SERVPERF (Service Performance) dimensions

5.3.4 *Organizational Objectives*

Organizational Objectives can be defined around five key areas, as shown in Figure 5.14. They include:

- Culture
- Leadership
- Talent/Capabilities
- Adaptability/Flexibility
- Workforce (loyalty, turn-over, etc.)

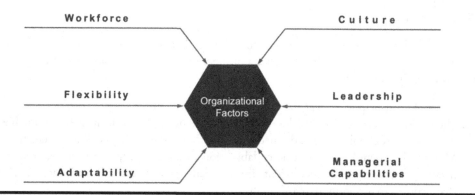

Figure 5.14   Organizational objectives factors

5.4 Understand Today

To ensure that the Strategic Objectives we set to define our future are Achievable and Realistic—but still ambitious and aligned with Society 5.0 and the future economies—we need to carry out a strategic diagnosis to understand where we are today. This is done by using strategic analysis tools such as SWOT analysis and Porter's five forces analysis, to name a few. However, these analyses need to be conducted in a way that moves away from the orthodox approach, thereby allowing to identify and prioritize critically important areas to leverage. I call this Strategic Analysis approach, the way to define the "Strategic Drivers".

Since this step is always used to answer questions about **Where We are Today**, it is important before we can move on to the strategy analysis tools, to define the "**WE**", which acts as the boundary of the strategic analysis to make it more relevant and actionable. For example, are "**We**" a business unit in a global company or the global company itself? For instance, General Electric (GE) has very strong connections with the US government, which can be put as a strength for GE global, but it means very little for GE Egypt. Therefore, "**We**" defines our playing field, which in turn impacts the strategy planning and, ultimately, the strategic decision-making.

Our today is defined by understanding the environment in which an organization is operating, together with the organization's interaction with it. This strategic analysis is carried out by using a variety of strategic analysis tools. The Chartered Institute for IT compiled a guide that includes 72 business analysis tools which include, for example [6]:

- SWOT analysis
- PESTEL analysis
- Porter's five forces analysis
- Competitor analysis framework
- Four Corners analysis
- Value chain analysis
- Early warning scans
- TOWS matrix

These analytical methods and tools are key to ensuring that consistency and an appropriate level of rigor are applied to the analysis. There are a number of important considerations to be aware of when using analytical tools:

1. The tool must help to answer the question that the organization has asked.
2. The expected benefit of using the tool needs to be defined, and it must be actionable. The more clearly the tool has been defined, the more likely the analysis will be successful.
3. Many tools benefit from input and collaboration with other people, functions, or even organizations. There should be sufficient time for collaboration and advance warning given so that people can accommodate the analysis.
4. Proper use of analytical tools may be time-consuming. It is important to ensure that key stakeholders, for example, the board, senior directors, and company departments are aware of this. Otherwise, they may not be able to provide the necessary commitment to complete the analysis.

The aim of the analytical tool is to sharpen the focus of the analysis and to ensure a methodical, balanced approach. All analytical tools rely on historical, backward-looking data to extrapolate future assumptions. Therefore, it is important to exercise caution when interpreting strategic analysis results. Otherwise, the analysis may be unduly influenced by preconceptions or pressures within the organization which seeks to validate a particular strategic assumption.

5.4.1 SWOT Analysis—Simple But...

A SWOT analysis is a simple but widely used tool that helps in understanding the strengths, weaknesses, opportunities, and threats involved in a project or business activity.

It starts by defining the objective of the project or business activity and identifies the internal and external factors that are important to achieving that objective. Strengths and weaknesses are usually internal to the organization, while opportunities and threats are usually external.

However, despite its popularity and longevity, SWOT analysis lacks originality and can yield misleading results. When I discuss with executives and MBA students their experience with doing a SWOT analysis, they all agree with the fact that it is simple to use but not very useful or actionable. The following points summarize some of the critical shortcomings of the traditional SWOT analysis [7]:

- **Typical SWOT guidelines promote superficial scanning and impromptu categorizing instead of methodical inquiry.** They leave the false impression that noteworthy particulars can be spotted at a glance, and their likely impact is obvious and independent of context. Hence, they prompt analysts to reflexively equate the likes of stricter impending regulations with threats and rapid market growth with opportunities. Yet, circumstances that threaten some contestants usually extend opportunities to others, and many apparent opportunities evaporate when examined in light of the competitive context. In practice, most SWOTs are done using brainstorming sessions with the management team. This produces an analysis that is too qualitative without investing enough time to collect data to support it.
- **The SWOT framework does not readily accommodate tradeoffs.** For instance, Southwest Airlines' lack of customary in-flight meals should be regarded as a strength or weakness? From one aspect, no meals put Southwest at a disadvantage. However, serving meals would diminish Southwest's key advantage which is low cost. Aside from increasing the out-of-pocket cost, it will also increase the opportunity cost because more time would be used to service planes, leaving less revenue-generating flying time, thereby making the Southwest's no-meals policy too important to ignore. Moreover, categorizing Southwest's dearth of customary amenities as weaknesses while listing effects (lower costs) among strengths is confusing and implies that "rectifying" the apparent "weaknesses" would diminish corresponding strengths. In sum, tradeoffs and their consequences are among various strategically significant phenomena that are complex, dynamic, and systemic. They rarely can be depicted effectively by simplistic, static, taxonomic schemata, such as SWOT matrices.
- **SWOT guidelines commonly confuse accomplishments with strengths.** For example, market-share leadership is an accomplishment listed as a strength in Kotler's checklist [75]. Calling it a strength may seem appropriate because frontrunners must be doing something right; studies have shown direct correlations between market share and earnings. Nevertheless, reflexively equating market-share leadership with competitive advantage or strength is imprudent because the implied causal relationship between volume and advantage may no longer exist or may never have existed. When market-share leadership, early entry, or other accomplishments do seem to underlie current advantages, then the specific

advantages should be enumerated (e.g., cost leadership) and their sources noted (e.g., superior scale economies and bargaining power derived from market share).

■ **SWOT guidelines generally lack criteria for prioritizing/ranking SWOTs**. Hence, items are listed as if all were equally important and critical matters are often ignored

■ **It doesn't have a clear linking to the future/objectives**. Strengths/Weaknesses are typically not evaluated in terms of their **Importance** toward achieving the Strategic Objectives and Opportunities/Threats are not evaluated in terms of their **Likelihood of Occurrence**.

■ **The cross-linking between the four quadrants is not always done**. Hence, the TOWS matrix was later proposed to link the four quadrants of the SWOT. Strengths can be linked to Opportunities to provide SO strategies that define what strength can be used to take advantage of what opportunity. Similarly, ST, WO, and WT strategies can be developed. An elaboration on this TOWS matrix will be provided later in the chapter.

My proposal to address these serious shortcomings of traditional SWOT analysis in the context of understanding *Today*, is to combine a number of the available Strategic Analysis and Management tools to provide a more precise and actionable answer to the question of "Where Are We Today?"

My proposal is to combine the following traditional tools in a new way:

■ Strengths/Weaknesses Analysis should be done using the same Balanced Scorecard Perspectives used to set the Strategic Objectives that define the *Future*. So we should analyze the organization's Strengths/Weaknesses in the Financial, Market, Operations, and Organization dimensions. It can also be organized using a value chain analysis approach. Each element in the analysis needs to be evaluated on two scales: Performance and Importance.

■ Opportunities/Threats Analysis should be done at two levels. The macro-level uses the PESTEL Framework factors (Political, Economic, Socio/Demographic, Technological, Ecological, and Legal). The microlevel (also known as industry-level) can be analyzed using Porter's five forces model in combination with the Competitor Analysis framework proposed by Chen. Each element in the analysis needs to be evaluated on two scales: Impact and Probability of Occurrence.

■ The SWOT Analysis needs to be complemented with a TOWS matrix analysis, the Four Corners Analysis, and an Early Warning System.

■ Finally, this SWOT Analysis needs to be done by taking into consideration the evolution of Society 5.0 and the Future Economies.

5.4.2 EBOR Framework

I believe this integrated approach to Strategic Analysis can improve the quality of the foundation on which we can build our strategy. This approach can be summarized as shown in Figure 5.15. To differentiate it from the traditional SWOT, I propose labeling it as **Enablers, Blockers, Options, and Reactions (EBOR)** Analysis Framework.

The following section will provide an overview of the proposed **EBOR Strategic Analysis** framework and how the continuous use/update of it allows the organization to have a **Strategic Early Warning System** that helps in guiding its journey toward Making the Future Happen Today.

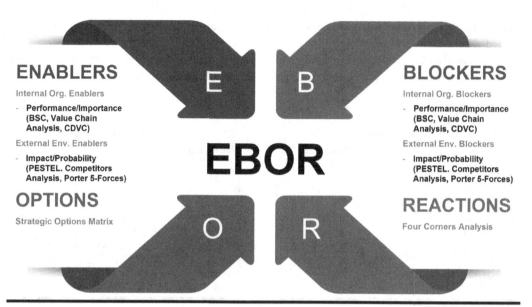

Figure 5.15 EBOR strategic analysis framework

5.4.2.1 Enablers and Blockers

Strategy Enablers and Blockers can be found both internally and externally. Hence, it is advised to organize the analysis based on these perspectives.

The **Enablers** will be defined as the items that score as follows:

- In the Internal Assessment items that have both **Fundamental Strength** and **High Importance**
- In the External Assessment items that have both **Very Positive Impact** and **High Probability**

The **Blockers** will be defined as the items that score as follows:

- In the Internal Assessment items that have both **Fundamental Weakness** and **High Importance**
- In the External Assessment items that have both **Very Negative Impact** and **High Probability**

5.4.2.1.1 Internal Assessment

The organization's performance is analyzed using the same four perspectives of the Balanced Scorecard used to develop the Strategic Objectives as discussed earlier. This includes the Marketing, Financial, Operational, and Organizational set of factors. Using those four dimensions/set of factors ensures the proper link of our assessment of *Today* with our definition of *Tomorrow*.

Each of the elements of those dimensions/factors can be assessed on a five-point performance scale: Fundamental Strength, Marginal Strength, Neutral, Marginal Weakness, or Fundamental Weakness. In addition, the importance of that factor for the defined Strategic Objectives is measured on a high, medium, and low scale. This is crucial since some of the factors can be performed with a high level of strength but may not hold significant importance when it comes to the future of the organization. Figure 5.16 shows the four dimensions/types of factors as per the Balanced Scorecard perspectives (Marketing, Financial, Operational, and Organizational) and

INTERNAL ENABLERS/ BLOCKERS	PERFORMANCE					IMPORTANCE		
	Fundamntal Strength	Marginal Strength	Neutral	Marginal Weakness	Fundamntal Weakness	High	Mid	Low
Marketing Factors								
Financial Factors								
Operations Factors								
Organization Factors								

Figure 5.16   Internal strategic enablers and blockers

two scales (Performance and Importance) of the internal analysis of the enablers and blockers [8]. Table 5.1 provides a comprehensive listing of the elements that can be considered for this analysis.

5.4.2.1.2 Value Chain Analysis (Basic and CDVC)

To better assess the operational factors for the organization, a deeper analysis of the company value chain can be done. Value chain analysis is based on the principle that organizations exist to create value for their customers. In the analysis, the organization's activities are divided into separate sets of activities that add value. The organization can more effectively evaluate its internal capabilities by identifying and examining each of these activities. Each value-adding activity is considered to be a source of competitive advantage.

The three steps for conducting value chain analysis are:

1. **Separate the organization's operations into primary and support activities**
   Primary activities are those that physically create a product, as well as market the product, deliver the product to the customer and provide after-sales support. Support activities are those that facilitate the primary activities (Figure 5.17).
2. **Allocate cost to each activity**
   Activity cost information provides managers with valuable insight into the internal capabilities of an organization.
3. **Identify activities that are critical to customer satisfaction and market success**
   There are three important considerations in evaluating the role of each activity in the value chain.
   – **Company vision.** This influences the choice of activities an organization undertakes.
   – **Industry type.** The nature of industry influences the type of activities undertaken by the organization.

Table 5.1 Internal Enablers and Blockers Analysis Elements

Internal Enablers and Blockers	Performance					Importance		
	Fundamental Strength	Marginal Strength	Neutral	Marginal Weakness	Fundamental Weakness	Hi	Mid	Lo
Marketing Factors								
1—Relative market share								
2—Reputation								
3—Previous performance								
4—Competitive stance								
5—Customer base								
6—Customer loyalty								
7—Breadth of product range								
8—Depth of product range								
9—Product quality								
10—Program of product modification								
11—New product program								
12—Distribution costs								
13—Dealer network								
14—Dealer loyalty								
15—Geographical coverage								
16—Salesforce								

(Continued)

Table 5.1 (Continued) Internal Enablers and Blockers Analysis Elements

Internal Enablers and Blockers	Performance					Importance		
	Fundamental Strength	Marginal Strength	Neutral	Marginal Weakness	Fundamental Weakness	Hi	Mid	Lo
17—After-sales service								
18—Manufacturing costs								
19—Manufacturing flexibility								
20—Raw material advantage								
21—Pricing								
22—Advertising								
23—Unique selling propositions								
24—Structure of competition								
Financial Factors								
25—Cost of capital								
26—Availability of capital								
27—Profitability								
28—Financial stability								
29—Margins								
Operations Factors								
30—Production facilities								
31—Economies of scale								

(Continued)

Table 5.1 (Continued) Internal Enablers and Blockers Analysis Elements

Internal Enablers and Blockers	Performance						Importance		
	Fundamental Strength	Marginal Strength	Neutral	Marginal Weakness	Fundamental Weakness		Hi	Mid	Lo
32—Flexibility									
33—Workforce									
34—Technical skill									
35—Delivery capabilities									
36—Supplier sourcing flexibility									
Services Factors									
37—Reliability									
38—Responsiveness									
39—Assurance									
40—Empathy									
41—Tangibles									
Organizational Factors									
42—Culture									
43—Leadership									
44—Managerial capabilities									
45—Workforce									
46—Flexibility									
47—Adaptability									

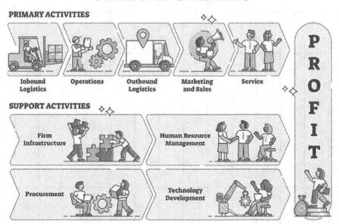

Figure 5.17   The basic value chain

 – **Value system**. This includes the value chains of an organization's upstream and downstream partners in providing products to end customers.

A more comprehensive approach to analyzing the primary activities in light of the VUCA world that we are living in today is the use of the concurrent digitalized value chain (CDVC) analysis model [9].

In CDVC, the organization value chain, as shown in Figure 5.18, is defined in six elements:

■ Design and portfolio management
■ Planning
■ Suppliers and sourcing management
■ Make (manufacturing)
■ Deliver
■ Sales and customer service

The model assesses the concurrency progression/maturity of the value chain along five levels:

■ Level 1: **Restored** (standards defined and foundations ensured)
■ Level 2: **In-Control** (standards adherence and performance to standards)
■ Level 3: **Responsive** (flexibility and speed, agile, simplified, and effective)
■ Level 4: **E2E Integration and Synchronization** (value chain end-to-end integration based on customer demand pull)
■ Level 5: **Real-Time Networks** (sales growth and value creation in interconnected network)

Most organizations today perform at levels 1 or 2, and investments are being made leveraging data and the digital economy models to develop E2E value chains that are responsive, integrated, and synchronized (levels 3 and 4). Society 5.0 and the future economies provide real opportunities for the development of Real-Time networks. Hence, organizations today should assess their capabilities against this future benchmark and develop their plans to reach Level-5 maturity in the future.

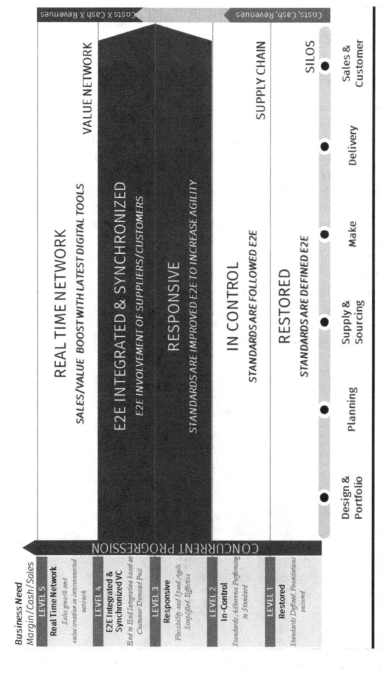

Figure 5.18 CDVC [9]

Ultimately, the output of the Internal Assessment provides the organization of clear undersetting of the Internal Enablers and Blockers as follows:

- The **Internal Enablers** are items that have both **Fundamental Strength** and **High Importance** toward achieving the organization's future strategic objectives
- The **Internal Blockers** are the items that have both **Fundamental Weakness** and **High Importance** toward achieving the organization's future strategic objectives

5.4.2.1.3 External Assessment

Similarly, the opportunities and threats of an organization are analyzed based on the impact of macro- and microenvironmental forces. Macro-environmental forces consist of non-industry-specific aspects in the organization's surroundings that have the potential to affect the organization's strategies. Their impact is less direct on the organization and the organization has a more limited impact on these elements of the environment.

Microenvironmental forces influence the organization directly. It includes suppliers that deal directly or indirectly, consumers and customers, and other local stakeholders. Together these two factors consolidate to form the external assessment. Figure 5.19 summarizes the key macro- and microenvironment elements.

The impact analysis of each of these forces on an organization is determined by indicating whether the impact is very positive, positive, neutral, negative, or very negative. Besides, the probability of occurrence of these factors on an organization is analyzed through a high, medium, or low probability (see Figure 5.20).

Table 5.2 provides a listing of the elements that can be considered for this External Enablers and Blockers analysis at the macro- and micro business environment levels.

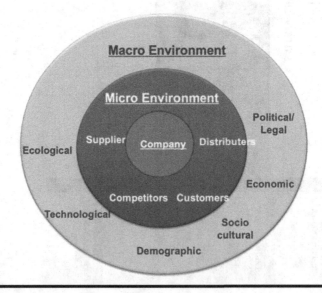

Figure 5.19   Macro- and microenvironment

EXTERNAL ENABLERS/BLOCKERS	IMPACT					PROBABILITY		
	Very Positive	Positive	Neutral	Negative	Very Negative	High	Mid	Low
Macro-Environment Forces (PESTEL)								
Micro-Environment Forces (Porter 5-Forces)								

Figure 5.20 External strategic enables and blockers

Table 5.2 External Enablers and Blockers Analysis

External Enablers and Blockers	Impact					Probability		
	Very Positive	Positive	Neutral	Negative	Very Negative	Hi	Mid	Lo
Macro-Environment Forces								
Political								
Economic								
Socio/ Demographic								
Technological								
Ecological								
Legal								
Microenvironment Forces								
Customers and/or distributors (buyers)								
Existing competitors								
New competitors								
Substitutes								
Suppliers								

5.4.2.1.4 Macro-Environment Analysis—PESTEL

All organizations need to identify external factors within their environment that could have an impact on their operations. Many of these will be things that the organization has no control over, but the implications of which need to be understood.

A popular tool for identifying these external factors is the PESTEL Analysis, which can be used to help you consider political, economic, social, technological, ecological, and legal issues. As organizations become more globalized, expanding their existing borders, the PESTEL technique ensures that they thoroughly question each of these factors and consider their impact.

The PESTEL Analysis provides a framework that enables you to investigate your external environment by asking questions about each factor and discussing the likely implications. These are the types of questions you would ask:

- **What are the key political factors?**
- **What are the important economic factors?**
- **What cultural/sociodemographic aspects are most important?**
- **What technological innovations are likely to occur?**
- **What current and impending legislation may affect the industry?**
- **What are the ecological/environmental considerations?**

How you categorize each issue raised is not important when using the PESTEL technique because the aim of this tool is simply to identify as many factors as possible. For example, whether you classify an impending government regulation as a Political or Legal issue is not important. The only thing that matters is that it is identified as potentially having an impact on your organization.

The PESTEL tool is a powerful technique for analyzing your environment, but it should represent just one component of a comprehensive strategic analysis process. The PESTEL factors, combined with external microenvironmental factors and internal drivers, can be classified as Enablers or Blockers in our proposed EBOR Analysis.

- **Political Factors**

    It is always advisable to keep abreast of potential policy changes in any government because even where the political situation is relatively stable, there can be changes in the policy at the very highest level, and these can have serious implications.

    This may result in changes in government priorities, which in turn can result in new initiatives being introduced as well as changes to trade regulations or taxation. These can include changes in:
    - **Employment laws:** An example of the complexity of those issues is the handling of GIG workers in the future and how current laws lack clarity on those issues. Uber case with their captains is an interesting model to watch about the future evolution of employment laws.
    - **Consumer protection laws:** Here again, most existing consumer protection laws have not evolved to address the challenges of the online consumer. Hence, our external environment analysis should clearly include this as we move toward the digital economy.
    - **Environmental regulations:** The 2021 UN Climate Change Summit (COP26) held in Glasgow tried to send another wake-up call to the world about the importance of responsible business practices to save our world ... as Greta Thunberg put it: **We don't**

have Planet B. So, your strategy should address this Net-Zero plans to see how it can enable or block your strategic moves.

- **Taxation regulations:** Governments are keen on taxing new revenues/incomes such as money made by online influencers and bloggers, Facebook shops sales, and other informal economy players. Those new tax policies are crucial for SMEs (small and medium enterprises) strategies.
- **Trade restrictions or reforms:** Both trade wars and trade cooperation agreements are part of the economic systems of today and are expected to evolve in the future. Africa as the last frontier for development and growth is targeted today by trade agreements with many world trade powers such as China and Russia.
- **Health and safety requirements:** Moving from the traditional definition of physical health and safety, regulations are evolving to address mental, emotional, and psychological health and safety too. The debate about Facebook/Instagram and their impact is prompting regulatory action in the United States that can be followed in other parts of the world.

■ **Economic Factors**

These issues include assessing potential changes to an economy's inflation rate, taxes, interest rates, exchange rate, trading regulations, and excise duties. In terms of operational efficiency, you would need to consider factors such as unemployment, skills levels, availability of expertise, wage patterns, working practices, and labor cost trends. When trying to determine the economic viability of a market, we also need to look at such issues as the current cost of living for the target market as well as the availability of credit and finance. A good reference to start with for such economic indicators is the CIA World Factbook https://www.cia.gov/the-world-factbook/. Other international economic organizations such as the World Bank Open Data Sources https://data.worldbank.org/, the International Financing Corporation www.ifc.org, and the OEDC https://www.oecd.org/ can provide very valuable reports and statistics on those economic factors for the macro-environment analysis.

■ **Cultural-Social-Demographic Factors**

Cultural-Social-Demographic factors that need to be considered are those that have an impact on your market. These include issues such as:

- Age distribution
- Population growth rate
- Employment levels
- Income statistics
- Education and career trends
- Religious beliefs
- Cultural and social conventions

We have been talking for a while about the Aging of the Population as a mega trend that we need to study for any future strategy. This issue can be a great enabler for developing economies but a great blocker for developed economies. Countries like China had to change their one-child per family policy to encourage its people to have more babies to compensate for the effect of the aging population. Europe which is commonly described as the Aging Content is greatly concerned about this issue. Old policies related to migrants are being challenged now due to the social and cultural implications that complicate this policy. I believe that the use of Robotics and the advancement of Industry 4.0 policies in the future have those demographic shifts as one of their underlying drivers. A very good resource to consult on the demographic shifts is the Population Pyramid website https://www.populationpyramid.net/

■ **Technological Factors**

This element has become a key factor for organizations in assessing and listing issues that could have a potential impact on their operations and that could be critical to its long-term future. The pace of change in technology is becoming more rapid, and often changes that impact your market come from unexpected sources. Technological factors can be broadly divided into three areas: company value chain, customer experience, and infrastructure. For example, by exploiting opportunities to update or alter their production technology, an organization can gain market share, thereby attaining a strong competitive advantage. Such activities include:

- Automation
- Improved quality of parts and the end product
- Better visibility of operational performance to achieve significant cost savings
- Better connectivity to use outsourcing to control costs and offer greater flexibility

Technological advances have also allowed organizations much greater freedom of choice when deciding how best to manage their operations, streamline their workflow, and eliminate operational bottlenecks.

■ **Environmental Factors**

The issues surrounding environmental protection have become increasingly important in recent years as the implications of under-regulated economic activity are seen today. This has become more significant with globalization as the impact of an organization's actions may be felt outside of its native country and may incur unquantifiable financial penalties.

As discussed earlier many courtiers are changing their energy policies to address the global warming threats. Issues such as renewable energy storage technologies are transforming businesses such as TESLA. The advancement of **Green Hydrogen** technologies is the hottest thing in renewable energy these days. Their impact on countries and industries dependent on Natural Gas will be significant.

Other environmental factors are those that relate to the weather, climate, and geographical location. For example, natural disasters or weather cycles such as monsoons may create too high a risk for operating in a particular region.

■ **Legal Factors**

The list of legal factors should include current and impending legislation that may affect the industry in areas such as employment, competition, unemployment rate, competition, and health and safety. Recent years have seen a significant rise in the number of regulatory bodies that have been set up to monitor organizations' observance of legislation relating to all areas of operations, including consumer protection, employee welfare, waste disposal, and how their earnings and investments will be taxed. There are also trading restrictions, quotas, and excise duties to consider.

The impact of technology on the individual has led to legislation being introduced which aims to protect privacy and ensure organizations have to gain permission before emailing or contacting the consumer. For example, the EU **General Data Protection Regulation (GDPR)**, which governs how personal data of individuals in the EU may be processed and transferred, went into effect on May 25, 2018. GDPR is comprehensive privacy legislation that applies across sectors and to companies of all sizes. Organizations need to give careful thought to the type and nature of potential legislation that governments could introduce to curb what is often seen as the invasive side of the rapid growth of technology.

5.4.2.1.5 Microenvironment Forces

The microenvironment, also known as the industry-specific environment, provides the second level of analysis for the External Enablers and Blockers. One of the most famous tools to perform this analysis is Porter's five forces model. In addition to analyzing the power of Buyers and Suppliers, this model includes three elements related to competitors (current, future, and substitutes). Hence, I believe that this model quality can be better enhanced by first using the Competitors Analysis Framework proposed by Chen in his 1996 article in the *Academy of Management Review*. The next section provides an overview of this framework.

■ **Competitors Analysis Framework**
   As shown in Figure 5.21, the framework used dimensions to classify the company competitors: market commonality and resource similarity, and used two levels, high and low. This classification framework identified four quadrants that can define the relationship between competitors to better plan future moves [10].

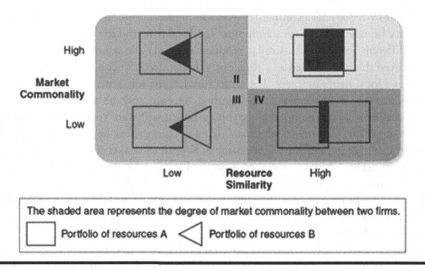

Figure 5.21   Competitors analysis framework [10]

Quadrant I represents a competitor with high market commonality and high resource similarity from the focal firm standpoint. Simplifying but without loss of generality, the focal firm and the competitor are competing in the same markets with similar products to satisfy the same need. Hence competition between them can only be in price, and competition brings margins down. This quadrant will be called "**Mutual Forbearance**" and the competitor in it "**twin**". A focal firm with the competitor in this quadrant will not want to attack the competitor but will retaliate if the competitor attacks. Customers see those two companies as direct competitors without a great degree of differentiation, for example, detergents produced by P&G (e.g., Ariel and Tide) versus those produced by Henkel (e.g., Persil).

Quadrant II represents a competitor with high market commonality and low resource similarity from the focal firm standpoint. The focal firm and the competitor are competing in the same markets with different products to satisfy the same need. Hence competition between them is about different value propositions. This quadrant will be called "**Differentiation**" and the competitor in it "**Different**". A focal firm with a competitor in this quadrant will want to attack the competitor. Customers can see those two companies as substitutes. For example, Google Due and Facebook Messenger are competing with Vodafone and Orange (global mobile operators) in the international calling market, and WhatsApp is competing with the mobile operators in the messaging market.

Quadrant III represents a competitor with low market commonality and low resource similarity from the focal firm standpoint. The focal firm and the competitor are competing in different markets with different products. Hence any action undertaken by them is not deemed as a threat or a direct attack. This quadrant will be called "**Perfect Competition**" and the competitor in it "**Common**". The term Perfect here refers to the fact that competition is not a threat at this point, and the firm resources can be allocated to issues other than countering competitors' actions. A focal firm with the competitor in this quadrant will neither want to attack the competitor nor retaliate for any action the competitor undertakes.

Quadrant IV represents a competitor with low market commonality and high resource similarity from the focal firm standpoint. The focal firm and the competitor are competing in different markets with similar products to satisfy the same need. Hence competition between them is deemed as a threat or a direct attack since the competitor could easily enter a focal firm's markets. The same way that the focal firm could enter the competitor's markets. This quadrant will be called "**Ocean**" and the competitor in its "**Future**". A focal firm with a competitor in this quadrant will want to attack the competitor. In this quadrant, customers might see that the competitors don't compete now but that might change in the future. For example, Korean carmakers (such as Hyundai and Kia) don't consider Chinese carmakers (such as JAC and MG) as competitors now, but this can change in the near future.

Using this Competitors Analysis framework can help focus Porter's five forces analysis, as will be discussed in the next section.

■ **Porter's Five Forces**

Porter's five forces of competitive position analysis was developed in 1979 by Michael E. Porter of Harvard Business School as a simple framework for assessing and evaluating the competitive strength and position of a business organization.

This model is based on the fact that there are five forces which determine the competitive intensity and attractiveness of the market. Porter's five forces help to identify where power lies in the business situation. This is useful in understanding both the strength of an organization's current competitive position and the strength the organization may look to move into. Figure 5.22 shows the five forces and their determinants that can be assessed as they apply to the organizational environment. The Regulatory Intervention dimension (such as de/regulation) was later added to the model, and other dimensions such as the competitor's level of innovativeness, exposure to globalization, and the threat of digitalization were proposed to improve the quality of the model. Our discussion will focus on the key five forces since the proposed additional dimensions can be incorporated as needed into the existing model.

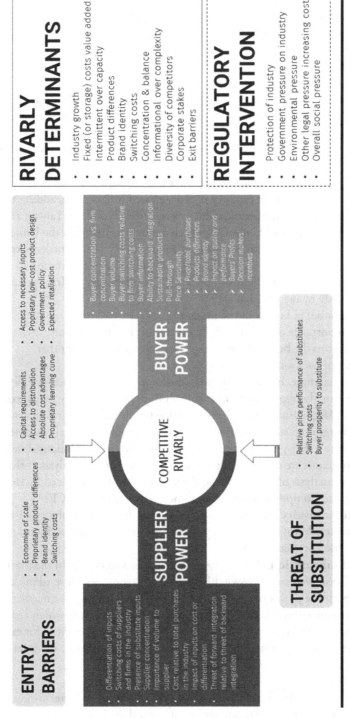

ENTRY BARRIERS

- Economies of scale
- Proprietary product differences
- Brand identity
- Switching costs
- Capital requirements
- Access to distribution
- Absolute cost advantages
- Proprietary learning curve
- Access to necessary inputs
- Proprietary low-cost product design
- Government policy
- Expected retaliation

SUPPLIER POWER

- Differentiation of inputs
- Switching costs of suppliers and firms in the industry
- Presence of substitute inputs
- Supplier concentration
- Importance of volume to supplier
- Cost relative to total purchases in the industry
- Impact of inputs on cost or differentiation
- Threat of forward integration relative to threat of backward integration

COMPETITIVE RIVARLY

BUYER POWER

- Buyer concentration vs. firm concentration
- Buyer volume
- Buyer switching costs relative to firm switching costs
- Buyer information
- Ability to backward integration
- Sustainable products
- Pull-through
- Price Sensitivity
  - Price/total purchases
  - Products differences
  - Brand identity
  - Impact on quality and performance
  - Buyers' Profits
  - Decision makers incentives

THREAT OF SUBSTITUTION

- Relative price performance of substitutes
- Switching costs
- Buyer prosperity to substitute

RIVARLY DETERMINANTS

- Industry growth
- Fixed (or storage) costs value added
- Intermittent over capacity
- Product differences
- Brand identity
- Switching costs
- Concentration & balance
- Informational over complexity
- Diversity of competitors
- Corporate stakes
- Exit barriers

REGULATORY INTERVENTION

- Protection of industry
- Government pressure on industry
- Environmental pressure
- Other legal pressure increasing cost
- Overall social pressure

Figure 5.22   Porter's five forces and their determinants [9]

The five forces are:

1. **Supplier power**. An assessment of how easy it is for suppliers to drive up prices. This is driven mainly by factors such as:
   - Supplier Concentration: The number of suppliers of each essential input
   - Differentiation of Inputs: The uniqueness of their product and services
   - The relative size and strength of the supplier
   - Switching costs from one supplier to another
   - Threat of forward integration

   Other determinants are shown in Figure 5.22 to aid in further analysis of this force. A very recent example of how this supplier power force might represent a threat is a shortage in Computer Chips supply to the automotive industry. It has been reported that chip shortage could cost automobile makers worldwide a loss of US$60.6 billion in revenues in 2021 alone.

   The Semiconductor Industry Association (SIA) says that about 75% of global semiconductor manufacturing capacity is concentrated in East Asia, adding that the production of the most advanced semiconductors is entirely located in Taiwan and South Korea. Companies in the Quad Countries, which comprises Australia, the United States, Japan, and India, are putting great focus on resolving supply chain bottlenecks for this crucial component to reduce the threats posed by this supplier concentration in the Far East.

2. **Buyer power**. An assessment of how easy it is for buyers to drive prices down. This is driven mainly by factors such as:
   - The number of buyers in the market
   - The importance of each individual buyer in the organization
   - The cost to the buyer of switching from one supplier to another
   - Threat of backward integration

   For example, having a few large customers might be operationally very attractive but it can also represent a major threat of not being properly managed. Losing one of the key large customers can be devastating for the company and its sustainability. Also, low-margin pressures imposed by large high-profile powerful customers can limit the company's ability to invest in its future strategy and continuous development. Other determinants are shown in Figure 5.22 to aid in further analysis of this force.

   The analysis of the following three forces can be enhanced by the data analyzed using the Competitors Analysis Framework developed by Chen.

3. **Competitive rivalry**. The key driver is the number and capability of the competitors in the market. Many competitors, offering undifferentiated products and services, will reduce market attractiveness.

4. **Threat of substitution**. Where close substitute products exist in the market, it increases the likelihood of customers switching to alternatives in response to price increases. This reduces both the power of suppliers and the attractiveness of the market.

5. **Threat of new entry**. Profitable markets attract new entrants which erode profitability. Unless incumbents have strong and durable entry barriers to entry, for example, patents, economies of scale, economies of scope, capital requirements, or government policies, the profitability will decline to a competitive rate.

Although Porter's five forces analysis is typically used to determine the competitive intensity and therefore the attractiveness of a market, it is suggested here to use it to identify the External Enablers and Blockers for the firm's future strategy. To demonstrate

Force	Determinants for Competitive Pressure	Threat to Profits (Low threat=0 / Medium=5 / High= 10)		Trend
		Present	Future	
Competitive Rivalry	Industry Growth	4.00	5.00	↗
	Industry Profitability	2.00	5.00	↗
	Competition concentration	2.00	3.00	↗
Threat of New Entrants	Informational over complexity	7.00	7.00	=
	Undifferentiated products	6.00	6.00	=
	Switching costs to competitors	9.00	9.00	=
Threat of substitutes	Brand Loyalty	8.00	8.00	↗
	Importance of strong distribution	5.00	5.00	=
Supplier's Power	Investment in promotion	3.00	3.00	=
	Diversity of competitors	7.50	9.00	↗
Buyer's Power	Average	5.35	6.00	↗

Figure 5.23   Five-forces analysis to identify enablers and blockers [9]

how to perform this analysis, Figure 5.23 provides an example of how the determinants of Competitive Rivalry can be scored on a scale from 0 to 10 (low threat = 0, medium threat = 5, high threat = 10) as related to its level of Threat to Profits both *Today* and in the *Future*. This analysis provides the view that Competitive Rivalry is an Enabler or a Blocker and its trend too.

Determinants of other forces (buyers, suppliers, new entrants, and substitutes) can also be analyzed using the same approach presented above. In order to determine which force has the highest impact, the average score for each of the forces is calculated by computing the average of determinant scores for both the present and the future.

The average score of each force is compared against a set of thresholds to identify the threat level. These thresholds are set as follows:

- High threat (above 7)
- Medium–high threat (5–7)
- Medium–low threat (3–5)
- Low threat (below 3)

Ultimately, the output of the External Assessment provides the organization of clear undersetting of the External Enablers and Blockers as follows:

- The **External Enablers** are items that have both **Very Positive Impact** and **High Probability of Occurrence**
- The **External Blockers** are the items that have both **Very Negative Impact** and **High Probability of Occurrence**

The first level of our understanding of where we are *Today* can be summarized by combining all internal and external Enablers and Blockers that are clearly linked and aligned with the Balanced and SMART Strategic Objectives translating the Strategic Direction agreed on with different stakeholders.

5.4.2.2 *Options and Reactions*

Identifying the Strategic Options and Competitors' Reactions to the organization's strategic moves is a crucial step prior to defining the final detailed strategies for the firm to follow. In this step, Strategic Options can be identified by matching the internal and external Enablers and Blockers using the Options matrix. The Competitors' Reactions can be identified using Porter's Four Corners Analysis.

5.4.2.2.1 Strategic Options Matrix

A Strategic Options matrix can add real value to an organization, helping to take strategic planning one step further. Figure 5.24 is an example of a Strategic Options matrix.

A Strategic Options analysis enables an organization to match its Internal Enablers (IE) and External Enablers (EE) to develop "maxi-maxi" strategies (IE/EE)—those with the greatest potential for success. For example, Internal Enabler such as high brand recognition or customer loyalty could be combined with the External Enabler of a growing market to launch a new product or service.

	Internal ENABLERS (IE)	Internal BLOCKERS (IB)
External ENABLERS (EE)	**IE/EE** Strategic Options to use the Internal Enables (IE) to take advantage of the External Enablers (EE)	**IB/EE** Strategic Options to remove the Internal Blockers (IB) to take advantage of the External Enablers (EE)
External BLOCKERS (EB)	**IE/EB** Strategic Options to use the Internal Enables (IE) to minimize the External Blockers (EB)	**IB/EE** Strategic Options to remove the Internal Blockers (IB) to minimize the External Blockers (EE)

Figure 5.24 Strategic Options matrix

On the other extreme, it highlights the organization's vulnerability to External Blockers (EB) based on its Internal Blockers (IB) and facilitates the development of strategies that minimize these and avoid threats (EB/IB)—"mini-mini" strategies. For example, such strategies could include developing strategic alliances or a more drastic strategy could be to withdraw from a specific market altogether.

In between, mini-maxi (IB/EE) and maxi-mini strategies (IE/EB) are designed to remove Internal Blockers, utilizing External Enablers, and minimize External Blockers utilizing Internal Enablers. An example mini-maxi strategy (IB/EE) is that an organization may have identified an External Enabler to outsource some aspects of its business operations, overcoming the Internal Blocker of lack of specific skills within the organization.

It's important to remember that an Options Analysis will not point to which specific strategy to adopt, but it does focus attention on the areas where the action is required and give some indication of the nature of those actions.

5.4.2.2.2 Reactions—Four Corners Analysis

Developed by Michael Porter, the Four Corners Analysis is a useful tool for anticipating competitors' reactions and moves. It emphasizes that the objective of competitive analysis should always be on generating insights into the future [11].

The model can be used to:

- Develop a profile of the likely strategy changes a competitor might make and how successful they may be
- Determine each competitor's probable response to the range of feasible strategic moves other competitors might make
- Determine each competitor's probable reaction to the range of industry shifts and environmental changes that may occur

The "Four Corners" refer to four diagnostic components that are essential to competitor analysis: Drivers, Current Strategy, Management Assumptions, and Capabilities. Figure 5.25 shows the Four Corners aligned in two dimensions: Motivation (Drivers and Management Assumptions) and Actions (Current Strategy and Capabilities).

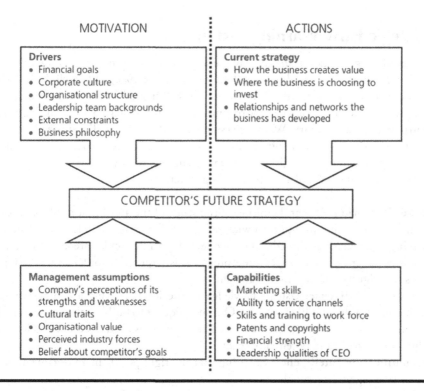

Figure 5.25   Four Corners Analysis [11]

Most of the organizations carry out basic competitor analysis and have an appreciation for their competitor's strategies. However, motivational factors are often overlooked and yet are generally the key drivers of competitive behavior. Understanding the following four components can help predict how a competitor may respond to a given situation.

Motivation—Drivers. Analyzing a competitor's goals assists in understanding whether they are satisfied with their current performance and market position. This helps predict how they might react to external forces and how likely it is that they will change strategy.

Motivation—Management Assumptions. The perceptions and assumptions that a competitor has about itself, the industry, and other companies will influence its strategic decisions. Analyzing these assumptions can help identify competitors' biases and blind spots.

Actions—Current Strategy. A company strategy determines how a competitor competes in the market. However, there can be differences between the "intended strategy" (the strategy that is stated in annual reports, interviews, and public statements) and the realized strategy (the strategy that the company is following in practice as evidenced by acquisitions, capital expenditure, and new product development). Where the current strategy can yield satisfactory results, it is reasonable to assume that an organization will continue to compete in the same way as it currently does.

Actions—Capabilities. The drivers, assumptions, and strategy of an organization will determine the nature, likelihood, and timing of a competitor's actions. However, an organization's capabilities will determine its ability to initiate or respond to external forces.

5.5 Strategic Early Warning System

To ensure that the organization is insightfully guided during its journey toward the future and that its strategy is continuously informed by a good understanding of *Today* and a well-defined *Future*, the strategic objectives should be regularly reviewed, and the EBOR analysis framework should be actively used and updated. This process provides the organization with a Strategic Early Warning System.

The purpose of Strategic Early Warning systems is to detect or predict strategically important events as early as possible. They are often used to identify the first scene of attack from a competitor or to assess the likelihood of a given scenario becoming a reality.

The seven key components of an early warning system are [11]:

- **Market Definition**: A clear definition of the scope of the arena that needs to be examined.
- **Open System**: Ability to capture a wide range of information on relevant competitors
- **Filtering**: Information which has been collected for a particular arena needs to be filtered according to significance. Expert interpretation is required in order to identify particular events that signify strategic moves and shifts.
- **Predictive Intelligence**: Using knowledge of the forces driving a competitor to predict which direction they are likely to take. One technique is to build likely scenarios and actively seek the signals that confirm the scenario. The predictions need to be assessed for their probability of occurring and potential impact.
- **Communicating Intelligence**: Ensuring that the right people in an organization receive a regular briefing on key signals.

- **Contingency Planning**: Events that have a high potential impact or probability of occurring may merit contingency plans, for example, a change of strategy or mitigating actions.
- **A Cyclical Process**: The process of scrutinizing information for new warning signals should never stop. While the emphasis is on emerging threats and opportunities, the process should be flexible enough to tackle unexpected short-term development too.

References

1. DiversityBestPractices.com - Strategic Savvy, pp. 31–44. https://seramount.com/
2. Murphy-Scanlon, J. (2010). How to be a Strategic Thinker: 5-Steps to Being Strategically Savvy. Strategies-Direct Limited. https://www.strategies-direct.com/
3. https://corporatefinanceinstitute.com/resources/knowledge/finance/financial-ratios/
4. Baroncelli, C., and Ballerio, N. (2016). *WCOM (World Class Operations Management): Why You Need More Than Lean*. Springer.
5. Rodrigues, L. et al. (2010). Comparison of SERVQUAL and SERVPERF metrics: An Empirical Study. *The TQM Journal*, 23(6), 629–643.
6. Cadel, J., Paul, D., and Turner, P. (2010). *Business Analysis Techniques: 72 Essential Tools for Success*. BCS The Chartered Institute of IT.
7. Valentin, E. K. (2005). Away With SWOT Analysis: Use Defensive/Offensive Evaluation Instead. *The Journal of Applied Business Research*, 21(2), 91–105. https://www.researchgate.net/publication/239580501_Away_with_SWOT_analysis_Use_DefensiveOffensive_Evaluation_instead
8. Kotler, P. (1988). *Marketing Management: Analysis, Planning and Control*. Longman Higher Education.
9. EFESO Consulting Tool Kit. www.efeso.com
10. Chen, M. J. (1996). Competitor Analysis and Interfirm Rivalry: Toward a Theoretical Integration. *Academy of Management Review*, 21(1), 100–134.
11. Downey, J. (2007). Strategic Analysis Tools. The Chartered Institute of Management Accountants (CIMA). https://www.cimaglobal.com/Documents/ImportedDocuments/cid_tg_strategic_analysis_tools_nov07.pdf.pdf

Chapter 6

Making the *Future* Happen *Today*

Moving from the strategic analysis phase with its myriad set of frameworks that I tried to integrate in a more actionable way requires that we investigate new approaches to formulate the strategy that allows organizations to *Make the Future Happen Today*.

This chapter will review two important approaches to developing strategies: Design Thinking and the Innovation Framework. Both concepts have proven to be useful approaches to better improve the outcomes of the strategy development process. Using Design Thinking and the Innovation Framework led me to propose a new integrated **Balanced Strategy Development (BSD) Model**. This new model provides a strategy that is driven by **Insights, Culture, Operations**, and **Digitization**.

6.1 Design Thinking

Design is transforming the way leading companies create value. The focus of innovation has shifted from being engineering-driven to design-driven, from product-centric to customer-centric, and from marketing-focused to user-experience-focused. For an increasing number of CEOs, design thinking is at the core of effective strategy development and organizational change.

The biggest driving force is the accelerated rate of change in business and society caused by advances in technology. As companies become more digital-driven and the rate of change increases, so does the complexity. Most companies are optimized to execute and solve a stated problem. Creativity is about **finding the problem worth solving**. An absence of a scalable creative framework encourages incremental innovation in lieu of disruptive innovation. As companies strive for disruptive innovation, they must find ways to inject and scale creativity across their organizations.

Design thinking is our best tool for sense-making, meaning-making, simplifying processes, and improving customer experiences. Additionally, design thinking minimizes risk, reduces costs, improves speed, and energizes employees. Design thinking provides leaders with a framework for addressing complex human-centered challenges and making the best possible decisions concerning the following six areas [1]:

DOI: 10.4324/9781003280941-10

- Redefining value
- Reinventing business models
- Shifting markets and behaviors
- Organizational culture change
- Complex societal challenges such as health, education, food, water, and climate change
- Problems affecting diverse stakeholders and multiple systems

> Design Thinking is a human-centered approach to innovation that draws from the designer's toolkit to integrate **the needs of people**, the **possibilities of technology**, and **the requirements for business success**
>
> **– Tim Brown**

Design, it seems, is now everywhere—it is no longer just the purview of designers. The non-design world has come a long way since the work of Professor John E. Arnold over 60 years ago to bring the disciplines of mechanical engineering and business administration more closely together around the ideas of design thinking. Examples now abound of corporate managers and engineers making design thinking central to their business operations, from conservative organizations hiring Chief Design Officers (CDO) to "professionals" talking about personas and point-of-view statements. However, hiring design studies graduates, sending employees to design-thinking courses, and setting up cross-functional teams is not enough for an organization to become "designerly". To make a difference to the kinds of products and services that get routinely implemented in the market, design thinking needs to be integrated into the organization's strategy. This is the only way that design can move from thinking to action, from lab formulation to strategic implementation across marketing, sales, and operations. We call the integration of design thinking into organizational strategy "**Design-Led Strategy**".

Design thinking needs to be integrated with strategy because firms wrestle with the problem of product–market fit. This problem relates to how organizations construct products that are relevant to their customers. In 2019, Liedtka and Kaplan [2] noted that "understanding the job customers are trying to do and the problem they have doing it" is a strategic issue. It is crucial for competitive advantage as it mobilizes the organization's strategy toward products that offer greater value than existing alternatives.

Product–market fit is particularly acute in innovation contexts, where organizations must either reimagine existing products and services or create new offerings. Dougherty has argued that the creative linkages needed here between market and technology are challenging because there is a lack of knowledge spanning both contexts. Metaphors, drawings, and gestures play a crucial role in transforming tacit knowledge into articulable knowledge so that shared understanding emerges between what customers want "out there" and what managers can do "in here". Design thinking offers a way to constitute such knowledge processes, focusing not only on the discursive aspects of knowledge translation but also on the visual, sensory, and material means through which market-oriented concepts are rendered interpretable.

6.1.1 From Design Thinking to Design-Led Strategy

Design thinking has emerged over the last 60 years as a method for collecting and analyzing the market and customer-level data, using tools that are visually instantiated, such as personas and sketching, and physically instantiated, such as prototypes and customer observation. Design thinking originated in engineering as a way for engineering construction to become more embedded within its physical environment and has evolved into being part of design studies as a discipline in its own right. However, it is being increasingly embraced by business managers as an empathetic way to understand the market environment and advance strategic management. Liedtka and Kaplan suggest that design practices improve strategy development in several ways by enabling businesses to see opportunities differently and learn through prototyping. This enables a portfolio approach to innovation by exploring a range of "bets" and accommodating greater emotional engagement in strategy making. Figure 6.1 depicts the design practices that improve strategy development.

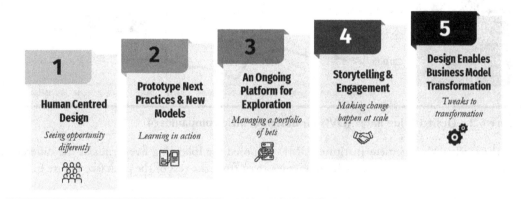

Figure 6.1   Design practices that improve strategy development [2]

This intersection between design thinking and strategic management has gained attention in recent times [3]. Several of the world's leading strategy consulting firms now integrate design into their strategy offering. Boston Consulting Group now has a design function called BCG Digital Ventures. McKinsey & Company operates McKinsey Design to complement its strategic services and bought Lunar, a top design firm known for its work with clients like HP, Apple, and SanDisk, as well as Stockholm-based design firm Veryday. ADAPT@Bain® is Bain & Company's advanced digital and product team, which combines design-thinking approaches, such as human-centered design and prototyping, with software engineering, digital marketing, and advanced analytics. Booz Allen Hamilton draws on design thinking by building a rich understanding of experiences to identify strategic opportunities for innovation and build solutions that not only matter to people but also fit with the business and are technically feasible. The proliferation of design roles at a C-suite level is further evidence that design thinking is gaining attention at a more strategic vantage point in organizations. Covering a range of industries, CDOs (Chief Design Officers) are employed in a diverse range of companies including 3M, ANZ Bank, Apple, Electrolux, Hyundai, Johnson & Johnson, Lloyds Banking Group, PepsiCo, and Philips. At Lloyds Banking Group, the CDO appointment was cited as a "strategy for transforming for success in a digital world" at Lloyds Banking Group and as building capability around "strategic design" at ANZ Bank, one of Australia's "big four" banks.

When design principles are applied to strategy and innovation, the success rate for innovation dramatically improves. Design-led companies such as Apple, Pepsi, IBM, Nike, Procter & Gamble, and SaP have outperformed the S&P 500 over a ten-year period by an extraordinary 211%, according to the 2015 Design Value Index created by the Design Management Institute and Motiv Strategies as shown in Figure 6.2. Design thinking, if executed properly and strategically, can impact business outcomes and result in real competitive advantages [4].

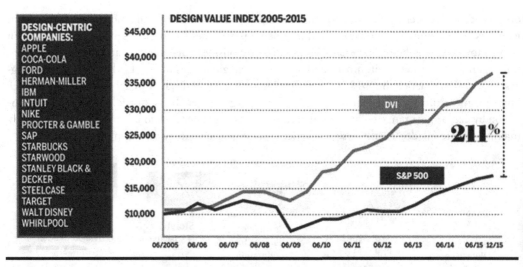

Figure 6.2 Design value index (DVI) for design-centric companies [4]

The Design Management Institute (DMI) proposed the following five trends as the differentiators that set these Design-Centric companies apart from the rest of the pack (see Figure 6.3):

- Training at scale
- Customer co-creation
- Savvy use of senior and support management
- Infusing the brand
- Acknowledging, praising, and repeating

Figure 6.3 Five trends for design-centric companies

6.1.1.1 Training at Scale

All of the companies mentioned are working very hard to train hundreds of their employees about the value of design and how design thinking works in practice. Along with this commitment, many are turning design thinking inward to help the organization itself get better at its own internal issues that may include functional strategies and tackling vexing departmental problems.

6.1.1.2 Customer Co-Creation

We've seen co-creating with customers as a trend for quite a while now, but it is worth noting that the *Design-Centric* companies have taken this practice to the next level by using tangible and somewhat costly structures (e.g., SaP's co-innovation labs, GE's Menlo, and 3M's innovation centers) to formally promote co-creation with their customers using design-thinking methods and mindsets as well as hiring staff and devoting employee time to drive these types of efforts.

6.1.1.3 Savvy Use of Senior and Support Management

Long ago when designers and business people weren't so good at understanding design and how it needs to operate, design managers were often left to their own devices with meager budgets to grow their design functions in staff and influence all by themselves. Talk about pushing a boulder up a hill. Today it's different. Virtually all of the *Design-Centric* companies enjoy a seat at the table with their leadership team members as well as getting enabling support to run design operations from legal, HR, and finance departments. This is a clear indication that the status and perception of the value of design is permanently shifting in a positive and more influential direction.

6.1.1.4 Infusing the Brand

"In a world that is moving from TV-centric to one where we are a topic in the conversation, we need to earn the right to be part of the conversation. And you earn that right by being relevant", reflects PepsiCo Chief Design Officer Mauro Porcini. Corporate brand management has never been more challenged to maintain relevance. For this reason, many of the *Design-Centric* companies are playing a very big role in the look, feel, application, and evolution of how their corporate brands are used and displayed across the globe.

6.1.1.5 Acknowledge-Praise-Repeat

It was remarkable to me how, without prodding, many of the *Design-Centric* design managers brought up the practice of lavishly acknowledging and praising their internal functional partners such as engineering, marketing, and supply chain for the work they do in bringing designs to life and launch. Are we seeing a new, largely unspoken, design best practice emerging? Yes, and that's because the design can do many things, but in the end, it is a team sport.

6.1.2 Design Thinking Model—E 6²

Mindshake's Innovation and Design Thinking Model **Evolution 6²** was developed by Katja Tschimmel between 2012 and 2015. In 2017, the model received a refreshment in its design and tool distribution. The model is used today in public and private innovation projects (training and coaching), start-up accelerator programs, entrepreneurial education, master classes, and research projects [5].

The model is called **Evolution 6²** for the following reasons:

- **Evolution**, because the creative process is an evolutionary process, iterative, and interactive (people and situations). The graphic design shows that each E-phase of the model is related to the others in iterative cycles
- **E6**, because the model is divided into six phases, all of which begin with E: Emergence, Empathy, Experimentation, Elaboration, Exposition, and Extension

■ **E6²**, because in each phase of the process, moments of divergence (Exploration), and convergence (Evaluation) occur, making it symbolically six squared

Figure 6.4 shows the model phases and the tools that can be used in each phase.

Digital Thinking Model
Evolution 6²

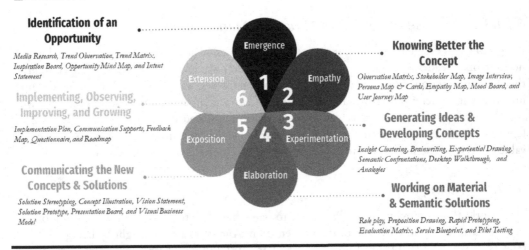

Identification of an Opportunity

Media Research, Trend Observation, Trend Matrix, Inspiration Board, Opportunity Mind Map, and Intent Statement

Implementing, Observing, Improving, and Growing

Implementation Plan, Communication Supports, Feedback Map, Questionnaire, and Roadmap

Communicating the New Concepts & Solutions

Solution Stereotyping, Concept Illustration, Vision Statement, Solution Prototype, Presentation Board, and Visual Business Model

Knowing Better the Concept

Observation Matrix, Stakeholder Map, Image Interview, Persona Map & Cards, Empathy Map, Mood Board, and User Journey Map

Generating Ideas & Developing Concepts

Insight Clustering, Brainwriting, Experiential Drawing, Semantic Confrontations, Desktop Walkthrough, and Analogies

Working on Material & Semantic Solutions

Role play, Proposition Drawing, Rapid Prototyping, Evaluation Matrix, Service Blueprint, and Pilot Testing

Figure 6.4   Evolution 6² Design Thinking Model [5]

The model phases are defined as follows:

1. **Emergence**: Identification of an opportunity
2. **Empathy**: Knowing better the context
3. **Experimentation**: Generating ideas and developing concepts
4. **Elaboration**: Working on martial and semantic solutions
5. **Exposition**: Communication of the new concept and solutions
6. **Extension**: Implementing, observing, improving, and growing

For a detailed review of the tools used for each phase, you can check https://www.minds hake.pt/.

The **Evolution 6²** model is guided by five principles to ensure its successful implementation for design-led strategy development.

1. Human-Centered Approach

    Products and services should be experienced from the user's perspective. "Real" people's needs and desires are at the center of the whole design-thinking process.

2. Collaboration

    Design thinking is a collective and participatory process. As many stakeholders as possible should be included throughout the phases of the process.

3. Experimentation

    Design thinking gives space to think in variety and of many possibilities. Some may not succeed. Playful thinking, making mistakes, and learning by doing are important parts of every creative process. Without some failures, nothing really new will emerge.

4. Visualization

Images have the power to synthesize and clarify ideas in an internal and external dialogue. Quick prototyping helps the learning process and improves the initial ideas. The visualization of concepts simplifies what seems complex and fosters connections between ideas.

5. Holistic Perspective

Every product, service, or media message belongs to a system of interactions and interdependent entities. The wider context and environment of an artifact, service, or business model should be considered in every innovation process.

6.1.3 Strategy Needs More Than Just Design Thinking

Despite the importance of greater integration between design and strategic management, the fit is not straightforward. To start with, the challenges of bringing new ways of thinking into organizations are substantial and not ones that the discipline of design studies has really engaged with. For managers, these challenges arise from the way in which knowledge is created and translated with organizations and into day-to-day strategy making. Cohen and Levinthal, for example, argue that much of the knowledge managers gain about their market emerges from observation and know-how (i.e., tacit knowledge) rather than codified forms of expertise that might be delivered through standard training or workshops. This places a premium on the ability of executives to change their cognitive mindset, empathize with their customers, and observe the unexpected. This is a difficult attribute to develop for two reasons. First, senior executives in charge of the firm's strategy may live a very different life from their customers, thereby making their connection with customers in the "outside" world, and the frontline of practice, difficult. The founder of Facebook, Mark Zuckerberg, for example, is allegedly himself not a customer of Facebook, instead deferring his day-to-day interactions with the product he created to staff in his office. Very few senior leaders at the helm of universities continue to teach students or write research papers as their responsibilities for the institution's strategy grows. Although it is good practice for senior executives to consume the products and services they sell, when this does not take place, executives need to find other ways to understand what it is like to walk in the shoes of their customers.

Second, even as senior executives make use of design-thinking methodologies to bridge the gap between their own and customers' experiences, the sheer variety and difference of data this introduces can increase cognitive load and make strategic decision-making difficult. Design thinking goes beyond verbal data (for example, through customer interviews) to introduce visual data (for example, through contextual observations of how customers use products or services) and material data (such as the development of prototypes). Nike, for example, overlaid data on shopping experiences with emotional journey mapping to help design the integrated digital app-based and physical shopping experience of their recently opened Nike Live concept in Melrose, Los Angeles. This visual and material data are immensely valuable in enriching a manager's understanding of how products and services are used by customers in real life. But it can also be overwhelming for inexperienced senior executives. Moreover, as strategists, senior executives need to go beyond just making sense of this new kind of visual and material data. They need to triangulate it and then interpret it in relation to traditional strategy tools that provide guidance over when and how to balance tensions versus make tradeoff choices. This means that integrating design thinking into strategy not only involves a multimodal approach, which goes beyond what design studies offer but also requires managers to transform their approach to strategy by integrating multiple and more varied types of data that can advance an organization's strategic ends.

Given not only the importance but also the challenges of integrating design thinking and strategic management, strategy scholars have sought to tackle the synergies between the two fields by examining different aspects of the strategy function. Each aspect brings a different strategic focus to the fore.

Three types of aspects were reviewed [3] (see Figure 6.5):

■ Design and cognitive aspects of strategic management
■ Design and structural aspects of strategic management
■ Design and organizational culture aspects of strategic management

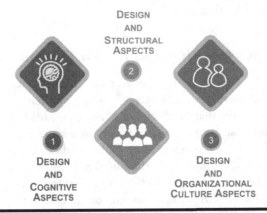

DESIGN
AND
STRUCTURAL
ASPECTS

2

1

DESIGN
AND
COGNITIVE
ASPECTS

3

DESIGN
AND
ORGANIZATIONAL
CULTURE ASPECTS

Figure 6.5 Design thinking and strategic management integration aspects

- **Design and Cognitive Aspects of Strategic Management**

    Strategic management literature has taken a cognitive perspective, focusing on the thinking side of design and how this influences the decision-making of strategists. Within this stream of work, Martin has argued that having managers who apply design thinking by blending analytical thinking and intuitive thinking is a means for firms to gain a competitive advantage. Liedtka similarly focuses on the cognitive elements, showing how strategic thinking can enable more synthetic, dialectical, and adductive strategies to emerge compared with traditional, hierarchical decision-making.

    Other work emphasizing the cognitive elements of design thinking focuses on tools themselves and how these guide particular ways of knowing and solving problems. Dong, Garbuio, and Lovallo show how these tools can inform behavioral characteristics. They argue that managers can develop a set of "generative sensing capabilities" that allow them to generate hypotheses about observed events and, through doing so, make decisions that improve a firm's dynamic capabilities.

- **Design and Structural Aspects of Strategic Management**

    A second stream has focused on how design thinking influences strategy from a structural perspective. This work is concerned with where design thinking should be located within the organizational structure and also considers how design can be elevated to a strategic level in organizations. For example, in 53 interviews across 12 companies, Micheli, Perks, and Beverland identify the following six practices that elevate the structural positioning of design in organizations: (1) Top management support, (2) leadership of the design function, (3) generating awareness of design's role and contribution, (4) inter-functional coordination, (5) evaluation of design, and (6) formalization of product and service development processes. They suggest that strategic design is more effective when designers operate cross-functionally because it enables designers to better balance the role of design champions alongside commercial considerations.

The structural perspective on design and statement management also considers the effects on firm performance and strategic decision-making when designers reside outside the organization. For example, Calabretta et al. examined seven cases involving design consultancies influencing their clients' strategies by contributing to their innovation agendas. Finally, the structural stream is also interested in how design thinking is "managed" within the firm. Perks, Cooper, and Jones, for example, found that design had different effects on firm performance when it was organized top-down as a functional specialism, or as part of new product development, compared with when it operated cross-functionally as a way to integrate multi-functional teams

- **Design and Organizational Culture Aspects of Strategic Management**

The third stream of work has focused on how design thinking shapes organizational culture, giving more attention to the process elements of strategy. This work is less focused on structural design choices and more attuned to how design thinking shapes the flow of activities over longer periods of time. For example, John Body, in a study of the Australian Tax Office, found that the use of design-thinking tools instigated new routines that allowed teams to collaborate that had previously not worked together. This allowed for "shared understanding" to emerge across interdisciplinary teams, thereby opening up new forms of working. Similarly, Vetterli and colleagues found that design thinking helped to challenge ways of working in the IT division at Deutsche Bank. In their case, design thinking served as a powerful legitimating approach that allowed managers to challenge and discuss underlying assumptions about "the right way to work".

Beyond design thinking influencing ways of knowing and working in organizations, design can also play an integrative role between functional areas at odds with each other by contributing practices that complement existing organizational approaches. Rather than focusing merely on the cognitive aspects of design thinking, this stream gives attention to the process of "designerly" ways of thinking influencing the rest of the organization. The enculturation of design helps overcome factors that prevent the design from achieving strategic relevance in organizations, such as transcending different mental models and managers' lack of design appreciation

These three streams of work reflect different ways of conceptualizing strategy—as cognition, as structure, and as a process—and give emphasis to different kinds of aims and contributions related to how design thinking and strategic management are related.

6.1.4 Four Practices of Integration in Design-Led Strategy

Design thinking brings rich customer-centric data about an organization's position in the market inside the organization. However, these data need to be taken further by managers in order to yield insights into how they influence the organization's strategizing. As noted, there are four different ways in which managers interact with "design-thinking" data and then use it in their interactions with each other to advance a new product–market insight for the organization's strategy (see Figure 6.6) [3].

We observed how the use of design thinking influences strategy making through the manipulation of two dimensions. One dimension we call the **"Dynamism of Materials"**. Design thinking generates a range of different materials—from personas to Point-of-View problem statements through to raw customer data—that need to be interpreted in the context of the strategic issues facing the organization. Managers use these materials in one of two ways: Either statically, by treating the content independently of other visuals at hand, or dynamically, by collating and (re)

DYNAMIC

Simulating

Description: Involves managers engaging concurrently with multiple, user-derived materials

Impact: Enables managers to triangulate the design content with user- inspired feedback to produce richer customer insights

Description: Involves managers organizing & creating materials to build collective understanding of design & strategy problems

Impact: Enables managers to rapidly deepen understanding of issues and generate shared solutions to complex problems

Collaborating

DYNAMISM OF MATERIALS

Reviewing

Description: Involves managers empathetically reflecting on materials and interrogating on materials and interrogating the details of design content

Impact: Improves managers understanding of design content, facilitates design iterations & enables better contribution to subsequent discussion

Description: Involves managers engaging in free-flowing discussion not centred around design materials

Impact: Enables managers to negotiate alternative understandings of strategic issues and gain alignment by making sense of organizational challenges

Conversing

STATIC

INDIVIDUAL

ENGAGEMENT CONTEXT

COLLECTIVE

Figure 6.6   Four practices of integration in design-led strategy [3]

combining the materials at hand and even generating new materials so that insights could emerge at their intersection. These two alternate practices create different kinds of openness in terms of how managers engage with design-thinking content.

The second dimension we call the "**Engagement Context**". Managers engage with the design-thinking data either individually (by reflecting on the data themselves) or collectively (by discussing their interpretation of the design-thinking data with others), thereby unleashing a third interpretive path. In this respect, design-led strategy from a practice perspective prompted different degrees of engagement in terms of who was involved in the strategy process.

The combination of the two dimensions of "Dynamism of Materials" and "Engagement Context" provide four practices: Reviewing, Simulating, Conversing, and Collaborating. The next section will review each practice and how it can be used to develop a design-led strategy.

6.1.4.1 Reviewing

Design thinking puts much emphasis on the quality of data collected from customers, with data capturing customers' emotional responses to prototypes and prototype use in context, an important principle for data collection. In the words of prominent design-thinking practitioner Gianfranco Zaccai, "You have to know your customers not as statistics but as human beings". However, from a Strategy-as-Practice perspective, the customer data is not as important as how internal managers go on to engage with the data for enhanced understanding. It was imperative that managers had time during strategy workshops to "sit with" the design-led data. Often, this involved surfacing a single material—such as a strategy document or a piece of customer data—and reviewing its significance in the context of a strategy conversation. This practice is labeled "reviewing" and is coded as an individual practice involving static materials. In a case of a Bank that used design thinking to revise its strategy, managers had a wide-ranging discussion about what customers expect from their banks "as partners" based on raw customer data. This led to a number of insights about the kinds of reminders that customers expect from their banks to help them save money or make investment decisions. As this conversation came to an end, the meeting chair shared a one-page document that summarized the discussion to date, noting the customer value propositions of a product that the bank was considering developing. This prompted participants to review the materials and evaluate them in light of prior discussions about the customer. Did the proposed document prima-facie respond to customer concerns covered in the immediate prior discussion? Were there other issues that needed attention but were not discussed?

What is the consequence of enacting a reviewing practice? It was found that "reviewing" opened up the richness of the ensuing strategy discussion by shifting the conversational focus. When each of the participants had a chance to review the same material, each was able to compare the others' points proactively. It is argued that reflection-in-action is a key attribute of how professional knowledge comes into being. Unlike technical rationality, "learning from experience" arises from reflecting on actions at the moment in order to surface differences and work through diverse understandings. Using static materials is a useful way to deliberately trigger such reflection. Reviewing materials in the context of discussions about customer needs forced participants to actively reflect on those customer needs. Building on the finding that user research provides insights which help clarify a design problem, it was found that reviewing practices prompt reflective strategy conversations by giving direct attention to strategy materials and artifacts from the customer's perspective.

In an interview, a Design Lead explained that he regularly used single-page summaries of key design concepts in order to trigger reflections, which prompted colleagues to "come back with better summaries" once they understood the main design elements. In this way, reviewing the summaries enabled managers to understand the savings concept of the digital app—overall savings requirements that take into account personal savings goals as well as a buffer for unplanned spending—and enable a better contribution to subsequent discussions and design iterations. However, in meeting segments where participants did not review materials (such as the moments before a review practice was enacted), the strategy discussions took on a different character. Participants often contributed their own perspectives to the discussion without reflecting on a shared theme or common reference point. This shows how design-led strategy from a practice perspective can sensitize the focus of strategy making to reflective learning activities.

6.1.4.2 Simulating

Managers sought to empathetically simulate their end user's experience of their product or service in real time. This is usually labeled as a re-creation of the user's experience, a "simulating" practice, which was an individual practice with dynamic materials. It was individual in the sense that managers wanted to reproduce the customer's experience of a product or service for themselves. At the same time, it was dynamic because it was a multimodal experience, bringing together different types of visual, verbal, and sensory data over time to re-create a real-life activity undertaken by a customer rather than a summary of the strategy discussion (as in the reviewing practice). The physical setup of design workshops was very much organized to enable this kind of dynamic with multiple materials or types of data.

An example of this is when managers meet in a design studio to project the app on a computer screen and "walk through" the different aspects of the product under development. One group of managers, acting as customers, were sitting in front of a screen while another manager pressed different buttons on a connected device to move the image forward and backward between screen projections based on the managers' desired product journey. This re-created the experience of a user using a smartphone. This layout of materials is dynamic since there are multiple screens on display, and participants are able to interact with the materials by moving back and forth in an immersive way.

Effect of the practice. Simulating opens up strategy practice because it provokes managers to form an empathetic engagement with the customer experience, thereby making the market context immediately appraisable. Design-led strategy from a practice perspective, therefore, moves from being a rational activity to also being an emotional one so far as empathy is recognized as a legitimate means of changing the strategy. In the above example, this immersive experience enabled one of the participants to realize that the error messaging on the app was too small to read for some customers. This resulted in a change request to the design team to adjust the app.

In an interview, a Digital Product Owner explained the effectiveness of the simulating practice: "The prototypes are really effective at conveying [to Executives how] user feedback is shaping the product". A key attribute of a simulating practice, then, is not only the more interactive nature of the practice but also the extent to which it allows managers to experience what the strategy feels like "on the front line". This enacts a narrowing of the product–market gap. This allows managers to have a more multifaceted connection with their market and alter their strategy directions through the different ideas, values, assumptions, and emotions this elicits about customers' problems. The ability of senior managers to deliberately construct these sensemaking contexts becomes crucial in design-led strategy. This builds on Knight and Paroutis' insight within a media company where senior managers shaped the interpretative context experienced by lower-level managers, thereby helping them to deal with contradictory demands. Simulating, therefore, builds on this in a design-thinking context and supports more balanced a strategy-making process by ensuring bottom-up user perspectives moderate top-down managerial concerns

6.1.4.3 Conversing

Design thinking has a focus on materials. However, there are times when materials are not a feature of the discussion. Instead, strategists discuss their conceptions of the strategic challenges in a free-flowing manner. This is labeled as "conversing", which is a collective practice in the context of static materials. These moments are significant as they allow the managers to move away from "the data" and discuss the practical realities of the challenges they face at an interpersonal level based on their unit, organizational, and/or occupational backgrounds.

Although instances of conversing arose throughout workshops, they were particularly prevalent at the start when managers provided background updates, contextualized the purpose of the workshop, and discussed challenging priorities that needed to be taken into account beyond the data. For example, when a manager reconvened a workshop between the strategists and designers over a month hiatus, he grouped everyone together in a meeting and prompted a dialogue around what each person was doing and what needed to be addressed in the meeting. In this respect, the materials were static, but the practice was collective in the sense that each managers' response informed the others. For example, as the group settled on what needed to be implemented, each actor contributed different qualifying statements to test their understanding. Conversing was particularly important in enabling collective reflection and getting agreement between participants with diverse understandings of the strategy. In order words, this aspect of design-led strategizing amplified managers' attention to the real fit within product–market fit.

Collective rather than individual reflection exposes "prejudices and blind spots" and provides "a platform for articulating ideas and aspiration". Through vocalizing different views, participants are able to negotiate alternative understandings of a problem that leads to a more consensual solution. Often design thinking is about the customer data, but frequently implementing new products and services based on the customer data depends on negotiating complex political realities within the organizational strategy. This builds on work by Stigliani and Ravasi who found that the ability of individuals to notice and classify material issues enriched the interactive talk at the group level, thereby enhancing strategic influence. Conversing was more inclusive as a result of the design artifacts because it opened up discussions to more diverse and fully articulated opinions. For this reason, conversing frequently followed long technical discussions when design-led scenarios were developed, but their link back into the organization was unclear.

6.1.4.4 Collaborating

The fourth practice in relation to design-led strategy is labeled "collaborating". This was a collective practice, but one that also entailed dynamic materials. Participants not only engaged in a collective dialogue about the customer data but also (re)organized and created new materials to surface a collective understanding of design and strategy problems. These moments usually took place around a whiteboard, using text, Post-it notes, or other materials or around a computer where the comment functions on programs were used to add additional insights around a central design material.

For example, in one of the early stages of the design project, product managers and strategy managers sat down on a couch to detail all the research tasks that needed to be completed in order to conduct appropriate customer interviews, marketing validation, budget appraisals, and other activities to consider a new product and service. Different members of the team made proposals while a manager wrote these up verbatim on Post-it notes and stuck them on the whiteboard against a timeline. As these Post-it notes were stuck up, managers commented on their location on the timeline, leading to several of the Post-it notes being moved around. This was an iterative activity as managers moved between a conversation about the design project (collective practice), emergent materials capturing action points (dynamic materials), and amendments to the design project plan. This approach is similar to a design-thinking exercise called the Gallery Walk, in which the seemingly most important data collected are "galleried" on walls for managers to review individually before collectively interrogating.

This practice was especially useful when teams were dealing with complex issues that could easily be forgotten or lost in the conversational dialogue. Rather than trying to empathetically understand each manager's perspective (as in the conversing practice) the focus in collaborative translation was on generating a shared solution to a complex problem (e.g., how to prioritize the tasks in a project plan) by making connections between various ideas from disparate areas.

6.2 Innovation Framework—D6[4]

In the business environment, the most seminal contribution to the study of innovation has been "The Innovator's Dilemma" by Clayton Christensen. This year marks the 25th anniversary of its publication—a defining moment in how executives should think of disruptive innovation. The web was still in its infancy, the dot-com boom was just gathering pace, and communication technologies we now consider normal did not exist. In a survey of 821 executives across the globe conducted by PA Consulting, it was quite shocking to see that while 66% of executives confirm that their organizations will not survive without innovation, only 24% are fully confident that they have the defined skills and activities they need to innovate, and 50% don't believe their organization leaders fully display the vision and passion needed to make innovation happen. Figure 6.7 shows the findings of this PA Consulting "Innovation Matters" report [6].

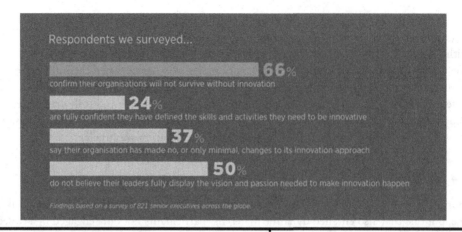

Figure 6.7   PA Consulting "innovation matters" survey

Looking at leading organizations today, one wonders about what businesses those organizations are really in. Is Amazon in retail, payments, devices, infrastructure, health, drones, or entertainment? Is Apple in devices, media, health, communications, software, wearables, retail, or payments? Is AT&T in telecoms, connected health, entertainment, cloud computing, or the connected home? Boundaries are blurring, and many organizations feel less in control of their destiny than ever before.

This makes using innovation in strategy more critical than ever. Hence, PA Consulting proposed a framework for innovation [6] to help organizations put in practice an innovation-driven strategy to complement their design-led strategy development.

The framework can be called the **Innovation D6⁴ Framework**. It has six stages supported by four practices. The six stages are:

1. **Desire**: Develop a clear aspiration and sense of purpose
2. **Discover**: Look outside and inside to develop ideas to support your purpose
3. **Define**: Scope out the opportunities and validate initial concepts against your purpose
4. **Design**: Develop the concept into a solution, prototype and iterate, and design supporting operating model
5. **Deliver**: Set up to deliver and launch in the marketplace
6. **Drive**: Lear, iterate, continuous improvement of value, and scale

The supporting four practices to practice innovation are:

1. Leadership
2. Funding
3. Engagement
4. Decision-making

Figure 6.8 provides a detailed description of the Innovation **D6⁴** Framework indicating the different stages (*What*: In dark gray text) and the tools that can be used for each stage (*How*: In light gray text) with the expected outcome/deliverable (*Goal*: In blue text).

LEADERSHIP

FUNDING

A FRAMEWORK FOR INNOVATION	WHAT?	HOW?	GOAL
DESIRE	Develop a clear aspiration & sense of purpose	• Strategy & brand analysis • Scenario planning options • Innovation dimension analysis • Disruptive strategy framework	A clear statement, quantifiable goals, and a strategy for engaging the organization
DISCOVER	Look outside & inside to develop ideas to support your purpose	• Technology trend analysis • Competitor & market insight • Consumer & employee analysis • Creativity tools • Ideation frameworks	The longest possible list of untested, unqualified ideas, initial assessment criteria & assumptions
DEFINE	Scope the opportunities and validate initial concepts against your purpose	• Customer desirability measures • Technical feasibility measures • Commercial reality measures	Evaluated, prioritized list of ideas, initial concept development. An innovation scorecard measuring ganist a clear definition of success
DESIGN	• Develop the concept into a solution, prototype, and literate • Design a supporting operation model	Agile methodolog - collaboration tools - Customer observatory - Market testing - Killer business cases - Governance options - Minimum desirable product	Rapid progress from idea to realistic proposition. Designed, developed & fully tested proposition (with business case, operating model, and go to market plan)
DELIVER	Setup to deliver and launch in marketplace	• Fully tested proposition • Operating model	Proposition launched to market and a plan for scaling fast
DRIVE	• Lean, literate, continous improvement of value • Scale	Learnings	Feedback, insight, and increased momentum for the next innovation

ENGAGEMENT

DECISION-MAKING

Figure 6.8   Innovation D6⁴ framework [6]

The **Innovation D6⁴ Framework** can easily be integrated with the **Evolution 6² (E6²)** Design Thinking Model discussed earlier to offer the organization a comprehensive approach to strategy development. My recommendation is that organizations use the best out of both models to fit their organization's capabilities and needs. Both models have many valuable tools to facilitate their application and can provide a great foundation for your organization's strategy development.

However, in order to unlock innovation within the organization, there are four pragmatic and actionable areas on which innovation leaders need to focus on in their quest to create breakthrough innovation (see Figure 6.9). These four key areas and the key aspects for each area based on the research study conducted by PA Consulting are [6]:

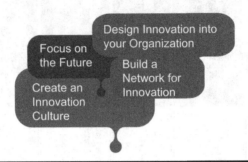

Figure 6.9   Four distinct areas to unlock innovation

6.2.1 Focus on the Future

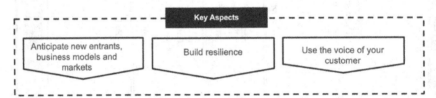

6.2.1.1 Anticipate New Entrants, Business Models, and Markets

Entire industries are being redefined by customer expectations and emerging technologies. Organizations without an innovation mindset and a clear sense of purpose are missing out.

New market entrants are ignoring decades of legacy processes and building customer-centric solutions that are better, faster, and cheaper than incumbent players. Consider legal or accountancy firms, where industry estimates suggest that 40–60% of fees could be related to work that is better delivered by artificial intelligence (AI). AI would be faster and reduce costs, and perhaps even be more accurate.

But are traditional firms prepared to reduce their billing rates, and pass on value, because parts of a project are now automated? If not, the price difference may be enough for some customers to try a new service. Create a decent customer experience, and industry economics and competitiveness could change forever.

New technologies can also mask what is really a change in the business model. When eBay was launched in 1995, it was seen as new technology. Yet the company merely enhanced an age-old process of matching buyers and sellers. Uber and Airbnb are other examples of companies using technology to disrupt existing systems. These peer-to-peer platforms may be using technology to deliver a service, but the real innovation is the change in the business model.

And technology can also create entirely new markets that did not exist previously. Snapchat allows people to communicate in a fleeting way using images and has created billions of dollars of value for the founders of the company. But five years ago, no one communicated this way.

6.2.1.2 Build Resilience

Innovating in this environment requires vision and resilience. Most business leaders know innovation is essential for long-term survival but struggle with forces that can stop innovation from becoming a reality in their organizations. So, how can you:

- Maintain your belief that innovation can transform your business?
- Battle learned behavioral and institutional inertia?

Successful innovation leaders actively use disruption stories as a catalyst to focus leadership attention and management debate toward digital, Agile, disruption, and innovation. Successful leaders use these stories to further build the case and organizational energy for innovation.

Fear is a basic human emotion, and fear of standing out or making a wrong decision will often influence executives considering the opportunity versus the risk of pursuing innovation, creating unhelpful learned behavior and institutional inertia.

In fact, our research by PA Consulting shows that 54% of organizations are rejecting the very disruptive ideas that may lead to the greatest success. Being bold and maintaining a belief and focus on innovation in the toughest of economic or business pressures is difficult but critical.

Individuals will fight innovation if they feel the disruption to their business puts their own personal power base at risk, particularly if the change proposed is so dramatic that the entire company may need to be redesigned or divisions cannibalized to allow an innovative new service to flourish.

The focus required on short-term results, budgets, regulatory compliance, and the disciplines of management reporting can make maintaining this focus on innovation challenging. Our research also shows only 31% of respondents say their leadership teams prioritize innovation in any substantive way.

6.2.1.3 Use the Voice of Your Customer

As customers today—be that as consumers, citizens, or business professionals—we are more empowered than ever before, enabled by proliferating choice and hyperconnectivity. Technology and generational dynamics have changed the way we connect and relate to what is around us, placing us at the center of our own ecosystem of people and organizations that inform, inspire and influence us.

Innovation leaders are also increasingly focused on what customers really want in the long term rather than just features, brands, or experiences. Organizations that fail to recognize this fundamental shift—and the new power of the customer—risk a rapid decline in relevance and value to their customers.

Yet the opportunities are huge. Reorienting around the customer can be a powerful force to accelerate—and steer—innovation in your organization.

The organizations that will thrive in this world will be those that continuously innovate around the customer. They will be clear on their purpose and be led by people who understand that customer value is a core driver of future growth.

However, in order to create this kind of innovation we need to ask ourselves four critical questions:

- **Do we know what our customers need, both now and in the future?** Henry Ford did not just listen to what his customers wanted; he invented a new market for them. There are many new and disruptive scenario-planning techniques, and market scanning and technology foresight tools that will keep you ahead of potential threats and give you the sight of opportunities
- **How much time and attention are we spending at the board/leadership team on innovation?** Leaders need to create an environment in which to innovate. Tackling areas of inertia and resistance upfront through leadership interventions will help
- **How close are we to our customers' activities and environment?** Sophisticated data and analytics tools will give you immediate intelligence on your customers. But we also still find traditional techniques like focus groups to be critical of qualitative information and to create empathy
- **What does "Customer 4.0" mean for you?** It could be that your business design might change radically if you genuinely oriented your organization around your clients. Understanding the new universe of influences, and testing and improving your relevance with clients, requires a new mindset, skills, and tools

6.2.2 Design Innovation into Your Organization

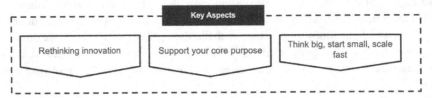

6.2.2.1 Rethinking Innovation

Innovation may be about improving the customer experience or using an entirely new business model. It may be a dramatic change to how you bring a product or service to market, or it may be centered on how you change how you work with your employees. All these areas of your organization have the potential to be improved through innovation.

6.2.2.2 Support Your Core Purpose

One of the most common mistakes an organization can make is to take an approach to innovation that is at odds with its core purpose. Fear of failure, a risk-averse culture, and overzealous risk management are just some of the reasons why organizations are reluctant to take the bold steps into the unknown that is essential for innovation.

Innovation leaders, on the other hand, are crystal clear on where they create value and align innovation priorities against this core purpose.

It can be as simple as wanting to:

- Be able to bring new products and services to market faster than the competition
- Have more customer accounts than any other provider
- Offer the best experience for our customers
- Be the simplest and leanest in our industry

When the purpose is clear and the goals are stated, then a path to innovation can be charted. It is important to find the right blend of innovation frameworks that support organizational goals. Some simple questions can help. Is the objective to:

- Use innovation techniques to solve specific issues?
- Empower people to come up with more radical ideas to solve complex problems?
- Extract more value from the ideas already alive within the organization?
- Build innovation into the DNA of the organization?

The innovation framework illustrated below will help you to create future value by setting goals, developing processes, and building the infrastructure to turn ideas into action. Such a strategic framework will enable employees to manage the inevitable tension between creativity and pragmatism that is always present when an organization moves from a more traditional hierarchy to innovation as a normal function of the business.

6.2.2.3 Think Big, Start Small, Scale Fast

Agile techniques are not new, but we are increasingly seeing innovation leaders using Agile thinking in all areas of their business. This enables them to achieve more, change faster, and improve adoption in a large organization.

You might not initially think of Rentokil as an innovation leader, but they managed to revitalize their business by using the "Internet of Things". Instead of physically checking pest management devices at sites on a regular basis, we worked with Rentokil to develop connected devices to collect, analyze and share data in the cloud. This allowed the company to operate more efficiently and improve services to their customers. Rentokil's ideas were rolled out, using an Agile approach. The solution now operates in 12 countries with unlimited scalability.

So, what can we learn from this? "Think big, start small, scale fast" works for many of our clients. Benefits from innovation crystallize sooner as ideas test and iterate. Pilots can be quick, valuable, and with the ability to scale.

Organizations that do not incubate ideas well because they cannot provide the right organizational environment to nurture and accelerate them to success. Organizational and IT architectures can support agility or constrain it. The right technology, processes, and commercial flexibility are all essential to supporting an Agile environment.

6.2.3 Create and Innovation Culture

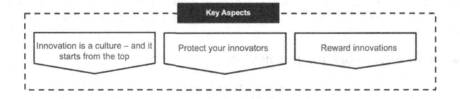

6.2.3.1 Innovation Is a Culture—And It Starts from the Top

Innovation takes great leadership. Yet we live in a time when many senior executives feel increasingly disconnected from the technological changes driving so much business and societal change.

One of the research findings of the research conducted by PA Consulting indicates that organizations are crying out for strong and inspiring leadership. In many organizations the one individual whose involvement would guarantee that innovation is prioritized—the CEO—is not leading from the front:

- 50% do not believe their leaders fully display the vision and passion needed to make innovation happen

If innovation is critical to survival and the strategic direction of organizations—as businesses say it is—then this needs to change. It is tougher than ever to lead in this environment. This is especially true when you have to make decisions on technology that is not fully developed or that you do not fully understand or use; if your competition is a company that did not exist a year ago; or in the context of an industry that is transforming out of all recognition.

Yet it is absolutely critical that leadership teams find a way to protect and nurture innovation in their organizations. Ultimately, only the CEO can give assurance that the company's approach to innovation is in line with its purpose. It is the senior leaders who can create momentum, break down internal silos and ensure changes are genuinely embedded into the organization.

6.2.3.2 Protect Your Innovators

Many organizations were historically created to control, not to inspire. Hierarchy and process create the ability for the company to repeatedly deliver a product or service to consistent standards. But this traditional structure may need to be challenged if you want to inspire innovation.

Often innovation thrives in the flatter structures and decentralized decision-making of an Agile business—protected by senior leaders but not waiting for them to set direction from above. There is no simple formula, but shielding your team can give them the space and time to find out what works for them.

6.2.3.3 Reward Innovations

Innovation leaders consider the entire employee value proposition and the environment for their people, not just the obvious levers of remuneration and performance management. Mastercard has sought answers to the challenges it faces around digitization by transforming the way it engages its employees to contribute ideas.

There are many examples of companies that have used systems that can capture ideas—involving people at every level of the organization in a process of constant improvement. We recently worked with a company that chose from a range of our creativity tools (designed to help organizations inspire and manage innovation pipelines) and ran an innovation competition.

6.2.4 Build a Network for Innovation

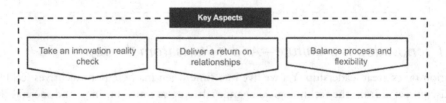

6.2.4.1 *Take and Innovation Reality Check*

Outside of your organization and strategy, there is a massive movement of open and permissionless innovation. Billions of pounds are invested every year in trying to find new and valuable products, solutions, and services. Start-ups, investors, and academia are conceiving, designing, and building new futures and innovations every day. This is something our innovation leaders recognize—61% say they are more likely to achieve success if they source some of their innovation from outside.

It is essential to dedicate some of your resources to being part of your external ecosystems. We see innovation leaders getting involved in building relationships, starting to understand, embrace and exploit the approaches, freedom, and investment this world enjoys.

It is easy to become bogged down in the formality of innovation, and the pressure to succeed and forget it can be fun and exciting.

6.2.4.2 *Deliver a Return on Relationship*

Organizations are realizing they cannot do everything themselves—and need to build an ecosystem of partners outside their organization. The difference in this year's research findings is that a far greater proportion of respondents are actually doing it—building a web of partnership, collaboration, and trust through formal and informal programs of work.

Now, over half of respondents believe they are more likely to achieve success if they also source innovation from outside the organization—bringing vision, ideas, experience, funding, and facilities.

Recognize there is a return on every dollar you spend, even if you fail to see a tangible return on investment. The return can take the shape of increased trust with a partner, new people skills for your team, or simply more confidence and momentum in your innovation efforts.

6.2.4.3 *Balance Process and Flexibility*

Probably, the greatest challenge is striking a balance in applying processes and procedures versus allowing employees and collaborators freedom to do things in new and inventive ways.

Methods for managing this challenge include partitioning the organization to create a "skunkworks" group or recognizing that flexibility best exists outside organizational confines and therefore sponsoring external innovation.

6.3 Innovation in Practice: Doblin 10 Types of Innovation

The Doblin 10 Types of Innovation framework is simple and intuitive. It is a useful tool you can use both to diagnose and to enrich an innovation you're working on or to analyze the existing competition. It makes it especially easy to spot errors of omission—missing dimensions that will make a concept stronger.

The 10 Types framework is structured into three color-coded categories: Configuration (blue), Offering (orange), and Experience (red)—see Figure 6.9 [7]. The types on the left side of the framework are the most internally focused and distant from customers; as you move toward the right side, the types become increasingly apparent and obvious to end users. To use a theatrical metaphor, the left of the framework is backstage; the right is onstage.

Figure 6.10 provides a definition of each of the ten types with an example to demonstrate the application of this innovation type.

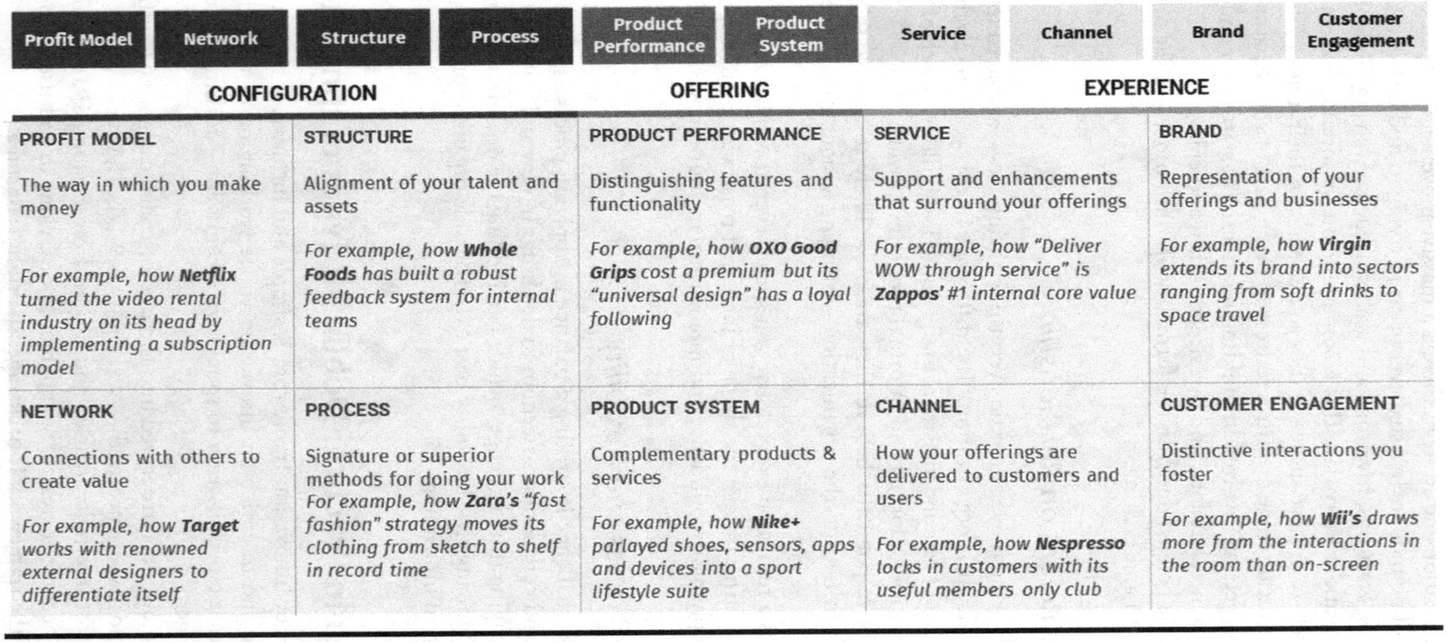

Profit Model	Network	Structure	Process	Product Performance	Product System	Service	Channel	Brand	Customer Engagement
CONFIGURATION				OFFERING		EXPERIENCE			
PROFIT MODEL The way in which you make money *For example, how **Netflix** turned the video rental industry on its head by implementing a subscription model*	**NETWORK** Connections with others to create value *For example, how **Target** works with renowned external designers to differentiate itself*	**STRUCTURE** Alignment of your talent and assets *For example, how **Whole Foods** has built a robust feedback system for internal teams*	**PROCESS** Signature or superior methods for doing your work *For example, how **Zara's** "fast fashion" strategy moves its clothing from sketch to shelf in record time*	**PRODUCT PERFORMANCE** Distinguishing features and functionality *For example, how **OXO Good Grips** cost a premium but its "universal design" has a loyal following* **PRODUCT SYSTEM** Complementary products & services *For example, how **Nike+** parlayed shoes, sensors, apps and devices into a sport lifestyle suite*		**SERVICE** Support and enhancements that surround your offerings *For example, how "Deliver WOW through service" is **Zappos'** #1 internal core value* **CHANNEL** How your offerings are delivered to customers and users *For example, how **Nespresso** locks in customers with its useful members only club*		**BRAND** Representation of your offerings and businesses *For example, how **Virgin** extends its brand into sectors ranging from soft drinks to space travel* **CUSTOMER ENGAGEMENT** Distinctive interactions you foster *For example, how **Wii's** draws more from the interactions in the room than on-screen*	

Figure 6.10 Doblin 10 types of innovation [7]

To use the ten types of innovation the following six principles need to be adopted by the organization:

- Understand all ten types
- De-emphasize reliance on products and technology
- Think about the three categories as well as the ten types
- Use enough of the types to make a splash
- Understand what the users really need
- Use the types that matter the most

Figure 6.11 elaborates on those six principles for the use of the ten types of innovation framework to put innovation into practice.

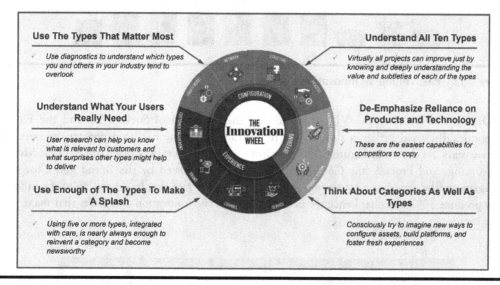

Figure 6.11   Principles for the use of the 10 types of innovation [8]

An important note about putting innovation in action is the shift that is taking place in the frequency of use of the different types of innovation. Historically, the volume of innovation efforts, as shown in the Pareto chart in Figure 6.12, was highly concentrated around Product Performance and Product System (the Offering category) innovations.

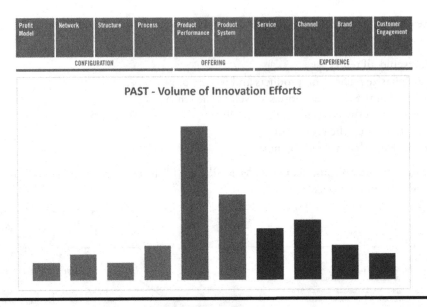

Figure 6.12 Past volume of innovation efforts

Due to the forces of the VUCA world and the evolution of Society 5.0 and the Future Economies discussed earlier, a shift in the innovation landscape has been progressing over the last few years. As shown in Figure 6.13, more innovation is now taking place in the Profit Model, Networking, and Process (the Configuration category), followed by the Brand and Customer Engagement (the experience category). This is driven by the fact that less than 2% of the innovations produce 90% of value; hence we need to focus on the innovation categories that maximize value creation.

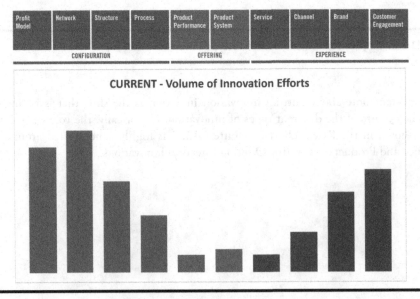

Figure 6.13 Current volume of innovation efforts

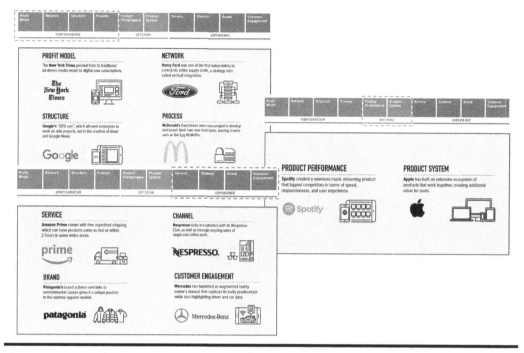

Figure 6.14   Companies with innovation-driven strategies

To conclude this section, it is worthwhile to show how different types of innovation have been used by different organizations. Innovation-driven strategies are not reserved only for technology companies. The examples in Figure 6.14 show that companies such as McDonald's, Ford, Google, Apple, and Patagonia have innovation as a common driver for their strategies.

References

1. Naiman, L. (2021). Design Thinking as Strategy for Innovation. https://www.creativityatwork.com/design-thinking-strategy-for-innovation/
2. Liedtka, J., and Kaplan, S. (2019). How Design Thinking Opens New Frontiers for Strategy Development. *Strategy & Leadership*, 47(2), 3–10.
3. Knight, E., Daymond, J., and Paroutis, S. (2020). Design-Led Strategy: How to Bring Design Thinking into the Art of Strategic Management. *California Management Review*, 62(2), 30–52. https://warwick.ac.uk/fac/soc/wbs/subjects/sib/people/sotirios_profile/knight_daymond_paroutis_20_cmr.pdf
4. Rae, J. (2016). Design Value Index. *Design Management Institute (DMI)*, 27(4),
5. Tschimmel, K. (2018). Toolkit Evolution 6^2 - An E-handbook for Practical Design Thinking for Innovation. Mindshake. https://www.mindshake.pt/
6. http://www2.paconsulting.com/rs/526-HZE-833/images/Innovation-Matters-Report.pdf
7. Keeley, L., Pikkel, R., Quinn, B., and Walters, H. (2013). *Ten Types of Innovation: The Discipline of Building Breakthroughs*. John Wiley & Sons, Inc.
8. Desjardins, J. (2020). 10 Types of Innovation: The Art of Discovering a Breakthrough Product. https://www.visualcapitalist.com/10-types-of-innovation-the-art-of-discovering-a-breakthrough-product/

Chapter 7

Balanced Strategy Development

7.1 Balanced Strategy Development (BSD) Approach

To ensure your arrival into the Future and capitalize on Society 5.0 and future economies your strategy needs to leverage four strategic dimensions as it needs to be driven by:

- Insights
- Culture
- Operations
- Digitization

Figure 7.1 shows how those four dimensions should be integrated into a holistic strategy since their interconnections, interdependencies, and impact on business performance are as important as each of them individually.

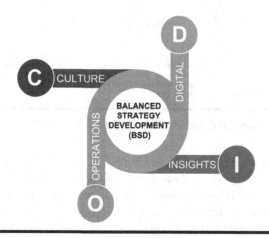

Figure 7.1   Balanced strategy development (BSD) dimensions

DOI: 10.4324/9781003280941-11

Digital is still considered the foundation and backbone for any strategy in the future. Leveraging digital tools can improve the company operations and organization culture. That will lead to new insights that can drive the company–customers interaction and to maximizing value creation for both sides. That is what I call a true win-win strategy.

Using this Balanced Strategy Development approach can ensure sustainable value creation for the different stakeholders, and that is the true essence of being strategy savvy.

The following sections will review the four dimensions and how we can use them to develop the organization strategy.

7.2 Insights-Driven Strategy

We are living in a world where *Data* is considered the new *Oil* ... companies that will learn how to manage their internal and external customer data to develop insights to drive their strategy, operations, and decision-making are those that will lead the way for the future business models.

IDC indicated in their study about "Worldwide Embedded and Intelligent Systems" that by 2020, the world will have more than 4 billion connected people, with US$4 trillion in revenue opportunities, more than 25 million mobile applications, and more than 25 million embedded intelligent systems—all this will generate 50 trillion GB of Data (see Figure 7.2) [1].

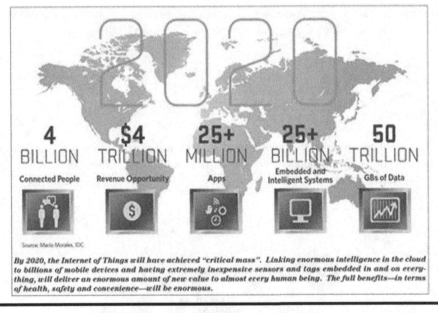

Figure 7.2   Worldwide embedded and intelligent systems by 2020

We are now moving toward the Internet of Things (IoT), where the physical and virtual worlds are integrated ... we are already seeing many devices and applications that are gradually becoming part of our life—such as smart homes, driverless cars, smart personal assistants, and industrial robotics. At the same time, many companies are working on commercializing the Internet of Everything (IoET). This is where people, applications, devices, sensors, and data are seamlessly integrated and used to generate revenue and create value.

This explosion of connectivity and data will require a different type of strategy development approach that can turn this data into valuable information that is used to create organizational knowledge that can be leveraged using new tools such as AI (Artificial Intelligence) and data science into customer *Insights*.

Figure 7.3 clearly indicates that the world has passed the Information Age and the knowledge economy and is now moving toward Insights-Driven Business Models as the foundation of future competitive advantage. But the figure also shows that Data is the foundation of this progression and evolution [2].

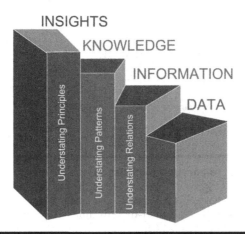

Figure 7.3   From data to insights

The consumer-buying world is being turned upside down, with new "paths to purchase", different ways of engaging with consumers, redefined roles for stores and brands, new approaches to assortments, consumer-driven supply chains, and dynamic networks of collaborating trading partners. For example, the traditional approach used to describe the consumer buying process using the **Funnel** metaphor has been replaced today with the **Loops** metaphor. As shown in Figure 7.4, the old metaphor ends with the consumer *Buy*, while the loops move the *Buy* to the middle of the process and extend to three new steps: Enjoy, Advocate, and Bond. This new loyalty loop management provides new levels of engagement with the customer and a continuous stream of data that can be used to generate insights that can inform and continuously improve our strategy development and implementation [3].

We're all aware of the underlying trends: Empowerment of consumers, an increasing pace of change in our lives, the growing amount of time we devote to social media, our greater reliance on these channels for information and advice that would once have come from brand owners, the immense trail of data that we now leave behind us.

Insights generated by this flood of data will be the most effective driver of business competitiveness in the near future. However, to get the insights in a cost-effective and timely manner, companies need a different approach. They must confront market changes head-on—recognizing, for example, that social media platforms such as Facebook and Twitter are more important to consumers than the information channels companies control themselves. To illustrate: A business may find that its e-mails and brochures increasingly end up in junk files and garbage bins, while consumers are congregating in their own online spaces to discuss or develop innovative ways of using its products. Add to this that social media is going increasingly "dark", taking place on private apps, and there will be no way to track where the conversation is going.

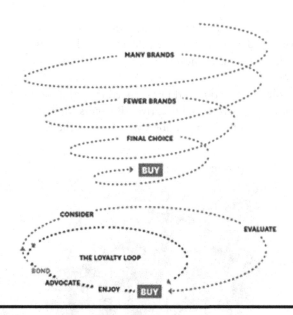

Figure 7.4 Consumer funnel to consumer journey [3]

In order to engage in these new consumer-driven value networks, you need not only new analytics tools but also a change to your operating model, working practices, skills, and culture. You need to be able to learn about the consumer from one minute to the next and make appropriate adjustments to what you're doing, including changing content "on the fly". Your teams will need to work in a whole new way—an extremely collaborative and dynamic one.

Our teams need to face today's digital-age consumers. Those consumers are more complex and better equipped to deal with salespeople. They are characterized by the following seven dimensions:

1. They are More **Knowledgeable**: Thanks to internet accessibility, user-generated content, and social media, the consumer today has access to many sources of information to learn about companies, products, and services from different sources and perspectives.
2. They are More **Demanding**: Consumers today have a new definition of *Value* that goes way beyond features and benefits. Sales teams need to focus on value propositions that can satisfy consumer demand.
3. They are More **Empowered**: Connected consumers have more options that allow them to compare and contrast differing offerings to choose the best. They have more channels to access information, products, services, and companies.
4. They are More **Collaborative**: Consumers today help each other and provide information, opinions, advice, and support that were traditionally provided by the salesperson.
5. They are More **Diverse**: Thanks to the globalization of markets and the consumerization of technology, consumers today share different experiences from different backgrounds and perspectives to enrich each other's purchase experience and make it more challenging for the sales team and the sales process adaptation to manage this diversity.
6. They are More **Interactive**: The prefiltration of User-Generated-Content (UGC) represents a whole new input to the company-customer communication process. This many-to-many communication requires continuous monitoring and evaluation by the sales team.

7. They are More on the **Move**: Sales teams need to learn how to manage this new AWATAD (Any-Where, Any-Time, Any-Device) shopping behavior of consumers that are constantly on the move.

This new level of consumer power in the digital age is based on four sources: Two individual-based power sources (demand and information-based power) due to higher level of accessibility and information availability and two dynamic and complex network-based power sources (network and crowd-based power) due to higher levels of connectivity and interactions on social media platforms [4]. Demand-based power is viewed as democratic voting power exercised by the consumer through different actions online, such as Facebook likes, YouTube views, Google searches, and Amazon purchases. Information-based power is related both to consumer content consumption and to content creation.

Network-based power comes from the consumer's ability to add value beyond the original content through content dissemination, content completion, or content modifications. Finally, crowd-based power comes from to pool, mobilize, and structure resources that can benefit the individual consumer and the groups he belongs to. This escalating level of consumer power needs to be managed across the different areas of customer touchpoints and interactions both in the physical and in the digital worlds. That led to the redefinition of when and where the customer and the sales team connect.

The see of data that is surrounding us today creates a new type of data that is known as big data and is characterized by the five Vs (see Figure 7.5):

1. **Volume—Scale of Data**: The sheer volume of data being generated every second
2. **Velocity—Analysis of Streaming Data**: The speed at which data emanating and changes are occurring

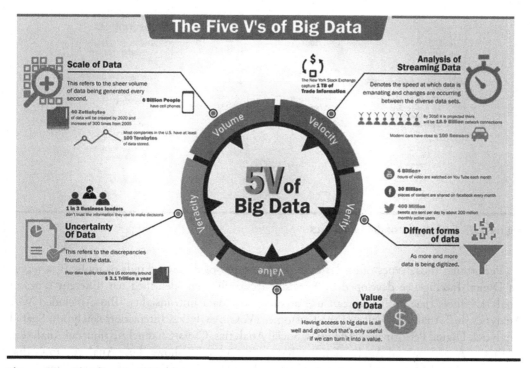

Figure 7.5   The five Vs of big data

3. **Verity—Different Forms of Data**: Text, images, voice, video, location, etc.
4. **Value—Value of Data**: Monetization of data
5. **Veracity—Uncertainty of Data**: Discrepancies found in the data

Using analytics on this to big data allows companies today to generate the needed insights to develop and drive their strategy. There are four types of data analytics, and they represent levels of maturity for the organization to try to achieve. Advanced technologies today allow all types/sizes of the organization to leverage the power of data in an economic way. Most organizations today can easily implement the first two levels (Descriptive and Diagnostic Analytics), but they need to work on learning how to use the higher two levels (Predictive and Prescriptive Analytics) to gain real insights.

1. **Descriptive**: Tells what is happening in real time
2. **Diagnostic**: Explains why things are happening
3. **Predictive**: Tells what likely to happen
4. **Prescriptive**: Defines what to do next

Figure 7.6 shows what those four types of data analytics are and how they rank in terms of complexity and value.

Figure 7.6 shows what those four types of data analytics are and how they rank in terms of complexity and value.

4 Types of Data Analytics

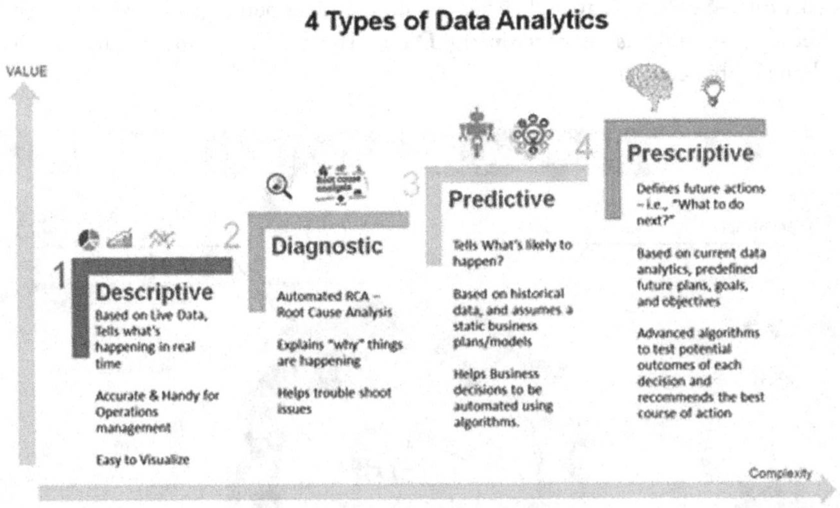

Figure 7.6 Four types of data analytics

Performing those types of analytics requires the use of different kinds of tools. In a report on Digital Intelligence developed by Forrester Research, they identified ten different types of Analytics Tools that businesses can use to turn their data into insights. Those included Web Analytics, IoT Analytics, Voice-of-the-Customer (VoC) Analytics, Interaction Analytics, Spatial Analytics, Digital Performance Analytics, Social Analytics, Cross-Channel Attribution Analytics, Predictive Analytics, and Application Analytics [5]. Figure 7.7 shows those Analytics tools that allow for using data to develop insights that can be used to optimize our customer interactions through Behavioral Targeting, Online Testing, and Recommendation Marketing across different digital touchpoints. This makes our customer management more relevant in different contexts and can truly influence consumer behavior to create a competitive advantage for the organization.

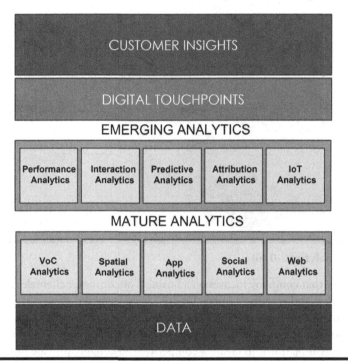

Figure 7.7   Data, analytics, touchpoints, and insights

Using analytics tools can help organizations answer some critical questions to develop insight-driven strategies. Figure 7.8 shows an example of five layers of **Web** Analytics 2.0 tools and the questions they answer. Clickstream analysis provides insights into **What** customers do online. Multiple Outcomes analysis provides insights into **How Much** customers do to convert and achieve their desired outcomes. Experimentation/Testing and Voice-of-Customer analysis provide insights into **Why** do customers do things. Finally, Competitive Intelligence analysis provides insights into **What Else** did customers consider. The five layers build on each other and provide valuable insights to effectively manage your organization's customer strategy [6].

Adding data from other sources such as Spatial Analytics tools that provide location-based data analysis and IoT Analytics that provide data from the devices customers use and interact with can provide very rich sources for your insights-driven strategy.

The insights achieved from the use of big data and different types of advanced Analytics Tools should be ultimately integrated into a Customer Strategy that articulates the distinctive value and experiences your company will deliver, along with the offerings, channels, operating model, and capabilities you will need. In a global survey conducted by Strategy of 161 executives, more than 80% indicated that having an insight-driven customer strategy is a crucial part of their organization strategy.

A well-designed customer strategy will coordinate many different functions, skills, and practices. For example, it should encompass data analytics; go-to-market and channel choices; and the delivery of products, services, and experiences. Ten principles are at the heart of any effective customer strategy. These principles are universally applicable, regardless of the industry a company

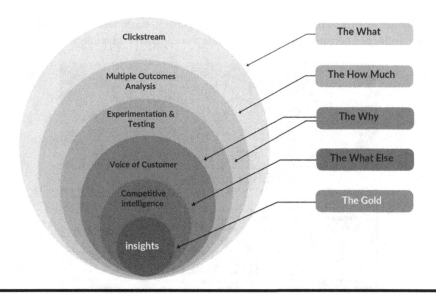

Figure 7.8 Web analytics 2.0 [6]

operates in, whether that company focuses on a business or consumer clientele, where it does business, or what products and services it offers. Figure 7.9 summarized those ten principles [7].

One example of how your organization can combine analytics, metrics, and customer strategy is the use of online communities to deliver sustainable business impact. Customer communities can provide a powerful platform to create a competitive advantage, provide bottom-line growth/

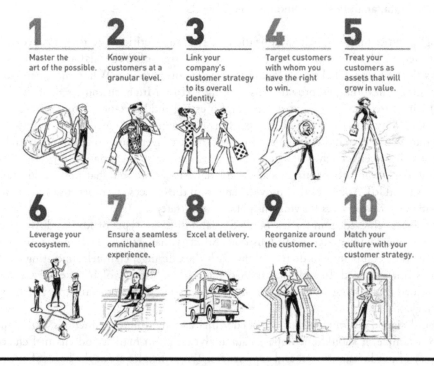

Figure 7.9 10 Principles of customer strategy [7]

savings, provide top-line growth/revenue, improve influence and operations, and improve business measures of success.

In a survey of more than 271 marketing professionals, 92% of respondents believe that their online customer communities have an impact on the business and 35% lack meaningful metrics to report success in business terms. Figure 7.10 shows a set of possible metrics that can be used by organizations to measure the impact of customer online communities at both the tactical and strategic levels. Those metrics are the basis for developing insights that can guide and drive your customer strategy [8].

Those metrics are organized into seven categories:

1. Community Vibrancy Metrics (CVM) that track the overall health and utility of the community
2. Engagement Metrics that track community relevance
3. Content Consumption Impact Metrics that track community content relevance and reach
4. Customer Support Impact Metrics that track the value of community as a support channel
5. Customer Retention/Satisfaction Metrics that track the correlation between community membership and customer retention
6. Marketing and Sales Metrics that track the impact of community on marketing and sales objectives
7. Business Integration Metrics (BIM) that track the impact of community on core operations

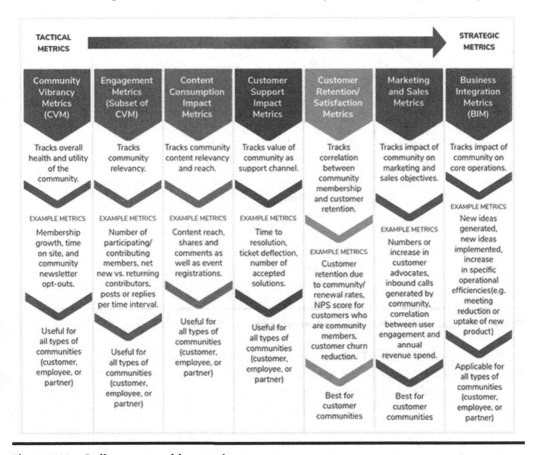

Figure 7.10 Online communities metrics

Those customer online communities provide just one example of how data is transforming the world of sales and marketing. Data-driven marketing/advertising. An integrated model that links the increased application of data-driven marketing with the expanded scope and role of marketing in the organization strategy proposes five layers of impact for an insights-driven strategy: Creativity, Relevance, Analytics Capabilities, Accountability, and Technology (see Figure 7.11).

7.2.1 Data-Driven Marketing

Data can impact creativity in advertising (more details on the impact of data and technology on advertising will be provided in the next section), the relevance of marketing activities for the customer (selling the right product to the right customer at the right time), the need for analytics capabilities in the organization, accountability by linking marketing outputs to firm-level financial outcomes, and technology adoption (such as AI/ML, mixed reality, blockchain, and IoT) to drive marketing [9].

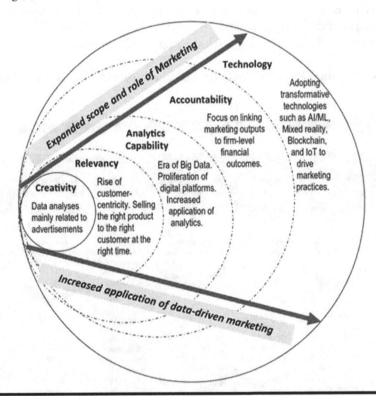

Figure 7.11   Data-driven marketing/advertising for insights-driven strategy [9]

Since advertising is crucial for customer strategy and it is witnessing a true transformation because of data and analytics, the following section will provide a review of how useful data, analytics, and insights can be used to drive your strategy and how customer concerns about the privacy and the security of their data might represent a challenge for this approach and how to address this challenge.

From the organizations' (advertisers) perspective, agility in directing and redirecting advertising spending to maximize the returns and show outcomes is of significant importance post-COVID-19. Scenario planning and agile monitoring of consumer behavior and advertising spending are the new priorities for advertising executives. Increased use of data and technology (such as predictive analytics, artificial intelligence, machine learning, and programmatically supported advertising buying models) is the new normal in advertising. In this new world of digital advertising, marketers who take action have the opportunity to create a significant and sustained competitive advantage for their organizations. They can harness the following benefits [10]:

■ Accelerate revenue growth
■ Create personalized consumer experiences at scale
■ Drive costs down
■ Generate greater ROI on campaigns
■ Get more actionable insights from marketing data
■ Predict consumer needs and behaviors with greater accuracy
■ Reduce time spent on repetitive, data-driven tasks
■ Shorten the sales cycle
■ Unlock greater value from marketing technologies

At the heart of this future advertising ecosystem are two critical issues: The use of online behavioral advertising (OBA) by advertising networks (i.e., companies that serve advertising on thousands of websites) and the use of ad blockers by consumers. This section will highlight some models that study those phenomena and their theoretical foundations.

7.2.1.1 Online Behavioral Advertising (OBA)

There are many definitions of OBA, which are also called "online profiling" and "behavioral targeting". Examples include:

■ Adjusting advertisements to previous online surfing behavior
■ A technology-driven advertising personalization method that enables advertisers to deliver highly relevant ad messages to individuals
■ The practice of collecting data about an individual's online activities for use in selecting which advertisement to display

These definitions and others have two common features: (1) The monitoring or tracking of consumers' online behavior and (2) the use of the collected data to individually target ads. Therefore, Boerman et al. defined OBA as "the practice of monitoring people's online behavior and using the collected information to show people individually targeted advertisements" [11].

In a simple example of OBA, an advertising network tracks a consumer's website visits. If a consumer visits several websites about cars, the network assumes the consumer is interested in cars. The network can then display ads for cars only to people (presumed to be) interested in cars. Consequently, when two people visit the same website at the same time, one may see car ads while the other (who had visited websites about furniture) may see furniture ads.

Online behavior can include web browsing data, search histories, media consumption data (e.g., videos watched), app use data, purchases, click-through responses to ads, and communication content, such as what people write in e-mails (e.g., via Gmail) or post on social networking sites. Currently, behavioral targeting mostly occurs when using computers or smartphones, but the borders between off-line and online are fading. Phrases such as the Internet of Things (IoT), ubiquitous computing, and ambient intelligence have been used to describe such developments. If objects are connected to the Internet, companies could use the data collected through those objects for OBA.

OBA differs from other types of online advertising because it aims at personal relevance, which often happens covertly. Similar to other forms of personalized advertising, such as location-based advertising and ads that include people's names, OBA uses personal information to tailor ads in such a way that they are perceived as more personally relevant. A new dimension to this personalization is the fact that the tracking of online activities, collection of behavioral data, and dissemination of information often happen covertly. This covertness may be harmful and unethical, as consumers are unaware of the persuasion mechanisms that entail OBA; it has led to a call for transparency. A study by PWC/IAB in 2021 about the digital ad ecosystem found that 76% of global consumers think that sharing personal information with companies is a necessary evil, and 36% say they are less comfortable sharing their information now than they were a year ago (Figure 7.12). Although advertisers can benefit from OBA, the practice also raises concerns about privacy. Therefore, OBA has received much attention from advertisers, consumers, policymakers, and scholars [12].

Data sharing¹

76%

of global consumers indicate they think "sharing my personal information with companies is a necessary evil in today's modern economy."

36%

of consumers say they are less comfortable sharing their information now than they were a year ago.

Figure 7.12   Consumer attitude toward data sharing [12]

Hence, to counter the proliferation of ad blockers and maintain advertising revenue streams, current industry initiatives are aimed to mitigate the most disruptive and annoying aspects of online advertising. Initiatives such as **LEAN (Light, Encrypted, Ad choices support, Noninvasive/ nondisruptive)** aim at improving advertisements' value to the viewer and minimizing interruption of the user flow. Although not yet a mandated requirement, these guidelines suggest limiting ad file size, restricting data usage, and assuring user choice and data security.

Another industry initiative—the IAB'S new **DEAL process (Detect, Explain, Ask, and Lift or Limit)**—is designed to help publishers apply appropriate tactics to address ad blocking based on their relationship with the audience. To date, none of these strategies has been overly successful. Subscription rates for the top US publishers barely top 7%, and among ad blocker users surveyed by Cortland (2017), 90% report that when encountering an ad-block wall that prevented them from viewing content on a publisher's website, 74% said they typically abandon the site rather than performing the steps required to allow the publisher to serve them ads (known as "whitelisting").

7.2.1.2 Futuristic Advertising Strategy

In order to formulate and realize the advertising strategy of the future, organizations need to look in greater detail at the following three macro factors, namely Customers' Demands, Advertisers'

Priorities, and Technological Advancements that will significantly determine the future of advertising strategy [13].

1. **Customer Demands**

    Personalized Communication: The recent advancement in digital technologies has evolved customer expectations for relevant messaging as they seek customized communication designed to address their specific needs. It is needless to say that customers truly value personalized communication as it is worth their time and effort. With the increasing availability of detailed customer data, the future of advertising will see more personalized communication within industry and markets. This, of course, needs to be balanced with the consumer concern discussed earlier about their privacy … don't over personalize.

    Relevant Messaging: Today brands try to seize every opportunity to broadcast their message to the consumer with the hope that consumers will not only become familiar with the brand but also make a purchase. Unfortunately, most of these efforts didn't achieve substantial results due to the irrelevance of the message and pose a significant threat to the effectiveness of advertising. Advertising is most likely to influence brand choice when the advertising message is most relevant and accessible.

2. **Advertisers' Priorities**

    Profitable Customer engagement: In recent times firms have realized the importance of having a profitable customer base instead of a large customer base. This has enabled the companies to shift from sales-centric philosophy to an engagement-centric that relies on maintaining lasting relationships with the customer.

    Data-Driven Advertising. The next wave of digital marketing is perceived to be predictive, with artificial intelligence emerging as a key in driving innovation in marketing. According to the survey commissioned by Forrester consulting, 84% of the marketers and agencies want to achieve marketing that learns and optimizes from each interaction with a customer [96]. The survey highlights the five fundamentals that will drive the future of predictive data-driven marketing:

    — **Customer recognition**: Today customers use multiple devices and it is quite important for firms to recognize individuals across these devices in order to understand their customer journey and offer a personalized and tailored experience.

    — **Nonlinear customer journey**: The proliferation of digital devices means that the customer journey is made up of an infinite combination of channels and touchpoints; hence, marketers must gain a holistic view of customer interactions.

    — **Real-time decision-making**: In order to provide relevant and personalized experiences, marketers need to be able to act on insights drawn in real time. This means that the action of deriving insights from the data and executing the marketing strategies need to take place simultaneously.

    — **AI-based intelligent decision-making**: Artificial intelligence and machine learning have emerged as solutions to tackle problems associated with processing large amounts of data and to draw actionable insights rapidly.

    — **Using first-party data over third-party external data**. Only first-party data can provide marketers with differentiated insights as compared to third-party data which is onerous and difficult to validate.

    Permission Marketing/advertising. Permission marketing is an approach where a marketer seeks customer permission before sending a marketing message. The key objective of permission marketing is to have an authentic engagement with the consumer without breaching their privacy.

Experiential Advertising. Experiential advertising focuses primarily on facilitating the consumers to experience the brand. In this form of advertising, the firm engages directly with the consumer and encourages them to help evolve the brand. This is feasible today because of recent advances in the use of virtual reality (VR) and augmented reality (AR) tools in advertising.

Capturing Customer Feedback. Advertisement is deemed to be effective only when it delivers the message that it was intended to deliver. Regular feedback from the consumers can help marketers to adjust their message accordingly.

3. **Technological Advancements**

Media convergence. Media convergence is the merging of mass communication outlets— print, television, radio, the internet along portable and interactive digital technologies through various digital media platforms. To reap the maximum amount of benefits future firms should use a data-driven strategy to identify the most effective mix of available media channels.

Social Media. Social media has fundamentally changed the way organizations communicate and has dramatically changed the advertising landscape. The rise of social networking sites has changed the power dynamics on the web giving consumers the power to control, process, and act upon the information that has been shared with them. The proliferation of user-generated content (UGC) due to social media platforms has changed the world of communications forever.

Smart Technologies. Brands are turning technology into a way to attract and engage consumers in new and innovative ways. Advertising embracing technologies have proved to have greater impact and more sophisticated ways to reach their target audience and gain great social connection and product value. The creativity in using digital technologies is considered a very effective way of breathing life into advertising campaigns.

In 2017, Pepsi introduced a new tactic of advertising, with the amount of time youth are spending on their smartphones, Pepsi decided to use this technology to create the ad. Carrying their message of "Let's Complete Our Gathering" bridging the gap between the slogan and reality, in order to view the ad, three smartphones are required to be placed next to each other for full view. The strategy was to actually use the smartphone technology to enjoy this advertising experience that would not be complete without the gathering of family or friends. The ad was divided into three sections, as mentioned, each part is seen on one smartphone, without having the other two smartphones, the picture would be incomplete. Figure 7.13 shows the ad using three smartphones to demonstrate how it became known as the first-ever multiscreen mobile ad.

The ad aims to bring together people and unite them, and this was clearly reinforced by the technology used to compel the people to unite, considered as a reality check to make the people realize that they are actually now together enjoying time with one another, the ad was able to shift smartphone technology from being an individualistic used tool to a collective social experience.

Heading into the future, futuristic technologies such as the use of the Internet of Things (IoT) and augmented reality will truly transform the advertising sector offering consumers the most immersive experience and allowing them to engage with products experientially. According to the Interactive Advertising Bureau (IAB), 65% of the people owning at least one Internet of Things (IoT) device say that they are willing to receive ads on IoT screens.

Figure 7.13   Pepsi advertisement as seen with three smartphones

These figures are quite promising, and marketers should continue to integrate the Internet of Things within their marketing strategies as tomorrow's prospects for IoT as a marketing platform seems very bright.

7.2.2 Insights-Driven Business to Drive Value

Companies accelerate their journey toward becoming an insight-driven business by not a narrow point-solution but a practice-proven approach that brings together business, data, analytical tooling, and technology platforms in small iterative steps while, in parallel, working toward the end game.

This involves a four-step approach [14]:

■ Igniting the journey
■ Demonstrating business value
■ Scaling the capability
■ Growing the insight-driven business using the framework shown in Figure 7.14.

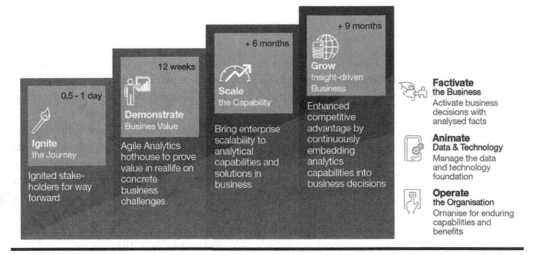

Figure 7.14   Insights-driven business to dive value [14]

This approach packages these three incremental phases together with three streams that reinforce each other:

- **"Factivate" the business ("activate with facts")**: It is focused on embedding analytics into core processes and your people's work by understanding your business personas, with T-shaped teams that are up-skilled in advanced data science and analytics
- **"Animate" the required data, platform, and advanced analytical tooling**: This is about bringing together all relevant data (internal and external data, structured and unstructured) to deliver real-time insights at the point of action
- **"Operate" the organization by building enduring capabilities and benefits**: Ensure consistent and scalable services-led delivery which is open innovation and industrialization. Use a hybrid funding model (both CAPEX and OPEX, mix of subscription, "pay-as-you-go" and custom-flex)

This is an end-to-end approach that combines bespoke business solutions and industrialized IT solutions, while taking into account the cultural aspects of moving data into the heart of decision-making.

7.2.2.1 Benefits of Becoming an Insight-Driven Business

Insights-driven business can reap the following benefits [14]:

- Build outstanding customer and consumer experiences—engaging effectively across multiple channels such as consumer-driven value networks
- Generate significant cost savings—through scalable industrialized business insights development, usage-based pricing, and unparalleled flexibility and security
- Increase productivity and performance—enabling staff to work more effectively so that marketers can optimize their media/advertising activity and content in real time
- Balance consumer choice and personalization against privacy requirements—dealing fairly with customers and avoiding stiff penalties for data breaches
- Achieve the appropriate balance of investment—in product mix, store promotions, or wider trade activities
- Keep your finger on the pulse of innovation—to remain efficient, agile, and aware of emerging trends

In a study by Capgemini Consulting about the benefits of insight-driven business for consumer products and retail companies, they suggested that insight-driven marketing can increase sales by 3% to 9%, insight-driven sales can reduce costs by 10% to 30%, and insight-driven supply chain can improve working capital by 10%.

Finally, continuously assess your analytics maturity to make sure that you are building your capabilities to become insights-driven strategy champions. Figure 7.15 provides an example of a tool that can be used for this maturity assessment [15]. The ADOPT Analytics Maturity Framework helps you plan your journey to leverage data as a strategic asset. It provides insight into an organization's scalable infrastructure for an analytics culture and program. The framework includes five categories that measure and assess analytics competencies including the people, processes, and technologies that align to support an information-driven culture. The five dimensions it measures are analyst, data, optimization, performance, and technology. They are measured on a five-point scale from Entreat to Expert.

Analytics Maturity

	ENTRANT	EVOLVING	EMERGING	EMPOWERED	EXPERT
ANALYST	• Analysts not identified or viewed as strategically important • Analysts quantify but do not interpret or explain	• Analysts identified but work in silos • Analysts quantify and link variables (e.g. relationship between procedure cost and avoidable events)	• Analysts identified and classified by skill level, expertise, and tools used • Analysts interpret needs of decision-makers and help design analytic output	• Analysts actively developed with learning, specialization, and an optimized structure • Analysts create advanced visualizations that support predictive analytics	• Highly skilled analysts use creativity and imagination to develop new meanings from data and metrics • Analysts create analysis and visualizations to help identify strategy and tactics
DATA	• Data sits in transaction systems and used inefficiently and/or redundantly	• Redundancies in data and metrics • Data stewardship and data quality validation that needs to be identified	• Data actively managed and developed, with providers involved in metric development	• Data & metric lifecycle actively managed • Data quality accountability is assumed • Data acquisition strategies developed	• Data quality and consistency is universal across the organization • Data acquisition developed where needed to meet strategic initiatives
OPTIMIZATION	• Leadership has not sustained an analytics program and is not sure where to begin	• Pockets of organizing analytics in development (i.e. department reports). But analytics not effective and efficient	• Analytics function actively managed and well led, expectation of utilizing technology • Analytics represents source of "truth" for entire organization	• Data shopping eliminated • Leadership supports and enforces analytic governance tools, structures, and processes	• Analytics shape business strategy – from descriptive to predictive to prescriptive • Analytics alignment communicated and demonstrated by leadership
PERFORMANCE	• Performance metrics incomplete and/or don't reflect strategy	• Performance metrics in development but conflicts/redundancies may exist	• Active management of metrics creation and accountability • Use of benchmarks, targets, and trends	• Active management of metrics creation, accountability, and alignment to strategic goals • Metrics used to identify performance gaps	• Robust performance improvement model using analytics, with new metrics continually developed to advance performance
TECHNOLOGY	• Analytics technology not implemented or not used efficiently • Data and metrics distributed via many different methods (email, print)	• Analytics technology implemented but not maintained or used effectively • Some data and metrics actively distributed via business intelligence	• Data acquisition and aggregation tools in place, maintained • Self-service business intelligence tools in place and utilized • Data housed once and used many times	• Data transformation tools used, maintained • Apps evaluated for data used/produced; redundancies eliminated • Advanced analytics tools required to achieve business goals	• Technology and applications are used to improve/advance the organization's competitive position and actively used for decision making

Figure 7.15 ADOPT analytics maturity model [15]

7.3 Culture-Driven Strategy

Corporate culture means different things to different people. It is emotional, ever-changing, and complex. Culture is human, vulnerable, and as moody as the people who define it. In general, most culture definitions have two common factors. First is that culture is *shared* among a group of individuals; an individual alone cannot have culture. Second is that culture typically involves *values* and/or *expectations*.

There are two different levels of culture that need to be understood when we try to understand the relationship between strategy and culture: **Organizational culture** and **societal culture**. Organizational culture is defined as "a pattern of basic assumptions—invented, discovered, or *developed by a given group as it learns to cope* with its problems of external adaptation and internal integration". It is labeled as **Little-c culture**. Societal culture is defined as "customary beliefs and values that ethnic, religious, and social groups transmit fairly unchanged from generation to generation". It is labeled as **Big-C culture**.

These contrasting definitions of culture suggest several dimensions on which the **setting** (size of the group), **source** (events in the distant past, by ambient conditions at an organization's founding or by intentional interventions during the life of the organization), **content** (values and expectations), and the **process** of change of cultures (speed and intentionality) may differ [16].

Culture is an incredibly powerful factor in a company's long-term success. No matter how good a strategy is, when it comes down to it, people always make the difference. For example, in attempting to understand why Southwest Airlines persistently outperformed competitors, researchers turned to notions of shared values and expectations that lie at the core of culture. Culture has also been offered as an explanation for the differential success of mergers and varying levels of cross-national foreign direct investment by multinational firms.

Culture can be viewed as the roots of a tree (Figure 7.16). It is the hidden part that ensures the tree stands and is the source of feeding the whole tree. It gets manifested in organizational behavior (the visible part of the tree) that gets nurtured by the climate (the influence of the organization leadership). This metaphor is simple but powerful in demonstrating how important culture is for the organization's ability to achieve its objectives and provide the results (fruits of our labor). This culture is an important driver for strategy development and implementation.

The disconnect between culture and strategy has been proven to negatively impact the organization's performance. In a study done by McKinsey that surveyed 2,135 respondents, they

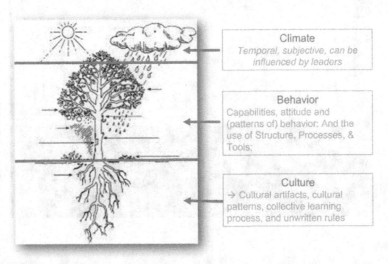

Figure 7.16   Culture, behavior, and climate

identified three types of cultures that have the highest correlation with an organization's negative economic performance [17] (Figure 7.17).

- Non-digital culture has a negative correlation of –0.47
- Siloed mindsets and behavior have a negative correlation of –0.44
- Aversion of risk has a negative correlation of –0.36

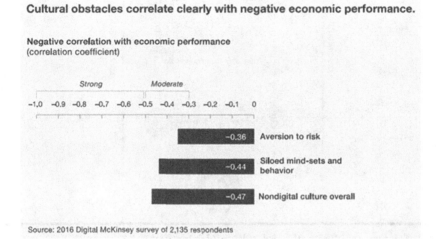

Figure 7.17   Cultural obstacles correlation to negative performance [17]

Hence, aligning strategy and culture is of paramount importance for organizational success. A strategy that is at odds with a company's culture is doomed. Culture trumps strategy every time— **Culture Eats Strategy for Breakfast (Peter Drucker).**

This alignment process assumes that strategy provides the organization with a *Guiding Path* and culture provides a *Driving Path* (as shown in Figure 7.18) [18]. This dual-path approach to integrating strategy and culture is similar to train tracks that keep the organization on its path to the future. Hence, a culture-driven strategy can be achieved when **Culture Meets (not Easts) Strategy for Breakfast**.

To keep it really simple, a business strategy focuses on "**what we do**" and "**where are we going**". Culture, on the other hand, focuses on the "**how**" and "**why**" **we do what we do** to operate as a team. Culture is created on the foundation of behaviors, rituals, and attitudes that are made collectively acceptable within an organization. It has a profound impact on how individuals make decisions and how they respond to challenges and adversity.

As an example, the high-performing organizations (HPO) culture model [19] provides the cultural dimensions that can drive the organization strategy. It is broken down into three dimensions: Creation of movement, capability to move, and moving together. Those dimensions are further delineated in six elements that can create a culture-driven strategy as follows (see Figure 7.19):

- Creation of movement
  - Inspiring leadership
  - Striving to be the best
- Capability to move
  - Workforce readiness
  - Adaptability and development

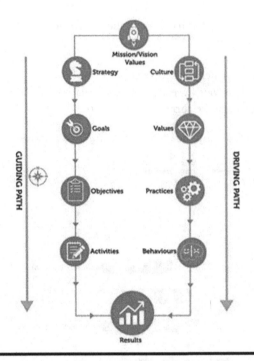

Figure 7.18 Strategy (guiding path) and culture (driving path)

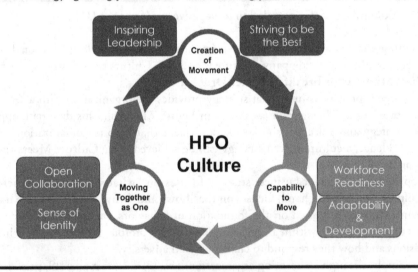

Figure 7.19 High-performing organization culture model

■ Moving together
  – Open collaboration
  – Sense of identity

Much like the chicken and the egg scenario of which came first, looking at organizational strategy and culture can prove problematic. It is useful for an organization to understand whether its strategy is foundational in leading toward a complimentary culture, or whether it is actually its culture that guides managers and executives to enact a suitable strategy. It has been widely touted for the previous 30 years or more that culture within an organization is a more powerful and useful force than strategy.

This is believed to stem from the growth and dominance of Japanese electronics and car manufacturers in the 1970s who embraced the ideal of the right organizational culture having a bigger impact on production and morale than the right strategy. In its most basic form, this is an assertion that happy workers who are all working toward the same goals and ideals are better than those who are unwillingly working toward the same strategy [20].

Figure 7.20 summarizes the key elements that differentiate the definitions and culture and strategy to try to answer the question of which of them is more important for sustainable business in the long run [21].

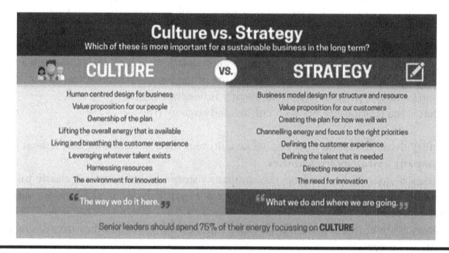

Figure 7.20   Culture versus strategy [21]

7.3.1 Cultivating Cultures and Strategies

While it may seem that culture takes priority over strategy, it is crucial to understand that not all organizations will be able to easily or effectively implement or cultivate a successful organizational culture. In organizations where there are already performance issues, it can be difficult to improve the culture due to employee disaffectedness. In such instances, it is down to successful strategy implementation to revitalize an organization to create a more receptive audience. Strategy is, therefore, a useful tool in creating organizational success, without which, it can be impossible to cultivate a good organizational culture. Such instances can be thought of as installing a new culture or uninstalling an existing culture in order to reinvent and realign an organization.

The work done by Kaul [22] has, in fact, highlighted that strategy precedes culture and that culture must be aligned to strategy. This is not to say that the role and importance of culture are superseded, as it is clearly fundamental in making an organization competitive. But for corporate-level strategy and strategy formulation, culture takes a back seat. It is when you look at functional- and operational-level strategic decisions that culture has a powerful influence. Culture also exerts an influence at the corporate level, as it guides and manipulates decisions made by top-level management unless they choose to ignore the embedded values of an organization.

A corporate-level strategy must, therefore, be considered as needing to bring about a strategy-culture fit. It is often the case that competitive advantage is lost due to a failing in organizational culture. Yet it can need a successful strategic recalibration in order to realign the failed culture.

Ultimately, organizational culture has a pervasive power that can lift an organization to leading the competitive charge. Organizational strategy, however, is the driving force that directs an organization on the right path from the outset. Neither can last without the other, but it is fundamental to implement a strategy which can benefit and boost the culture, rather than the other way around. Organizational culture and strategy are highly interrelated. It is generally accepted that once the organization changes strategy, it must align organizational culture with strategy, or face almost certain strategic failure. Behaviors that are intended to achieve strategic goals may be supported or impeded by the culture.

For better or worse, corporate culture has a major impact on a company's ability to carry out objectives and plans, especially when a company is shifting its strategic direction. Some studies have also indicated the significance of organizational culture in strategy implementation among other factors such as organization structure, work and information system, and essential business process.

Regarding the relationship between strategy and culture, the direction is viewed differently by different authors. Some studies view strategy as an outcome of organizational culture and maintain that strategic options are limited by the culture of the organization. Others maintain that an organization's strategic position may subsequently influence culture.

So, what is the relationship between culture and strategy [18]:

- Strategy drives focus and direction while culture is the emotional, organic habitat in which a **company's strategy lives or dies**
- Strategy is just the headline on the company's story—culture needs a clearly understood common language to embrace and tell the story that includes mission, vision, **values**, and clear expectations
- Strategy is about intent and ingenuity and culture determines and measures desire, engagement, and execution
- Strategy lays down the rules for playing the game, and culture fuels the spirit for how the game will be played
- Strategy is imperative for differentiation, but a vibrant **culture delivers the strategic advantage**
- Culture is built or eroded every day. How you climb the hill and whether it's painful, fun, positive, or negative defines the journey
- When culture embraces strategy, execution is scalable, repeatable, and sustainable
- Culture is a clear **competitive advantage**
- Culture must be monitored to understand the health and engagement of an organization

Finally, to demonstrate the linkage between the organization strategy and its cultures, a recent study conducted by Binda Gupta [23] examines the strategy and culture of 32 Indian organizations belonging to seven industry segments namely construction, banking, information technology (IT), pharmaceuticals, power, steel, and telecom.

The study used Miles and Snow strategy types that were classified as **defender, analyzer, prospector**, and **reactor**. Research over the years has investigated differences among these four strategic types with respect to a variety of internal factors, including innovation, management characteristics, organizational performance, and organizational design. The study also used Cameron and Quinn's categorization of organizational culture into four types: **hierarchy, clan, market**, and **adhocracy**. The two cultural variables used are stability and control versus flexibility and direction, and internal focus versus external focus.

Three basic questions regarding organizational strategy and culture were examined.

1. What is the dominant strategy across the industries in India, and are there significant differences in the strategy of organizations belonging to different industry segments?
2. Which is the most prevalent culture across the industries in India, and are there significant differences in the culture of organizations belonging to different industry segments?
3. It examined the linkage between types of business strategies and the culture of the organization

The contribution of the study lies in examining the differences in the culture and strategy of organizations belonging to different industry segments. The findings indicated that the most dominant strategy is the analyzer strategy and the most prevalent culture is adhocracy culture followed by clan culture across the industries in India. The study also points out there are significant differences in the strategy and culture of organizations belonging to different industry segments. The findings indicated that prospector strategy is most widely used by the telecom industry, and the most prevalent culture is adhocracy culture in organizations belonging to the telecom industry. Prospectors perceive a dynamic, uncertain environment and maintain flexibility to combat environmental change. The prospector seeks to identify and exploit new product and market opportunities.

Defender strategy was found most dominant in organizations belonging to the construction industry, and the most dominant culture was clan culture followed by hierarchy culture. The analyzer strategy was reported to be most frequently used by the IT sector, and the most prevalent culture is clan culture. Further, the organizations belonging to IT provide products, solutions, and services to client organizations. These factors may be some of the reasons for using the analyzer strategy in the IT industry.

Therefore, culture needs to be aligned with the strategic intent of the organization. Organizations seeking particular strategies need to consider whether their culture is favorable to, or can be changed to be favorable to, the desired strategy. As the organization's strategy evolves, managers need to create or modify systems and structures to install and reinforce the kind of culture needed to effectively implement the type of strategy selected. So, developing a culture-driven strategy can be achieved when *Culture Meets Strategy.*

7.4 Operations-Driven Strategy

An organization's operations function is concerned with getting things done, producing goods and/or services for customers. All business organizations are concerned with how they will survive and prosper in the future. A business strategy is often thought of as a plan or set of intentions that will set the long-term direction of the actions that are needed to ensure future organizational success. As discussed earlier, it is about "Making the Future Happen Today". These terms "Making" and "Today" indicate the clear link between strategy and operations.

Frequently the interrelationship between operations and corporate strategy is not easily grasped. The notion is simple enough—namely, that a company's competitive strategy at a given time places particular demands on its operations and, conversely, that the company's operations should be specifically designed to fulfill the task demanded by strategic plans. What is more elusive is the set of cause-and-effect factors which determine the linkage between strategy and production operations.

However, no matter how grand the plan, or how noble the intention, an organization's strategy can only become a meaningful reality, in practice, if it is operationally enacted. An organization's operations are strategically important precisely because most organizational activity comprises the day-to-day activities within the operations function. It is the myriad of daily actions of operations, when considered in their totality, that constitutes the organization's long-term strategic direction. The relationship between an organization's strategy and its operations is a key determinant of its ability to achieve long-term success or even survival. Organizational success is only likely to result if short-term operations activities are consistent with long-term strategic intentions and make a contribution to competitive advantage.

The traditional division of responsibilities, with a corporate strategy focusing on long-term thinking while operations focus on execution, will break down. The corporate strategy will maintain a critical role in growth strategy development, but the role will shift from the facilitation of individual opportunities to one more focused on network coordination. Strategy can identify growth opportunities that fall between silos, as well as opportunities for business units to collaborate on similar growth opportunities. This will involve strategy setting up mechanisms to create transparency throughout the organization, creating forums for businesses to collaborate, and providing training to develop the hard and soft skills necessary for collaboration. Strategy will help the business identify low-value or lagging projects to shut down to free up resources for more transformational, cross-cutting growth opportunities.

However, in order to stay competitive, we need to radically transform the operations due to the potential disruptive impact of the VUCA world, Society 5.0, and the future economies. These new radical innovations will not only support changes in the existing core business but also serve new product and service offerings, as illustrated in Figure 7.21.

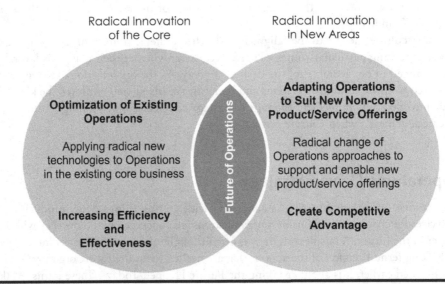

Figure 7.21   Radical innovation of operations [24]

The future of operations will be driven by applying radical new technologies to operations in the existing core business to increase efficiency and effectiveness, as well as applying the radical change of operations approach to support and enable new products/services to create new competitive advantages [24]. Operations will change their role from just being a strategy executor to a growth networker. These new operations of the future will be centered around eight essential core characteristics as shown in Figure 7.22.

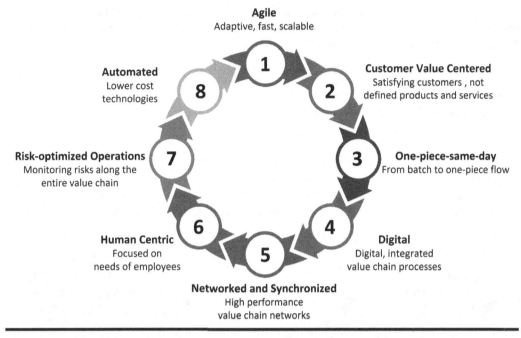

Figure 7.22   Operations of the future essential characteristics [24]

- **Agile**: Operations will be adaptive to change. This will include fast decision-making, scalability, fast time-to-market, and balanced value addition.
- **Customer Value-Centered**: Operations will shift the focus toward satisfying internal and external customers instead of delivering defined products and services. All operational functions will look at the total value to optimize the Total Cost of Ownership.
- **One-Piece-Same-Day**: Operations will change the focus from batch efficiency (trying to use scale effects by batch size optimization) to a one-piece flow production and same-day delivery to increase flexibility, e.g., 3-D printing to allow individualized products to be delivered efficiently to the client on the day they are ordered.
- **Digital**: The creation of more digital, real-time processes along the value chain to increase efficiency and reliability, along with digital integration of all relevant supply chain actors, while allowing for totally new business models and service offerings.
- **Networked and Synchronized**: Shifting Operations from high-performing autonomous units with a high degree of vertical integration toward a high-performing, highly synchronized, value chain network across single companies
- **Human-Centric**: Operations will focus on the capabilities and needs of the employee and create the appropriate work environment. For example, adapting the environment with better ergonomics to accommodate an aging workforce.
- **Risk-Optimized**: Operations will identify and monitor risks along the entire value chain to prepare for extraordinary events. This will be achieved by creating transparency for critical parts in the overall supply chain, not just for tier 1 suppliers.
- **Automated**: Greater automation than today. This is partly due to increasing wages in current low-cost countries and an increasing focus on quality, and also because lower-cost technologies will make automation and robotics increasingly affordable for any company.

To demonstrate how those characteristics can be applied, an integrated operational strategy framework for future operations management that includes four layers was proposed by Vinodh et al. in 2020. The four layers are (see Figure 7.23):

- Concepts
- Technologies supporting Industry 4.0
- Application domains in operations
- CI (continuous improvement) strategies

The developed framework includes lean principles to eliminate waste and make optimized process, LSS (Lean Six Sigma) to enable excellent product quality, Kaizen to enhance production process through continuous improvement, and integrate sustainability principle to eliminate or minimize environmental waste and make eco-friendly product to comply with government norms and regulations [25].

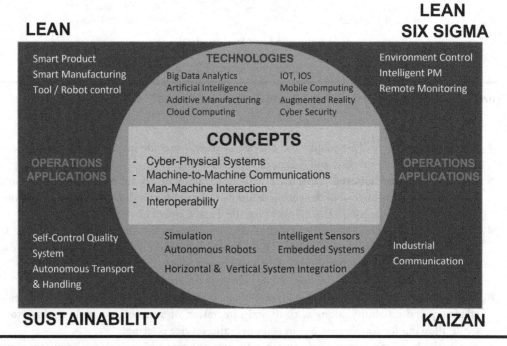

Figure 7.23 Integrated operational strategy framework

The above integrated strategy framework will help the organization achieve the following six strategic objectives to create competitive capabilities:

1. Cost: The ability to produce at a low cost
2. Quality: The ability to produce in accordance with the specification and without error
3. Speed/Agility: The ability to do things quickly in response to customer demands and thereby offer short lead times between when a customer orders a product or service and when they receive it
4. Dependability: The ability to deliver products and services in accordance with promises made to customers (e.g., in a quotation or other published information)

5. Flexibility: The ability to change operations. Flexibility can comprise up to four aspects: The ability to change the volume of production, time taken to produce, and mix of different products or services produced

6. Innovation: The ability to innovate and introduce new products/services, processes, profit models, customer experiences, etc.

In a study that examined the relationship between **business strategy**, **competitive priorities (capabilities)**, and **areas of operational decisions**, it was demonstrated that competitive priorities of business strategy and operational decision-making areas are the center bolt of alignment between business strategy and operations strategy. Areas of operational decisions include vertical integration, capacity, facility, product technology, and process technology. The proposed model was a bilateral type in which business strategy, on the one hand, determines operations strategy, and operational capabilities, on the other hand, determine business strategy [26].

7.4.1 Operations Strategy—Process

Slack proposed that operations strategy might come about in a top-down or a bottom-up process with regard to business and corporate strategies. Similarly, an operations strategy might be developed in response to market requirements (i.e., market-led) or be based on the capabilities of its operations resources (i.e., operations-led). As illustrated in Figure 7.24, this gives rise to four perspectives on operation strategy. Each perspective places a different emphasis on the nature of the operations strategy process [27].

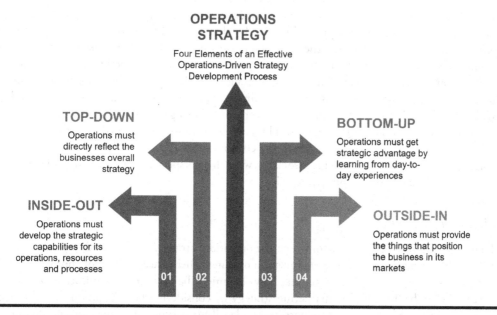

Figure 7.24   The four perspectives of operations strategy

7.4.1.1 Top-Down

The top-down perspective is one in which the operations strategy is derived from and is supportive of the organization's business strategy: An operations strategy that the organization uses to realize its business strategy. According to this perspective, the process of developing an operations strategy would follow the approach of identifying an operation's "task". The task for operations would be determined logically from the business strategy.

In a multi-business organization, the top-down perspective envisages operations strategy being linked to corporate strategy via the business strategy of each business unit. This then raises the question of whether it is possible to talk of a "corporate" operations strategy. If a corporate operations strategy means commonality in all aspects of operations, then this would only be possible if each business unit had similar business strategies and similar operations tasks. However, some might argue that a corporate operations strategy does not mean that every facet of operations must be the same in each business unit. Rather, operations decisions are considered holistically at the corporate level with a view to meeting corporate strategic objectives. A failure to do this means that operations decisions are taken only at the level of the business unit, with a view to meeting the immediate needs of that business unit. This can lead to operational competences being confined within individual business units, thereby restricting their future development, preventing their spread to other business units, and limiting opportunities for synergistic developments across the corporation. This can be particularly important in multisite, multinational enterprises.

7.4.1.2 Bottom-Up

The bottom-up perspective is one which sees operations strategy emerging through a series of actions and decisions taken over time within operations. These actions and decisions might at first sight appear somewhat haphazard, as operations managers respond to customer demands, seek to solve specific problems, copy good practices in other organizations, etc. However, they can build over time to form a coherent pattern recognizable as an operations strategy. The actions taken within this kind of strategy are likely to be characterized by a continuous series of incremental improvements rather than the large one-off technologically led changes that require large capital investments in new plant and machinery. The bottom-up perspective is one in which the organization learns from its experiences, developing and enhancing its operational capabilities as operations managers try new things out in an almost experimental fashion using their workplaces as a kind of "learning laboratory". Many of the manufacturing practices that are now considered leading edge (such as JIT, TQM, Statistical Process Control) were developed in just such a fashion by Japanese manufacturers responding to the constraints placed upon them in the aftermath of World War II. One of the problems associated with this perspective is that the organization may not recognize what its operations strategy is.

7.4.1.3 Market-Led

The market-led perspective is one in which the operations strategy is developed in response to the market environment in which the organization operates. There are a number of approaches in the operations strategy literature that suggest how this might be done. An organization's operations strategy should be linked to its marketing strategy by considering how its products and services win orders in the marketplace. It is possible to identify two types of competitive criteria in any market. Market qualifying criteria are those factors that must be satisfied before customers will consider making a purchase in the first place.

Order winning criteria, on the other hand, are the factors on which customers ultimately make their purchasing decision. For example, for many airline passengers, the order winning criteria is price, with criteria such as destination city, time of flights, and convenience of travel to and from airports being market qualifying criteria. For others, notably business travelers, the order winning criteria may be factors such as in-flight service or total travel time. Consequently, an operations strategy should be developed which will satisfy market qualifying criteria but excel at order winning criteria for the market segment that the operation wishes to serve.

7.4.1.4 Operations-Led

The operations-led perspective is one in which its excellence in operations is used to drive the organization's strategy. This fits with the resource-based view (RBV) of strategy that dominated the strategic management literature for many years. The premise of the RBV is that superior performance comes from the way that an organization acquires, develops, and deploys its resources and builds its capabilities rather than the way it positions itself in the marketplace. Thus, the process of strategy development should be based on a sound understanding of current operational capabilities and an analysis of how these could be developed in the future. This can then provide the basis for decisions about which markets are likely to be the best in which to deploy current and future capabilities, which competitors are likely to be most vulnerable, and how attacks from competitors might best be countered. These ideas involve undertaking an analysis of the resources that have underpinned the activities of a business unit over an extended period of time (at least the previous three to five years). Six resource categories, which are not mutually exclusive, are used: Tangible resources, knowledge resources, skills and experience, systems and procedural resources, cultural resources and values, network resources, and resources important for change. The resources are evaluated against three criteria: Value, sustainability, and versatility. Resources that individually or collectively score highly in these criteria are considered to be important resources. They are sources of existing or potential competitive advantage to the organization.

7.4.1.5 Key Recommendations for the Executives

Operations face a significant challenge to shape up for a future of technology disruption, innovation, and transformation. Today we see the following lessons and priorities as being important for operations executives to be able to support the development of operation-driven strategies for their organizations:

■ Build a dedicated function and supporting processes and systems within operations to scan for relevant trends and innovations and integrate plans on how to respond to new challenges and opportunities. Make use of the latest intelligence tools and approaches.

■ Be proactive in developing capabilities to meet future Operations requirements, including improvements in agility, customer-centricity, one-piece-same-day digitalization, network orientation, human-centricity, risk optimization, and automation.

■ Set stretch performance improvement targets that drive radical innovation and transformation in operations approaches, in addition to ongoing incremental improvements.

■ Promote creativity and innovation as a core value for operations, in addition to incremental efficiency and effectiveness, and reflect this in incentives and objectives.

■ Ensure that the operations organization develops a broader mix of individual skill sets and backgrounds to be able to master innovation and constant transformation in addition to safeguarding efficient and effective core operations.

Operations Management is no longer just about efficiency and effectiveness. In today's and tomorrow's business environment, those companies that focus only on "more of the same" are likely to suffer the consequences.

7.4.2 The Future of Operations—RPA and Industry 4.0

Two of the advancements that are reshaping the world of operations are the use of **Robotic Process Automation (RPA)**, and **Industry 4.0**. Both are gaining a lot of attention and are incorporated in most of the operations strategies that are developed to help organizations thrive in future economies.

RPA is software robots that act as virtual assistants for employees engaged in repetitive tasks associated with processes. While the word robot may produce a mental image of a human-like machine, an RPA robot is integrated across IT systems via the front-end, as opposed to traditional software, which communicates with other IT systems via the back-end. In practice, this means that the software robot uses IT systems exactly the same way a human would, repeating precise, rule-based steps, and reacting to the events on a computer screen, instead of communicating with the system's application programming interface (API). So, RPA is the technological imitation of a human worker, the goal of which is to tackle structured tasks in a fast and cost efficient manner. RPA is implemented through a software robot, which mimics human workers using software such as ERP systems or productivity tools [28].

For example, OpusCapita Group https://www.opuscapita.com/ is a Finnish company offering financial processes and outsourcing services to medium-sized companies and large corporations. OpusCapita particularly focuses on comprehensive purchase-to-pay and order-to-cash processes. In hopes to stay ahead of the curve in financial process automation, OpusCapita is betting on robotic process automation (RPA). According to OpusCapita's vision, after a brief "training" these virtual assistants will be able to carry the burden of routine tasks, allowing companies to reallocate human employees to more productive and creative tasks. Among other things, supervising and improving new digital coworkers could be one of such tasks. The challenge for OpusCapita is how to generate recurring revenues for RPA to replace its old revenue streams that were based on the business process outsourcing (BPO) model.

While RPA supports many back-office operations for organizations, Industry 4.0 is a strategy that promises enhanced production processes, while achieving significant economic and ecological benefits. Regarding the economic advantages, one of the main benefits of Industry 4.0 has to do with the capacity of smart factories to respond in a faster way to demand, influenced by the dynamics of the market. This flexibility results in a customized product, adding value to the outputs produced and leading to an efficient and successful business model and marketing strategy. Overall, Industry 4.0 enables the adjustment of production to the market needs and the customization of products in a fast-time delivery to market. These benefits are the result of real-time production and the virtualization of supply chains where all the stages of the production process can be digitized, generating autonomous factories, and self-manageable supply chains. This allows for the integration and interaction of the different production stages (R&D, design, production, and distribution), boosting the value chain for the new management and control system. In addition, this new process leads to more sustainable production with less waste and better utilization of raw materials.

Different countries have adopted different orientations to the use of Industry 4.0 in their national industrial strategies. For example, the United States focuses on using Industry 4.0 to drive radical innovation. The focus is on bringing digital innovation into the physical world by encouraging start-ups for IoT. In Germany, the focus is on engineering excellence. German manufacturers bring their engineering excellence into the digital world with visionary concepts integrating technology, society, and economy. In China, the focus is on speed. They try to develop a pragmatic application of quick wins and long-term strategy. Finally, Japan focuses on the ability to scale innovation by application. Figure 7.25 shows the global growth of Industry 4.0 initiatives and how companies should integrate this into their future operations strategies [29].

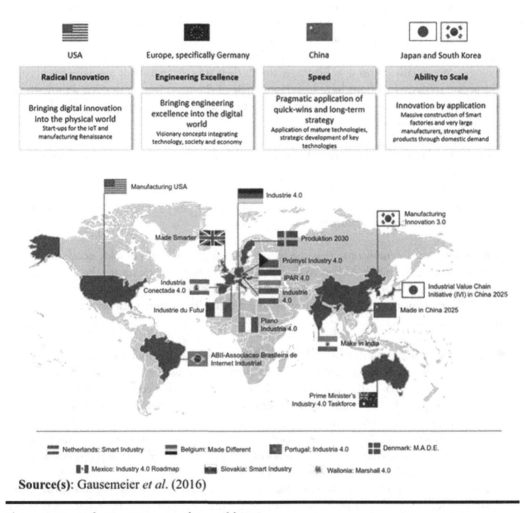

Figure 7.25   Industry 4.0 across the world [29]

7.5 Digital-Driven Strategy

Corporate strategy's day-to-day has historically revolved around facilitating strategic planning, sensing, and diagnosing emerging trends and helping business leaders prioritize growth opportunities. But strategy leaders are now rethinking their time spent in response to the dizzying pace at which digital technologies are transforming the business world. "Digital" theme is a foundational theme in the three strategies which we described above (insights, culture, and operations). This is not surprising at all since we have already referred to the *Digital Economy* as a transversal economy that acts as the enabler and influencer to the rest of the five economies in one way or several.

As digital technologies emerge and improve rapidly, firms face changing trade-offs in terms of their technology infrastructure and strategic direction. Hence, many of them adopt new digital technology and develop new business models and strategies. The literature on strategic alignment of IT suggests that firms need to synchronize these different domains of choice. We observe a strong positive association between the extent of strategy change and the stage of adoption of advanced digital technologies overall, suggesting a tight coupling between (technological) structure and strategy. We find that the adoption of new technologies may lead to a large and robust effect on strategy change: The more extensive the adoption, the larger the change in strategy. This result is robust to various specifications and across industries. However, we notice substantial differences across technologies, potentially pointing at heterogeneity in their strategic nature or maturity level [30].

Corporate strategy functions have historically helped the organization develop a growth-oriented strategic plan. Three trends are compelling corporate strategy teams to rethink this value proposition to the business [31]:

1. **Pervasive Digital Capabilities**: Digital capabilities permeate all aspects of business and operating models
2. **Asset Lite**: New products and services can be made, customized, and launched instantly
3. **Winners Take All**: The rise of platforms and network effects means companies that can create enough scale can secure most of the profits

Together these trends demonstrate that the pace of digital disruption is quickly accelerating and incumbents must make big, bold bets to stay ahead. Corporate strategy must take on the role of **"Digital Navigator"**, helping organizations sense digital disruption, re-envision themselves as truly digital companies and develop a pathway to get there. This comes with several implications for strategy leaders:

■ Strategy functions will shift from helping business leaders identify best-fit technology solutions for problems today toward focusing on identifying longer-term market shifts that drive a continually evolving digital portfolio. Technologies quickly become obsolete but market shifts are longer lasting, and corporate strategy is uniquely positioned to understand the implications for the digital portfolio
■ Strategists will help executives develop a new vision of the organization as a truly digital business, involving changes to all aspects of the business model: Value proposition, profit model, customer base, and business capabilities
■ Rather than supporting small scale digital pilots in isolated corners of the organization, strategy leaders and their teams will spearhead broader digital growth initiatives that cut across businesses and functions while finding smart ways to de-risk these projects and accelerate learning

In a survey conducted by PWC's Strategy and in their Global Digital Operations study [32], they identified eight key findings (see Figure 7.26):

■ Only 10% of global manufacturing companies are considered digital champions
■ Asia-Pacific is leading the way to digitization
■ Digital champions create value through an integrated customer solution ecosystem

- Digital champions serve customers by integrating operations, technology, and people ecosystems
- New technologies are implemented at a large scale to connect and collaborate along the end-to-end value chain
- Artificial intelligence (AI) is kicking off but will revolutionize the quality of operational decision-making
- Digitization will increase production in mature markets and customized manufacturing close to end-customer markets
- People are at the center of digital transformation

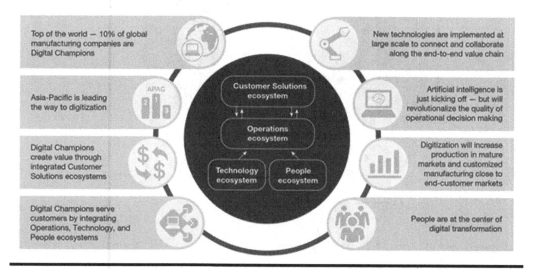

Figure 7.26   PWC global digital operations study

Developing a digital-driven strategy to become a digital champion requires the development of an integrated four-layer digital ecosystem. As shown in Figure 7.27, the four ecosystems are [32]:

- **Technology Ecosystem** that integrates new technologies with the organization IT architecture using different types of interfaces. This is the first foundational element
- **People Ecosystem** that integrates skills, mindsets and behaviors, relationships, and career development. This is the second foundational element.
- **Operations Ecosystem** that integrates digital R&D, product life cycle (PLC) management, after-sales services, connected logistics and distribution, smart manufacturing, and procurement 4.0. This provides the organization with integrated and continuous planning and connected execution. This is the solution enablement element
- **Customer Solitons Ecosystem** that integrates 12 customer-focused elements to provide individual solution, offering multichannel interaction. This is the customer value element. This provides personalization, customization for customer experiences that supports the organization's competitive advantage

Globally, only 10% of companies are considered digital champions, while digital innovators account for 27%, digital followers account for 42%, and digital novices account for 21%. So, there is great room for growth in digital maturity for organizations moving forward.

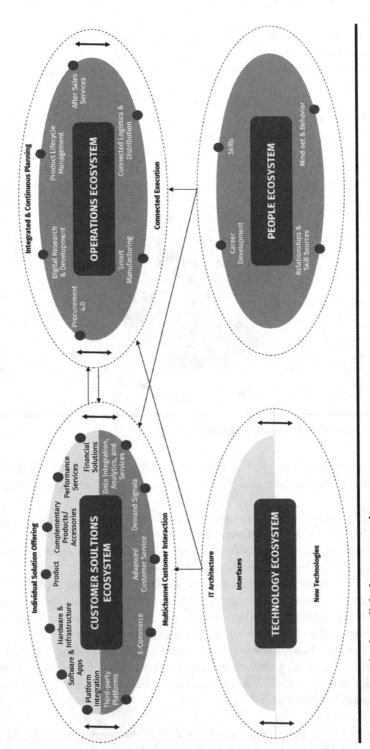

Figure 7.27 The four digital ecosystem layers

7.5.1 Digital Possibilities Must Shape Strategy and Strategy Must Shape Digital Priorities

Digital capabilities can help enable differentiation in several ways. As shown in Figure 7.28, companies focus their digital strategies on five key areas [17]:

- Marketing and distribution for better customer experiences
- New innovative products and services
- More efficient and effective processes
- Integrating their business ecosystem
- Integrating their supply chains

An interesting case for a digital champion that successfully implemented the four digital ecosystem layers that interact together to provide a digital-driven strategy for the organization is Li & Fung.

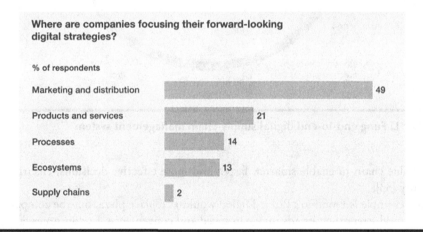

Figure 7.28   Focus of digital strategies [17]

Li & Fung creates customized, end-to-end supply chain and logistics solutions for brands and retailers worldwide. What sets them apart is their high degree of flexibility and scalability which is unrivaled in their industry. Millions of consumer goods pass through Li & Fung's supply chain every year. For that to happen, their global supply chain connects thousands of suppliers and vendors with leading brands and retailers, all with the goal of meeting consumer demand. They focus on managing complexity and risk to maximize your profitability.

Starting with product design and development and including everything from compliance to raw material and factory sourcing, manufacturing control, logistics, and more, they offer end-to-end services for all stakeholders in the consumer goods supply chain (see Figure 7.29).

Li & Fung is building a digital supply chain with innovative services and solutions to help their customers and suppliers navigate the digital economy. A fully digital global supply chain will enable them to be a catalyst for change, delivering data-driven insights for faster, smarter business decisions. Their goal is to fully digitalize each step of the supply chain so data can flow seamlessly, providing end-to-end visibility for our customers, suppliers, and other stakeholders. This means they can stay ahead of the disruption at retail, capture and share data across

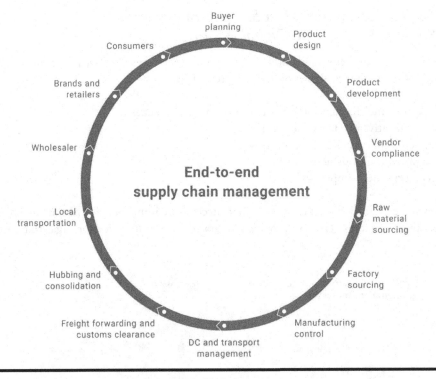

Figure 7.29   Li Fung end-to-end digital supply chain management system

the entire value chain to enable smarter, faster, and more effective decisions, ensuring business sustainability [33].

Another example is Domino's Pizza. Digital wouldn't replace pizza, but the company realized that digital could strengthen its advantage in speed and convenience. Its consumer-facing mobile app streamlined the steps for ordering and receiving a pizza (and capturing happy-customer feedback). An interesting fact is Domino's and Google both went public in 2004. If you'd invested a dollar in both, you'd have made more money with Domino's.

John Deere, in its agricultural business, began with use cases anchored in the jobs farmers were trying to optimize: Planting seeds optimally, adding just the right amount of nutrients, and putting the minimum amount of chemicals on their crops to prevent pests and weeds. This led to significant innovations—for example, the "see and spray" technology, which allows individual weeds to be identified through a combination of optical sensors and machine learning algorithms and then killed through highly engineered and individually controlled spraying nozzles. Company executives credit Deere's digital strategy with helping grow its net revenue by 19% year-over-year in fiscal Q1 2021.

ASICS has a global presence in the sports goods market with revenues of US$2.87 billion and 8,904 employees in 2020. In order to achieve further growth, the firm is strengthening its services in the digital area, aiming to become a "digital-driven company" as part of its corporate strategy. In addition to its business based on its current product line-up, ASICS also wants to provide personalized service to each customer and bring new value to their sports experience.

Capital One bank has steadily shrunk its branch network in recent years to invest more in digital channels, cloud computing, and machine learning to enhance customer experience. For instance, their Eno virtual assistant provides real-time fraud notifications and tokenization for secure online checkout. Due to the strength of its digital offerings, Capital One topped J.D. Power's 202 rankings for customer satisfaction among large retail banks.

Finally, China-based insurance giant PingAn transformed itself from a traditional insurance provider into a platform provider connecting more than half a billion users to financial, health, real estate, auto, and other services. They developed a FinTech Software-as-a-Service (SaaS) that provides digital lending, small business financing, and inter-bank trading solutions to more than 450 financial institutions. Their health-care affiliate Good Doctor provides online patient consultation and pharmacy delivery services, and their Autohome platform is China's largest car-shopping site. Those adjacent services help feed users into PingAn's core insurance services. As users search for cars on Autohome, for instance, PingAn gives them financing and insurance quotes. The digital platform strategy has paid off: PingAn is now the world's second-largest insurer by market capitalization.

In conclusion, Deloitte reported in their 2021 Executive Digital Transformation Survey that higher-maturity businesses that consider their digital strategy the central pillar of their business strategy were about twice as likely as lower-maturity ones to report net profit margins and annual revenue growth significantly above their industry average.

But the question here is **How** to make this digital transformation happen before it's too late. Time is running out!!

As executives look to deepen and broaden the digital reinvention of their own companies, they may benefit from a structured process grouped around discovering, designing, delivering, and de-risking their digital investments [17] (Figure 7.30).

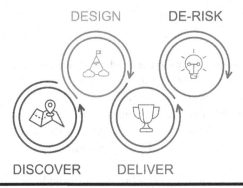

Figure 7.30   Structuring your digital reinvention

1. **Discover: Shape your digital ambition, strategy, and business case**

In this phase, companies develop a clear view of where value is being created and destroyed as the basis for a clear business strategy. That requires an analysis of their business, sector, customer behavior trends, and the larger economy to identify and quantify both threats and opportunities. These kinds of digital opportunity scans should be sorted by short- and long-term pockets of value.

At the same time, companies need to engage in a sober analysis of their own digital capabilities and resources. Capabilities that build foundations for other key processes and activities (e.g., modular IT and agile technology platforms) are particularly important.

With this understanding in hand, companies then determine what their strategic ambition is, whether retooling the existing business or something more radical, such as plunging into a new market or innovating a business model. They develop a detailed roadmap for addressing capability gaps and recruiting, developing, incentivizing, and retaining the necessary talent. The goal is to develop a tight business case for change based on facts.

2. Design: Create and prototype breakthrough experiences

Actually, acting on a digital ambition can be daunting. It has been found that the most successful companies start by focusing on the most important customer journeys, then work back from there to design and build out breakthrough customer experiences. Using design thinking and skills, these companies define each journey, looking especially for the pain points and potential missed connections. The change team can then map out, screen-by-screen, models for a new interface. In this phase, the company must avoid getting caught in endless rounds of planning but instead rapidly build prototypes, translating concepts into minimum viable products (MVPs) to test and iterate in the market before scaling.

This phase also includes building out rapid delivery approaches and an IT infrastructure that blends the legacy systems with microservices and modular plug-and-play elements). While agile IT has become standard, more digital businesses are embracing DevOps (integrated development and operations teams) and continuous delivery so that software can be developed, tested, and deployed quickly to consumers and end users.

On the organization side, the fluid nature of cross-functional collaboration, rapid decision-making, and iterative development means that the business should focus on the enablers for this kind of teamwork. This includes effective metrics and scorecards to evaluate digital performance and incentive structures to drive the right behaviors, mindsets, and outcomes. The CDO at one multinational pharma company addressed this issue by establishing a Digital Council, which was tasked specifically with breaking down organizational silos to enable transformational change across all business lines. The initiative was credited with significantly contributing to a 12% increase in sales.

3. Deliver: Develop a network of partners who can rapidly scale your ambition

Getting the speed and scale necessary for a reinvention increasingly requires an ecosystem of external teams, partners, suppliers, and customers. In practice, this means working with a mix of platform players, delivery specialists, and niche players. These are the relationships that companies can call on to provide specific skills and capabilities quickly. This reality has made ecosystem management an important competency, especially understanding how to find and plug into the right mix of complementary capabilities.

As companies push to scale their digital reinvention throughout the organization, the crucial role of seasoned change managers comes into focus. These leaders not only play "air traffic controller" to the many moving parts but also have the business credibility and skill to solve real business problems. They must maintain an accelerated pace of change and drive accountability across the business. The change leaders will look across the entire enterprise, examining the organizational structure, data governance, talent recruitment, performance management, and IT systems for areas of opportunity, making decisions that balance efficiency and speed with the outcome.

The "agility coach" is an example of this type of role. This person has strong communication and influencing skills, can create and roll-out plans to support agile processes across the business, and can put in place KPIs and metrics to track progress.

4. De-risking: Structuring the process to minimize risk

One of the most common reasons digital transformations fail is that the organization develops "change exhaustion" and funds start to dry up. To mitigate this risk, it's important to focus on quick wins that not only build momentum but also generate cost savings that can be reinvested in the next round of transformations. Many companies choose to invest first in "horizontal" components, such as business-process management (BPM) layers or central administration platforms that can be shared across many initiatives, while balancing them with more "visible" elements to provide the proof of concept.

Technology risks, especially cyber security, will also require increased attention as companies digitize more operations and processes. Organizations can mitigate these risks by automating tests on software, establishing systems in which failures can be rolled back in minutes, and establishing build environments in which fixes can be made without putting significant parts of the business at risk. Senior leaders in particular need to focus on the structural and organizational issues—from building cybersecurity into all business functions to changing user behavior—that hamper the ability to manage cyber risk.

One risk senior leaders often overlook is losing ownership over sources of value. These might include the company's data, customer relationships, or other assets. Having a clear understanding of where the value is coming from allows businesses to navigate ecosystem relationships profitably. In evaluating which partners to work with, the bookseller mentioned above, for example, declined to work with a storefront partner because it feared losing its most valuable asset: Its direct relationship with its customers.

References

1. IDC. (2015). Worldwide Embedded and Intelligent Systems 2015–2020 Market Forecast.
2. Dinana, H. (2019). Insight-Driven Sales Management, Modern Perspectives in Business Applications. Syed Abdul Rehman Khan and Selay Ilgaz Sümer, IntechOpen. 10.5772/intechopen.84806; https://www.intechopen.com/chapters/65939
3. Edelman, D. (2010). Branding in the Digital Age: You're Spending your Money in All the Wrong Places. *Harvard Business Review*, December 2010.
4. Labrecque, L., vor dem Esche, J., Mathwick, C., Novak, T. P., and Hofacker, C. F. (2013). Consumer Power: Evolution in the Digital Age. *Journal of Interactive Marketing*, 27(2013), 257–269.
5. McCormick, J. (2016). *TechRadar: Digital Intelligence, Q2 2016: Tools and Technology: The Digital Intelligence Playbook*. Forrester Research, Inc.
6. Kaushik, A. (2009). Web Analytics 2.0: The Art of Online Accountability and Science of Customer Centricity. Sybex, 1st edition (October 26, 2009).
7. Ripsam, T., and Bouquet, L. (2016). 10 Principles of Customer Strategy. *PWC-Strategy & Strategy + Business*, Winter 2016(85).
8. DiMauro, V., Fish, J., and Burke, K. (2017). The Business Impact of Online Communities. Leader Networks. https://www.researchgate.net/publication/314174120_The_Business_Impact_Of_Online _Communities
9. Shah, D., and Murthi, B. P. S. (2021). Marketing in a Data-Driven Digital World: Implications for the Role and Scope of Marketing. *Journal of Business Research*, 125(2021), 772–779. https://doi.org/10 .1016/j.jbusres.2020.06.062
10. IAB. (2021). IAB Advertising Spend and Revenue Research. https://www.iab.com/topics/ad-revenue/ ?spend=1
11. Boerman, S., Kruikemeier, S., and Zuiderveen Borgesius, F. (2017). Online Behavioral Advertising: A Literature Review and Research Agenda. *Journal of Advertising*, 46(3), 363–376.
12. PWC. (2021). Digital Ad Ecosystem: Galvanizing a Reset for Future Consumer-centric Success. https://www.pwc.com/us/en/industries/tmt/library/iab-digital-ad-ecosystem-2021.html
13. Dinana, H. (2021). Advertising in the Age of Ad Blockers, Moving Businesses Online and Embracing E-Commerce: Impact and Opportunities Caused by COVID-19. Tereza Semerádová and Petr Weinlich. 10.4018/978-1-7998-8294-7; https://www.igi-global.com/chapter/advertising-in-the-age -of-ad-blockers/292345

14. Capgemini. (2017). Becoming an Insight-Driven Business. https://www.capgemini.com/ro-en/wp -content/uploads/sites/21/2017/08/becoming_an_insight_driven_business_the_journey_for_con- sumer_products_and_retail_companies.pdf

15. Change Healthcare. (2018). Leveraging Data as a Strategic Asset: The ADOPT Framework to Direct a Successful Analytics Strategy. https://cdn2.hubspot.net/hubfs/498900/ADOPT%20Analytics %20guide%20v1r4%20(180129).pdf

16. Gibbons, R., Siegel, J., and Weber, R. A. (2021). Strategy Meets Culture (for Breakfast): Understanding the Relationship and Highlighting its Potential. *Strategy Science*, 6(2), 111–118. https://doi.org/10 .1287/stsc.2021.0138

17. Bender, M., and Willmott, P. (2018). Digital Re-invention: Unlocking the How. Digital/McKinsey. https://www.mckinsey.com/~/media/McKinsey/Business%20Functions/McKinsey%20Digital/ Our%20Insights/Digital%20Reinvention%20Unlocking%20the%20how/Digital-Reinvention _Unlocking-the-how.pdf

18. Rick, T. (2013). What is the Relationship Between Corporate Culture and Strategy. https://www.torben- rick.eu/BLOG/STRATEGY/RELATIONSHIP-BETWEEN-CULTURE-AND-STRATEGY/#:~ :TEXT=SO%20WHAT%20IS%20THE%20RELATIONSHIP,COMPANY'S%20 STRATEGY%20LIVES%20OR%20DIES&TEXT=CULTURE%20IS%20A%20CLEAR%20 COMPETITIVE,AND%20ENGAGEMENT%20OF%20AN%20ORGANIZATION

19. EFESO Consulting. (2012). High Performance Organization (HPO) Culture Model.

20. Strategic Direction. (2019). Does Culture Override Strategy? Looking at the Role and Power of Organizational Culture and Strategy. *Strategic Direction*, 35(3), 21–22. https://doi.org/10.1108/SD -12-2018-0247

21. Corporate Edge. (2020). 4 Reasons Why You Need a Strategy for Your Culture. https://corporate -edge.com.au/ce-author/4-reasons-why-you-need-a-strategy-for-your-culture/

22. Amarjeev, K. (2018). Culture vs Strategy: Which to Precede, Which to Align? *Journal of Strategy and Management*. https://doi.org/10.1108/JSMA-04-2018-0036

23. Gupta, B. (2011). A Comparative Study of Organizational Strategy and Culture Across Industry. *Benchmarking: An International Journal*, 18(4), 510–528.

24. Schreiber, B., Brundin, N., Eagar, R., and Tappenbeck, D. (2014). Anticipating the Operations of the Future: Operations Management and the Disruptive Change in Operations. *Arthur D. Little, Prism*, 2(2014), 66–74.

25. Vinodh, S., Antony, J., Agrawal, R., and Douglas, J. A. (2021). Integration of Continuous Improvement Strategies with Industry 4.0: A Systematic Review and Agenda for Further Research. *The TQM Journal*, 33(2), 441–472. https://doi.org/10.1108/TQM-07-2020-0157

26. Shavarini, S. K., Salimian, H., Nazemi, J., and Alborzi, M. (2013). Operations Strategy and Business Strategy Alignment Model (Case of Iranian Industries). *International Journal of Operations & Production Management*, 33(9), 1108–1130. 10.1108/IJOPM-12-2011-0467

27. Slack, N. (2017). *The Operations Advantage: A Practical Guide to Making Operations Work* (1st Edition). Kogan Page.

28. Asatiani, A., and Penttinen, E. (2016). Turning Robotic Process Automation Into Commercial Success – Case OpusCapita. *Journal of Information Technology, Teaching Cases*, 6, 67–74.

29. Erro-Garces, A., and Aranaz-Nunez, I. (2020). Catching the Wave: Industry 4.0 in BRICS. *Journal of Manufacturing Technology Management*, 31(6), 1169–1184.

30. Van Zeebroeck, N., Kretschmer, T., and Bughin, J. (2021). Digital "is" Strategy: The Role of Digital Technology Adoption in Strategy Renewal. *IEEE Transactions on Engineering Management*, 1–15.

31. Gartner. (2018). Strategy Action Plan.

32. Geissbauer, R., Lübben, E., Schrauf, S., and Pillsbury, S. (2018). Digital Champions: How Industry Leaders Build Integrated Operations Ecosystems to Deliver End-to-End Customer Solutions. PWC Strategy & Global Digital Operations Study 2018.

33. Li & Fung. (2021). Creating the Supply Chain of the Future. https://www.lifung.com/supply-chain -innovation/our-business/

Chapter 8

Putting Strategy in Action

8.1 Executional Excellence

We all know that strategy is crucial to business growth, but strategy ultimately gets you nowhere without proper execution. Unfortunately, that appears to be a problem for many organizations around the world.

A few years ago, a survey of more than 400 global CEOs found that executional excellence was the biggest challenge facing corporate leaders in the United States, Asia, and Europe, topping a list of some 80 issues. Execution beats out all other challenges, including innovation, geopolitical instability, and top-line growth [1]. Other studies have found more evidence of the problem of execution, with two-thirds to three-quarters of large organizations saying they struggle to implement their strategies. Moreover, McKinsey research tells us, for example, that 70% of change efforts fall short of desired results [2]. The financial losses implied by statistics like these are massive, and corporate leaders have taken notice of that. Today's senior leaders realize that implementation is at least half of the leadership challenge when it comes to improving performance via strategic change. There are many clear signs of how difficult it is to successfully execute strategies, but they don't reveal why execution is such a problem.

One approach to address those strategy implementation challenges revolves around the fact of narrowing down the factors instead of building a more comprehensive framework to incorporate all of them. There has been a variety of ideas based on the best practices of successful companies that talk about focusing only on the strategically important parameters. Chris Zook and James Allen, in their books *Profit from the Core: Growth Strategy in an Era of Turbulence* and *Repeatability: Build Enduring Business for a World of Constant Change*, provided an effective way to focus on the subset of strategic parameters. Similarly, *Blue Ocean Strategy* by W. Chan Kim and Renee Mauborgne represented rewarding forms of strategy formulation in order to create uncontested market space.

This focus on strategically important parameters starts with alignment around the Strategy Big Idea that paves the path from Strategy to Execution [3].

Business leaders know that great strategies with great execution produce winning companies. They also know that winning companies are far outnumbered by mediocre ones. What they may not realize is that it's the path from strategy to execution that often separates the two.

The typical path goes something like this: You start by setting your goals. These could be financially oriented (grow earnings a certain amount by so-and-so year) or strategic (become the leader in the this-or-that market). Then you prioritize the actions that will get you there: Invest here, cut there, reorganize this, and buy that. And then you implement like mad: Align the organization around your goals and priorities, review your progress quarterly, reward performance accordingly, and so on. Of course, some companies are much better than others in following this track.

Take Cardinal Health https://www.cardinalhealth.com/, one of the world's largest distributors of pharmaceuticals. The company started out as a food distributor, but its founder and then CEO, Bob Walter, decided in the early 1980s that he would make a better living by distributing high-margin drugs instead of low-margin food. That sounds like a typical move from an unattractive market to a more attractive one. And if that's all it was, it may not have amounted too much. But Walter had a big idea. At the time, the distribution of medicines was well established, but it was also highly fragmented among numerous local players. This made the sourcing of prescription drugs exceedingly complex for nationalizing pharmacy retailers and regionalizing hospital groups. Walter's idea solved that problem. He created the "prime vendor model" whereby Cardinal would aggregate the supply of drugs from the pharmaceutical manufacturers on behalf of a pharmacy retailer or hospital group. This breakthrough idea brought much-needed, rational consolidation to a fractured system. He saw a big problem, resolved to crack it, turned a simple but novel idea into an innovative strategy, and overcame the many barriers (including initial resistance from both suppliers and buyers) to execute that strategy. And over the course of about 20 years, he turned a mediocre food distribution business into a healthcare company worth over $US20 billion [3].

We can find something similar in the history of most winning companies. When Howard Schultz bought out the original founders of Starbucks, he turned the company from a local coffee roaster into a global brand by doing something most people (including Starbucks's founders) thought was foolhardy: Offering people in the United States high-quality coffee drinks at a "third place" between office and home. The strategy was based on a simple idea inspired by how many Italians live their social lives in their country's espresso bars. Similarly, when Rose Marie Bravo took over as chief executive of Burberry Group in 1997, she turned a staid British raincoat maker into a global fashion powerhouse with an idea that few people thought would work: "doing what Gucci did, at Burberry". And Jochen Zeitz, who became chief executive of Puma in 1993 at the age of 29, turned a struggling sports-shoe business into a leading sports apparel company with the then-radical idea of serving "people who like to wear sporting clothing because they like the look" rather than just athletes.

Walter, Schultz, Bravo, and Zeitz could have generated all the goals, actions, and implementation discipline that any "world-class" executive would have wanted, but that would not have been enough to create a winning enterprise. Instead, they designed innovative strategies based on novel ideas they owned unconditionally, and their commitment to those ideas enabled them to lead their companies through thick and thin to execute their strategies. In other words, their path was Problem-Idea-Strategy-Leadership, not Goals-Strategy-Initiatives-Implementation, as illustrated in Figure 8.1.

This tells us that mastering the strategy-to-execution challenge starts by asking two questions:

1. What is the big problem your company or business is trying to solve?
2. What's the big idea you have for solving it?

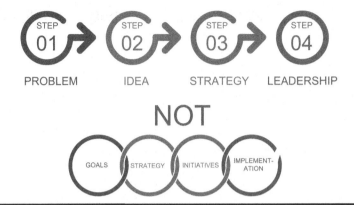

Figure 8.1 Strategy to execution path

If you have compelling answers to these questions, you can proceed to the next two:

1. What strategy does your company or business have for commercializing its big idea?
2. Do your company's leaders own the idea as if it was their own?

Unfortunately, too many companies cannot make it past the first two questions. When that's the case, they inevitably slide into a form of sleepwalking through an endless cycle of goals-actions-implementation—a cycle that's doomed to produce mediocrity. And that's no fun for the leaders or their organizations.

The path from strategy to execution should be energizing and inherently inspirational. You shouldn't need vision, mission, and purpose statements to have that kind of atmosphere. It won't work anyway. The fact is all companies (even the most "disciplined") are a mess when you look inside them, with runaway bureaucracy, spirited politics, dispiriting waste, and pointless meetings. These everyday realities will suck the joy and energy out of anyone. To overcome them, you need leaders who have an exciting idea that solves a big problem and a genuine commitment to seeing it through. This begets an organization with people who, even as they deal with the inanities of corporate life, intrinsically want to follow their leaders. That is how you master the strategy to execution challenges.

8.2 Eight Tough Questions to Ask about Strategy

Business leaders need to reframe their thinking in order to not only be successful but survive. They must let go of some commonly held "**truths**" and "**myths**" since these tend to hold them back—what they think they know, but don't. Companies often fail to address the tough questions about strategy and execution: Are we really clear, as a leadership team, about how we choose to create value in the marketplace? Can we articulate the few things the organization needs to do better than anyone else in order to deliver on that value proposition? Are we investing in those areas, and do they fit with most of the products and services we sell?

If your answer is yes to these and the other tough questions as listed in Figure 8.2, you're among the select few. However, in my experience, one of the biggest challenges in business today is that way too few companies are asking or answering these fundamental questions [4].

The eight tough questions to ask about strategy are organized in four levels and two ways. The four levels are about

- The way to play
- The capabilities system
- The product and service fit
- The coherence

Each of the levels needs to be asked in two ways. It should be asked if

- Can we state it?
- Do we live it?

Figure 8.2 states those eight questions for the organization to consider before they start their strategy implementation journey.

	CAN WE STATE IT?	DO WE LIVE IT ?
WAY TO PLAY	Are we clear about how we choose to create value in the marketplace?	Are we investing in the capabilities that really matter to our way to play ?
CAPABILITIES SYSTEM	Can we articulate the three to six capabilities that describe what we do uniquely better than anyone else? Have we defined how they work together in a system? Do our strategy documents reflect this?	Do all our businesses draw on this superior capabilities system ? Do our organizational structure and operating model support & leverage it? Does our performance management system reinforce it ?
PRODUCT AND SERVICE FIT	Have we specified our product and service "Sweet Spot"? Do we understand how to leverage the capabilities system in new or unexpected arenas ?	Do most of the products and services we sell fit with our capabilities system ? Are new products and acquisitions evaluated based on their fit with the way to play and the capabilities system ?
COHERENCE	Can everyone in the organization articulate our differentiating capabilities ? Is our company's leadership reinforcing these capabilities ?	Do we have right to win in our chosen market ? Do all of our decisions add to our coherence, or do some of them push us toward incoherence ?

Figure 8.2   Eight tough questions to ask about company strategy

Often, executives avoid questions they are not sure how to answer. Leaders and employees may feel that it's just not the right time to be asking them, perhaps rationalizing that the CEO has been at the helm of the company for a year or more and a strategy is already in place. They might feel that the time for asking these questions has already passed, and they don't want to come across as launching criticism. Some executives may, in fact, value the lack of strategic clarity because it allows them to pursue their own priorities. As for CEOs themselves, they often do ask these questions when they start in their roles, but they often feel constrained by the boundaries handed to them—either an incoherent portfolio or strong short-term pressure to meet targets that divert their attention.

If the executive team doesn't consistently address these questions, boards—who in many ways own the long-term strategic direction of the company—should at least ask management to provide answers, if not directly participate in finding those answers. However, most directors feel they are brought in way too late in the strategy process to have meaningful engagement. The result is that tough questions about the linkage between strategy and execution often go unaddressed.

8.3 The Eight Myths of Strategy Execution

A large-scale study was published by *Harvard Business Review* [1] to explain how complex organizations can execute their strategies more effectively. The research includes more than 40 experiments in which the researchers made changes in companies and measured the impact on execution, along with a survey administered to nearly 8,000 managers in more than 250 companies across 30 industries. The study included complex organizations in volatile markets such as financial services, information technology, telecommunications, and oil and gas, with one-third of them in emerging markets.

The study has produced valuable insights. The most important one is this: Several widely held beliefs about how to implement the strategy are just plain wrong. In this section, we debunk eight of the most pernicious myths and replace them with a more accurate perspective that will help managers effectively execute strategy. Figure 8.3 summarizes the eight myths and the following sections explain each of them and how to change the management mindset about them to improve strategy execution.

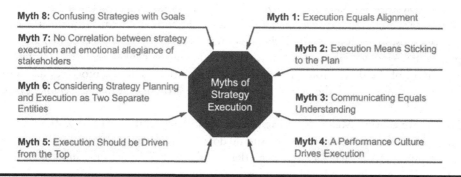

Figure 8.3   The eight myths about strategy execution

Myth 1—Execution Equals Alignment: In the survey, managers from hundreds of companies were asked to describe how strategy is executed in their firms. Their accounts paint a remarkably consistent picture. The steps typically consist of translating strategy into objectives, cascading those objectives down the hierarchy, measuring progress, and rewarding performance. When asked how they would improve execution, the executives cite tools, such as management by objectives and the balanced scorecard that are designed to increase alignment between activities and strategy up and down the chain of command. In the managers' minds, execution equals alignment, so a failure to execute implies a breakdown in the processes to link strategy to action at every level in the organization.

Despite such perceptions, it turns out that in the vast majority of companies that were studied, those processes are sound. More than 80% of managers say that their goals are limited in number, specific, and measurable and that they have the funds needed to achieve them. If most companies are doing everything right in terms of alignment, why are they struggling to execute their strategies?

To find out, survey respondents were asked how frequently they can count on others to deliver on promises—a reliable measure of whether things in an organization get done. About 84% of managers say they can rely on their boss and their direct reports all or most of the time. When we ask about commitments across functions and business units, the answer becomes clear. Only 9% of managers say they can rely on colleagues in other functions and units all the time, and just half say they can rely on them most of the time. Commitments from these colleagues are typically not much more reliable than promises made by external partners, such as distributors and suppliers.

When managers cannot rely on colleagues in other functions and units, they compensate with a host of dysfunctional behaviors that undermine execution: They duplicate effort, let promises to customers slip, delay their deliverables, or pass up attractive opportunities. The failure to coordinate also leads to conflicts between functions and units, and these are handled badly two times out of three.

Even though, as we've seen, managers typically equate execution with alignment, they do recognize the importance of coordination when questioned about it directly. When asked to identify the single greatest challenge to executing their company's strategy, 30% cite failure to coordinate across units, making that a close second to failure to align (40%). Managers also say they are three times more likely to miss performance commitments because of insufficient support from other units than their own teams' failure to deliver.

Whereas in companies that have effective processes for cascading goals downward in the organization, their systems for managing horizontal performance commitments lack teeth. More than 80% of the companies that were studied have at least one formal system for managing commitments across silos, including cross-functional committees, service-level agreements, and centralized project-management offices—but only 20% of managers believe that these systems work well all or most of the time. More than half want more structure in the processes to coordinate activities across units—twice the number who want more structure in the management by objectives system.

Myth 2—Execution Means Sticking to the Plan: When crafting strategy, many executives create detailed road maps that specify who should do what, by when, and with what resources. The strategic planning process has received more than its share of criticism, but, along with the budgeting process, it remains the backbone of execution in many organizations. Bain & Company, which regularly surveys large corporations around the world about their use of management tools, finds that strategic planning consistently heads the list. After investing enormous amounts of time and energy in formulating a plan and its associated budget, executives view deviations as a lack of discipline that undercuts execution.

Unfortunately, no Gantt chart survives contact with reality. No plan can anticipate every event that might help or hinder a company trying to achieve its strategic objectives. Managers and employees at every level need to adapt to facts on the ground, surmount unexpected obstacles, and take advantage of fleeting opportunities. Strategy execution, as we define the term, consists of seizing opportunities that support the strategy while coordinating with other parts of the organization on an ongoing basis. When managers come up with creative solutions to unforeseen problems or run with unexpected opportunities, they are not undermining systematic implementation; they are demonstrating execution at its best.

Such real-time adjustments require firms to be agile. Yet a lack of agility is a major obstacle to effective execution among the companies. In the survey when companies were asked to name the greatest challenge their companies will face in executing strategy over the next few years, nearly one-third of managers cite difficulties adapting to changing market circumstances.

It's not that companies fail to adapt at all: Only one manager in ten saw that as the problem. But most organizations either react so slowly that they can't seize fleeting opportunities or mitigate emerging threats (29%) or react quickly but lose sight of company strategy (24%). Just as managers want more structure in the processes to support coordination, they crave more structure in the processes used to adapt to changing circumstances.

A seemingly easy solution would be to do a better job of resource allocation. Although resource allocation is unquestionably critical to execution, the term itself is misleading. In volatile markets, the allotment of funds, people, and managerial attention is not a one-time decision; it requires ongoing adjustment. According to a study by McKinsey, firms that actively reallocated capital expenditures across business units achieved an average shareholder return 30% higher than the average return of companies that were slow to shift funds.

Instead of focusing on resource allocation, with its connotation of one-off choices, managers should concentrate on the fluid reallocation of funds, people, and attention. Fewer than one-third of managers believe that their organizations reallocate funds to the right places quickly enough to be effective. The reallocation of people is even worse. Only 20% of managers say their organizations do a good job of shifting people across units to support strategic priorities. The rest report that their companies rarely shift people across units (47%) or else make shifts in ways that disrupt other units (33%).

Companies also struggle to disinvest. Eight in ten managers said that their companies fail to exit declining businesses or kill unsuccessful initiatives quickly enough. Failure to exit undermines execution in an obvious way, by wasting resources that could be redeployed. Slow exits impede execution in more insidious ways as well: Top executives devote a disproportionate amount of time and attention to businesses with limited upside and send in talented managers who often burn themselves out trying to save businesses that should have been shut down or sold years earlier. The longer top executives drag their feet, the more likely they are to lose the confidence of their middle managers, whose ongoing support is critical for execution.

Myth 3—Communication Equals Understanding: The majority of the executives put a great deal of emphasis on "Communication" when it comes to effective strategy execution. Many executives believe that relentlessly communicating the strategy is a key to success. The CEO of one London-based professional services firm met with her management team the first week of every month and began each meeting by reciting the firm's strategy and its key priorities for the year. She was delighted when an employee engagement survey revealed that 84% of all staff members agreed with the statement "I am clear on our organization's top priorities". Her efforts seemed to be paying off.

Then her management team took the survey (survey designed by researchers from the MIT Sloan School of Management, the Hult International Business School, and Charles Thames Strategy Partners) which asks members to describe the firm's strategy in their own words and to list the top five strategic priorities. Fewer than one-third could name even two. The CEO was dismayed—after all, she discussed those objectives in every management meeting. Unfortunately, she is not alone. Only 55% of the middle managers that were surveyed can name even one of their company's top five priorities. In other words, when the leaders charged with explaining strategy to the troops are given five chances to list their company's strategic objectives, nearly half fail to get even one right.

In the great majority of surveyed companies, fewer than 10% of employees reported that they understood their company's strategy. The primary reason is that it is often too complex, not written in easy-to-understand language, too long, not focused, or never referred to. One business we work with had a 185-page strategic plan and numerous actions—and it sat in the bottom drawer and very little had been done to achieve any of the actions. Your strategy needs to be clearly communicated and visible to your team so that they understand their part in it. Clearly, employees who do not understand the strategy cannot link their daily activities to its successful execution.

Not only are strategic objectives poorly understood but they often seem unrelated to one another and disconnected from the overall strategy. Just over half of all top team members say they have a clear sense of how major priorities and initiatives fit together. It's pretty dire when half the C-suite cannot connect the dots between strategic priorities, but matters are even worse elsewhere. Fewer than one-third of senior executives' direct reports clearly understand the connections between corporate priorities, and the share plummets to 16% for frontline supervisors and team leaders.

Senior executives are often shocked to see how poorly their company's strategy is understood throughout the organization. In their view, they invest huge amounts of time communicating strategy, in an unending stream of e-mails, management meetings, and town hall discussions. But the amount of communication is not the issue: Nearly 90% of middle managers believe that top leaders communicate the strategy frequently enough. How can so much communication yield so little understanding?

Part of the problem is that executives measure communication in terms of inputs (the number of e-mails sent or town halls hosted) rather than by the only metric that actually counts—how well key leaders understand what's communicated. A related problem occurs when executives dilute their core messages with peripheral considerations. The executives at one tech company, for example, went to great pains to present their company's strategy and objectives at the annual executive off-site. But they also introduced 11 corporate priorities (which were different from the strategic objectives), a list of core competencies (including one with 9 templates), a set of corporate values, and a dictionary of 21 new strategic terms to be mastered. Not surprisingly, the assembled managers were baffled about what mattered most. When asked about obstacles to understanding the strategy, middle managers are four times more likely to cite a large number of corporate priorities and strategic initiatives than to mention a lack of clarity in communication. Top executives add to the confusion when they change their messages frequently—a problem flagged by nearly one-quarter of middle managers.

Myth 4—A Performance Culture Drives Execution: When their companies fail to translate strategy into results, many executives point to a weak performance culture as the root cause. The data tells a different story. It's true that in most companies, the official culture—the core values posted on the company website, say—does not support execution. However, a company's true values reveal themselves when managers make hard choices—and in the survey, it was found that a focus on performance does shape behavior on a day-to-day basis.

When companies are asked about factors that influence who gets hired, praised, promoted, and fired, most companies do a good job of recognizing and rewarding performance. Past performance is by far the most frequently named factor in promotion decisions, cited by two-thirds of all managers. Although harder to assess when bringing in new employees, it ranks among the top three influences on who gets hired. One-third of managers believe that performance is also recognized all or most of the time with nonfinancial rewards, such as private praise, public acknowledgment, and access to training opportunities. To be sure, there is room for improvement, particularly when it comes to dealing with underperformers: A majority of the companies that were studied delay action (33%), address underperformance inconsistently (34%), or tolerate poor performance (11%). Overall, though the companies in the sample have robust performance cultures—and yet they struggle to execute strategies. Why?

The answer is that a culture that supports execution must recognize and reward other things as well, such as agility, teamwork, and ambition. Many companies fall short in this respect. When making hiring or promotion decisions, for example, they place much less value on a manager's ability to adapt to changing circumstances—an indication of the agility needed to execute strategy—than on whether she has hit her numbers in the past. Agility requires a willingness to experiment, and many managers avoid experimentation because they fear the consequences of failure. Half the managers who were surveyed believe that their careers would suffer if they pursued but failed at novel opportunities or innovations.

Trying new things inevitably entails setbacks, and honestly discussing the challenges involved increases the odds of long-term success. But corporate cultures rarely support the candid discussions necessary for agility. Fewer than one-third of managers say they can have open and honest discussions about the most difficult issues, while one-third say that many important issues are considered taboo.

An excessive emphasis on performance can impair execution in another subtle but important way. If managers believe that hitting their numbers trumps all else, they tend to make conservative performance commitments. When asked what advice they would give to a new colleague, two-thirds say they would recommend making commitments that the colleague could be sure to meet; fewer than one-third would recommend stretching for ambitious goals. This tendency to play it safe may lead managers to favor surefire cost reductions over risky growth, for instance, or to milk an existing business rather than experiment with a new business model.

Myth 5—Execution Should Be Driven from the Top: In his best-selling book *Execution*, Larry Bossidy describes how, as the CEO of AlliedSignal, he personally negotiated performance objectives with managers several levels below him and monitored their progress. Accounts like this reinforce the common image of a heroic CEO perched atop the org chart, driving execution. That approach can work—for a while. AlliedSignal's stock outperformed the market under Bossidy's leadership. However, as Bossidy writes, shortly after he retired "the discipline of execution … unraveled", and the company gave up its gains relative to the S&P 500.

Top-down execution has drawbacks in addition to the risk of unraveling after the departure of a strong CEO. To understand why, it helps to remember that effective execution in large, complex organizations emerges from countless decisions and actions at all levels. Many of those involve hard trade-offs: For example, synching up with colleagues in another unit can slow down a team that's trying to seize a fleeting opportunity, and screening customer requests against strategy often means turning away lucrative business. The leaders who are closest to the situation and can respond most quickly are best positioned to make the tough calls.

Concentrating power at the top may boost performance in the short term, but it degrades an organization's capacity to execute over the long run. Frequent and direct intervention from on high encourages middle managers to escalate conflicts rather than resolve them, and over time, they lose the ability to work things out with colleagues in other units. Moreover, if top executives insist on making the important calls themselves, they diminish middle managers' decision-making skills, initiative, and ownership of results. In large, complex organizations, execution lives and dies with a group we call "distributed leaders", which includes not only middle managers who run critical businesses and functions but also technical and domain experts who occupy key spots in the informal networks that get things done. The vast majority of these leaders try to do the right thing. Eight out of ten in our sample say they are committed to doing their best to execute the strategy, even when they would like more clarity on what the strategy is.

Distributed leaders, not senior executives, represent "management" to most employees, partners, and customers. Their day-to-day actions, particularly how they handle difficult decisions and what behaviors they tolerate, go a long way toward supporting or undermining the corporate culture. In this regard, most distributed leaders shine. As assessed by their direct reports, more than 90% of middle managers live up to the organization's values all or most of the time. They do an especially good job of reinforcing performance, with nearly nine in ten consistently holding team members accountable for results.

But although execution should be driven from the middle, it needs to be guided from the top. Distributed leaders are hamstrung in their efforts to translate overall company strategy into terms meaningful for their teams or units when top executives fail to ensure that they clearly understand that strategy.

Conflicts inevitably arise in any organization where different units pursue their own objectives. Distributed leaders are asked to shoulder much of the burden of working across silos, and many appear to be buckling under the load. A minority of middle managers consistently anticipate and avoid problems (15%) or resolve conflicts quickly and well (26%). Most resolve issues only after a significant delay (37%), try but fail to resolve them (10%), or don't address them at all (12%). Top executives could help by adding structured processes to facilitate coordination. In many cases, they could also do a better job of modeling teamwork. One-third of distributed leaders believe that factions exist within the C-suite and that executives there focus on their own agendas rather than on what is best for the company.

Myth 6—Considering Strategy Planning and Execution as Two Separate Entities: For decades, we've often thought of leadership profiles in unique buckets—two popular varieties were the "visionaries", who embrace strategy and think about amazing things to do, and the "operators", who get stuff done. We intuitively knew that there must be leaders that span these areas, but in fact, few do. According to a global survey of 700 executives across a variety of industries conducted by Strategy&, the strategy consulting division of PwC, only 8% of company leaders were said to excel at both strategy and execution [5]. You may think that success can be achieved by excelling at either strategy or execution individually—that great visionaries can change how we see the world or that amazing operators can wind up outperforming competitors. But experience and research suggest that the days of keeping strategy and execution as separate topics are ending: We need leaders that can create big promises to customers, and help their organizations deliver on those promises.

Take Starbucks: CEO Howard Schultz created a very ambitious aspiration for the company, far more than just being a seller of coffee. He wanted Starbucks to be a "third place" for conviviality beyond home and the workplace. Visit a Starbucks anywhere in the world, and you will find the same consistently comfortable and welcoming ambiance. But he didn't get there simply by telling his staff to "be warm and friendly". Starbucks has been able to deliver on its promise because that promise is tightly linked to the company's distinctive capabilities. The feel of Starbucks stores isn't created merely by the layout and the décor—it exists because the people behind the counter understand how their work fits into a common purpose and recognize how to accomplish great things together without needing to follow a script.

Over many years, Starbucks has built a capability to foster a relationship-driven, "employees-first" approach. It was Schultz who famously said

> You can walk into [any type of retail store] and you can feel whether the proprietor or the merchant or the person behind the counter has a good feeling about his product. If you walk into a department store today, you are probably talking to a guy who is untrained; he was selling vacuum cleaners yesterday, and now he is in the apparel section. It just does not work.

Schultz made sure that Starbucks would be different: Workers are called "partners" rather than employees, and even part-time staff (in the United States) receive stock options and health insurance. At the height of the global financial crisis, when other companies were cutting HR costs wherever they could, Starbucks invested in staff training, including coffee tastings and courses that ultimately qualified employees for credit at higher-education institutions. Beyond employees, much of what you will see and experience at Starbucks has been well thought out to accomplish the company's mission, from the music played to the furniture selected. Even the bathrooms are strategic at Starbucks because they play a part in allowing customers to spend time in the "third place".

Leaders like Howard Schultz don't just have both visionary and operator skills—they deeply value the connection between the two skill sets. In fact, they see them as inextricably linked, since a bold vision needs to include both a very ambitious destination and a well-conceived path for execution that will get you there. This is ever more important today, where differentiating your company is so difficult. Differentiation increasingly requires more innovative thinking, and the use of very specific areas of expertise (like Apple's winning design, a capability that wouldn't have been prioritized in most technology companies before Steve Jobs).

Myth 7—No Correlation between Strategy Execution and Emotional Allegiance of Stakeholders: Managers are usually uncomfortable dealing with emotions in business settings, especially the all-important collective emotions—i.e., various emotions experienced by different stakeholder groups inside and outside the organization, including employees, customers, communities, and investors. However, as much as managers may want their intended strategy to succeed, they still find it difficult to accept that the fate of their best-laid plans depends on the emotional allegiance of these groups. Instead, they assume their communications—which often focus only on the intellectual "left brain" rather than incorporating the "right-brain", the seat of emotional engagement—will be heeded when their back is turned.

Executives who are receptive to the subtle, nonverbal signs of collective emotion are more likely to have the credibility required to lead strategic change. Sadly, such leaders are still few and far between. Over time, emotionally illiterate leadership gives rise to a change-averse corporate culture. While profits are high and the economic climate remains promising, the problem stays under the radar—much like the early stage of cancer. But when a change in course becomes necessary, senior leaders find that no matter how hard they try, transformation never takes root.

Consider what happened internally at Microsoft in a year or two just before the iPhone came out. Having gotten wind of Apple's impending game-changer, Microsoft chairman Bill Gates tasked then-CEO Steve Ballmer with creating a copycat device to forestall Cupertino's market dominance. Ballmer passed the word to his senior vice-presidents, each of whom had at his disposal thousands of engineers and an R&D budget running into the hundreds of millions of dollars. Their combined failure to produce an acceptable iPhone equivalent is the stuff of tech legend.

What went wrong? Despite their shared mandate, the departments didn't cooperate fully with one another. A big part of the problem, experts agree, was Microsoft's infamously cutthroat "stack ranking" system, which forced managers to grade employee performance on the curve. Regardless of individual performance, a certain percentage of staffers would always be ranked as "below average" or "poor". Low-ranking employees were ineligible for promotions and pay rises, and would sometimes be shown the door.

As a result of stack ranking, Microsoft's top talents were wary of and competitive with one another, seeking to surround themselves with employees who would make them look better by comparison. Any collaboration between them was stifled by the dehumanizing corporate culture.

Microsoft's story may be high-profile, but it is not unique. Wherever there is a lack of emotionally incisive leadership, employees will tend to fall back on the basic human instinct of self-preservation. Ironically, what is "survival mode" for employees may well spell the death of a corporate strategy.

INSEAD report [6] identified five main emotion-based barriers to strategy execution within organizations. Each one presents a major danger to transformational efforts by preventing the necessary sense of urgency and commitment to a common task from taking hold throughout the organization (Figure 8.4).

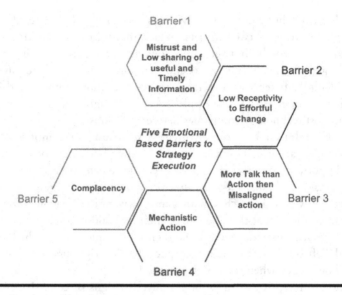

Figure 8.4   Emotion-based barriers to strategy execution

1. **Mistrust and Low Sharing of Useful and Timely Information**—A "politics first" mentality that prizes appearance management above action. This causes a situation where no one wants to be the bearer of bad news. As with Microsoft, Nokia and probably Volkswagen, problems will come to leaders' attention only when it is too late. Strategic alignment is further hindered by information-hoarding among players who see their colleagues as competitors.
2. **Low Receptivity to Effortful Change**—Effortful change (even when it's obviously beneficial, e.g., quitting smoking or staying on a diet) is easy to profess, difficult to do. Leaders must demonstrate their own willingness and ability to change before asking it of others.
3. **More Talk than Action, then Misaligned Action**—When leaders fail to inspire the collective toward a common goal, each team will tend to veer off in its own direction. It becomes impossible to integrate all the silos.
4. **Mechanistic Action**—When under high time and performance pressure, employees become creatures of habit rather than taking risks to become innovative.
5. **Complacency**—Confronted with the potential effort and risk of strategic change, the organization as a whole believes the status quo is good enough, so why do the hard work to change it?

Myth 8—Confusing Strategies with Goals: Many strategy execution processes fail because the firm does not have something worth executing. The strategy consultants come in, do their work, and document the new strategy in a PowerPoint presentation and a weighty report. Town hall meetings are organized, employees are told to change their behavior, balanced scorecards are reformulated, and budgets are set aside to support initiatives that fit the new strategy. And then nothing happens.

One major reason for the lack of action is that "new strategies" are often not strategies at all. A real strategy involves a clear set of choices that define what the firm is going to do and what it's not going to do. Many strategies fail to get implemented, despite the ample efforts of hard-working people, because they do not represent a set of clear choices.

Many so-called strategies are in fact goals. "We want to be the number one or number two in all the markets in which we operate" is one of those. It does not tell you what you are going to do; all it does is tell you what you hope the outcome will be. But you'll still need a strategy to achieve it.

Others may represent a couple of the firm's priorities and choices, but they do not form a coherent strategy when considered in conjunction. For example, consider "We want to increase operational efficiency; we will target Europe, the Middle East, and Africa; and we will divest business X". These may be excellent decisions and priorities, but together they do not form a strategy.

For instance, about 20 years ago, the iconic British toy company Hornby Railways—maker of model railways and Scalextric slot car racing tracks—was facing bankruptcy. Under the new CEO, Frank Martin, the company decided to change course and focus on collectors and hobbyists instead. As a new strategy, Martin aimed

- To make perfect scale models (rather than toys)
- For adult collectors (rather than for children)
- That appealed to a sense of nostalgia (because it reminded adults of their childhoods). The switch became a runaway success, increasing Hornby's share price from £35 to £250 over just five years

That's because it represented a clear set of just three choices, which fit together to form a clear strategic direction for the company. (Unfortunately, in recent years Hornby abandoned its set of choices, to quite disastrous consequences, where it was forced to issue a string of profit warnings and Martin was encouraged to take early retirement in 2014.) Without a clear strategic direction, any implementation process is doomed to fail.

8.4 Ten Principles of Strategy through Execution

Basic principles that make for good strategy often get obscured. Sometimes the explanation is a quest for the next new thing—natural in a field that emerged through the steady accumulation of frameworks promising to unlock the secret of competitive advantage. In other cases, the culprit is torrents of data, reams of analysis, and piles of documents that can be more distracting than enlightening. Ultimately, strategy is a way of thinking, not a procedural exercise or a set of frameworks. Excellence in strategy execution can be founded on the following ten principles as developed by PWC/Strategy& team and demonstrated by Figure 8.5 [7]:

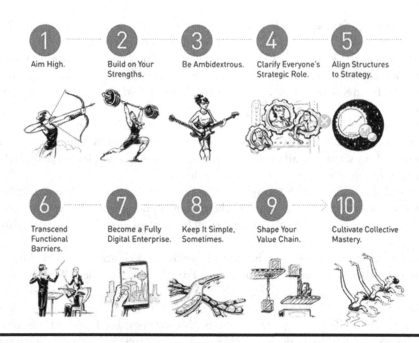

Figure 8.5   Ten principles of strategy execution [7]

1. **Aim High**: Don't compromise your strategy or your execution. Apple, for instance, has long been known for its intense interest in every aspect of product design and marketing, iterating endlessly until its notoriously demanding leaders are satisfied. The company's leaders do not consider execution beneath them; it is part of what makes Apple special.

   After the 1992 Olympics in Barcelona, a group of local political and business leaders realized, with some disappointment, that the event hadn't triggered the economic growth they had expected. So, they resolved to change the region's economy in other ways. Led by the mayor, the group created a common base of technologies and practices and set up training programs for local enterprises. By 2014, after two decades of persistent effort, the city had become a hub for research and technology companies. One legacy of the Olympics is a group of about 600 sports-related companies with a collective annual revenue of US$3 billion and 20,000 employees.

2. **Build on Your Strengths**: The more knowledge you have about your own capabilities, the more opportunities you'll have to build on your strategic enablers. So, you should always be analyzing what you do best, gathering data about your practices, and conducting post mortems. In every case, there is something to learn—about your operations, and also about the choices you make and the value you're able to deliver.

   Sometimes a particular episode will bring to light new ways of building on your strengths. That's what happened at Bombardier Transportation, a division of a Canadian firm and one of the world's largest manufacturers of railroad equipment. To win a highly competitive bid for supplying 66 passenger train cars to a British rail operator, Bombardier shifted its manufacturing and commercial models to a platform-based approach, which allowed it to use and reuse the same designs for several different types of railway cars. "Platforming", which was an operational strategy for the industry, required adjustments to Bombardier's supplier relationships and product engineering practices. But the benefits were immediate: Lower costs, less technology risks, faster time-to-market, and better reliability.

3. **Be Ambidextrous**: In business, it's the ability to manage strategy and execution with equal competence. In some companies, this is known as being "bilingual": Able to speak the language of the boardroom and the shop floor. In *The Self-Made Billionaire Effect: How Extreme Producers Create Massive Value*, John Sviokla and Mitch Cohen suggest using the word producers to describe ambidextrous individuals. Self-made billionaires, such as **Spanx** founder Sara Blakely, **POM Wonderful** cofounder Lynda Resnick, **Uniqlo** founder Tadashi Yanai, and **Morningstar** founder Joe Mansueto have this quality. They can both envision a blockbuster strategy and figure out in detail how to develop and sell it to customers. There are similarly ambidextrous people in every company, but they often go unappreciated. Find them, recognize and reward them, and give them opportunities to influence others.

4. **Clarify Everyone's Strategic Role**: The people in your day-to-day operations—wherever they are, and on whatever level—are continually called upon to make decisions on behalf of the organization. If they are not motivated to deliver the strategy, the strategy won't reach the customers. When the leaders of the General Authority of Civil Aviation (GACA) of Saudi Arabia decided to improve the way they ran the country's 25 airports, they started with the Riyadh airport. They had already outsourced much of their activity, redesigning practices and enhancing operations. But not much has changed. When analyzing the situation, the management teams found that problems were mainly due to operational silos that led to a large number of minor operational problems that when accumulated led to failure in GACA strategy execution. They stood in the way of the country's goal of becoming a commercial and logistics hub for Africa, Asia, and Europe.

5. **Align Structure to Strategy**: Set up your organizational structures, including your hierarchical design, decision rights, incentives, and metrics so they reinforce the company's identity: Your value proposition and critical capabilities. More generally, every structure in your organization should make your capabilities stronger, and focus them on delivering your strategic goals.

6. **Transcend Functional Barriers**: Great capabilities always transcend functional barriers. Consider Starbucks' understanding of how to create the right ambience, Haier's ability to rapidly manufacture home appliances to order, and Amazon's aptitude for launching products and services enabled by new technologies. These companies all bring people from different functions to work together informally and creatively.

7. **Become Fully Digital Enterprise**: Embrace digital technology's potential to transform your company: To create fundamentally new experiences and interactions for your customers, your employees, and every other constituent. Until you use technology this way, many of your IT investments will be wasted; you won't realize their potential in forming powerful new capabilities. For example, Under Armour began as a technologically enabled sports apparel company, specializing in microfiber-based synthetic fabrics that felt comfortable under all conditions. To keep its value proposition as an innovator, it aggressively expanded into fitness trackers and the development of smart apparel. The company developed clothing that will provide data that can both help athletes raise their game and point the way to design improvements. They partnered with IBM and Google to create an echo system for this new wearables platform. But the company did not keep up the pace with more formidable competitors (such as Nike, Apple, Fitbit, Gramin, and Withings) and is currently

withdrawing from this market. Becoming a fully digital enterprise in the age of VUCA is becoming really challenging for many organizations.

8. **Keep It Simple Sometimes (KISS):** Many company leaders wish for more simplicity: Just a few products, a clear and simple value chain, and not too many projects on the schedule. Unfortunately, it rarely works out that way. In a large, mainstream company, execution is by nature complex. The principle "keep it simple, sometimes" is itself more complex than it appears at first glance. It combines three concepts in one: First, be as simple as possible. Second, let your company's strategy be your guide in adding the right amount of complexity. Third, build the capabilities needed to effectively manage the complexity inherent in serving your markets and customers. Lenovo is a case in point for this application of this principle.

9. **Shape Your Value Chain:** No company is an island. Every business relies on other companies in its network to help shepherd its products and services from one end of the value chain to the other. As you raise your game, you will raise the game of other operations you work with, including suppliers, distributors, retailers, brokers, and even regulators. Since these partners are working with you on execution, they should also be actively involved in strategy. That means selling your strategy to them, getting them excited about taking the partnership to a whole new level, and backing up your strategic commitment with financing, analytics, and operational prowess. For example, when the Brazilian cosmetics company Natura Cosméticos began sourcing ingredients from Amazon rain forest villages, its procurement staff discovered that the supply would be sustainable only if they built deeper relationships with their suppliers. Beyond paying suppliers, they needed to invest in the suppliers' communities. The company has held to that commitment even during down periods.

10. **Cultivate Collective Mastery:** In a world where disruption has become prevalent, your company can't afford the time or expense of operating with bureaucratic internal operational rules and procedures that create frustration. The alternative is what we call collective mastery. This is a cultural attribute, often found in companies where strategy through execution is prevalent. It is the state you reach where communication is fluid, open, and constant. Many of the attributes of Silicon Valley companies owe a great deal to the high level of collective mastery.

In the end, the ten principles of strategy through execution will do more than help you achieve your business goals. They will also help build a new kind of culture, one in which people are aware of where you're going and how you're going to get there. The capabilities you build, and the value you provide, are larger than any individual can make them.

8.5 Four Pillars of Strategy Execution

Building on the lessons learned from the eight myths of strategy execution clarified by HBR and the ten principles proposed by PWC/Strategy&, I would propose the following four pillars as a good summary of the critical foundations for efficient and effective strategy implementation. They can really help organizations Put Strategy in Action. Those pillars are

1. Authentic Leadership and Corporate Values
2. Agility, Flexibility, and Resilience
3. Accountability
4. Cadence

Figure 8.6 summarizes those four pillars and the following sections will elaborate on them.

Figure 8.6   Four pillars of strategy execution

8.5.1 Pillar 1—Authentic Leadership and Corporate Values

Strong leadership with a clear vision and powerful corporate values can help organizations overcome the challenges presented by the VUCA business environment. However, genuine leadership is quite daunting to achieve amidst a rapidly changing and volatile business environment. It is due to this fact that in the past decade or so, several books, articles, and professional services have emerged on the scene in order to support effective leadership.

Leadership plays a key role from communicating and connecting your people to the vision and strategy, to creating accountability and generating momentum, through to having good meetings that maintain the essential communication and momentum to focus and execute the strategy. Research from Winsborough https://www.winsborough.co.nz/—New Zealand leadership consulting group shows that CEOs account for between 15% and 30% of the variance in firm performance. Bad CEOs bring firms like HP, Enron, Merrill Lynch, Yahoo, or the Royal Bank of Scotland to their knees and inflict misery and heartache on hundreds of thousands of employees, while good CEOs can inspire hope and create sustained performance lifts; take for example Rob Fyfe, the former CEO at Air New Zealand.

The leaders of the organization directly influence the motivation and inspiration of the team; this affects the discretionary effect of the team, their productivity, your customer service and loyalty, and your profitability. Good leadership is the critical multiplier for every business.

As your business grows, you will no longer be able to directly influence everything in the business and you have to learn to lead through others, systems, and processes. The specialist skills that you leveraged as you got started and grew the business will no longer be the mainstay of the skills and knowledge you need. You now need to be a generalist leader and trust other specialists in your business. The reality is you can't grow your business; only your people can—but you play the critical role in setting the example and framework for how others lead within your organization.

The success of any business is largely dependent on how its top leader inspires and leads its leaders. For businesses to thrive, executive-level leaders must know how to get the most from their senior managers, who in turn must drive performance throughout the organization—whether you have 30 or 3,000 people.

Simply put, great leaders know how to lead other leaders. Great leaders understand that by developing and positioning their leaders, they help guarantee the success of the business. Successful leaders change their mindset from growing followers to growing leaders, they develop relationship-based influence, they embrace being a generalist leader, they are skilled in the art of delegation of tasks and decisions, and they know how to best develop their leaders as individuals.

8.5.1.1 Leadership Starts with You

How can you expect to lead anyone else if you can't lead yourself? How can you expect to be given control over anything or anyone, if you can't control yourself? Increasingly, effective leadership is being defined by elements such as emotional intelligence, authenticity, credibility, and personal grounding. The leader's ability to connect with and inspire people are the critical components that define outstanding executive leader success.

Harold Hillman's model of "**The Balanced Leader**" helps demonstrate the basis for being an authentic leader. This starts with understanding and truly knowing yourself as a leader. This model highlights that an executive leader requires a mix of interpersonal and intrapersonal characteristics/behaviors to be seen as balanced. The model is presented in the shape of a circle (as shown in Figure 8.7, broken into intrapersonal and interpersonal characteristics [8].

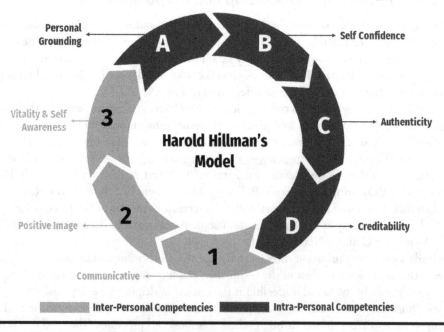

Figure 8.7   The balanced leader—Harold Hillman's model

The intrapersonal competencies are personal grounding, self-confidence, authenticity, and credibility. While the interpersonal characteristics that a leader needs to demonstrate are communication, positive image, vitality, and self-awareness. The balanced executive leader has developed skills across each of these areas.

Leaders need to understand that emotions are the cornerstone of inspiration. Every leader needs to understand that their, or anyone else's, emotions are highly contagious—whether positive or negative. As a leader, you must tune into your own emotions and be attuned to the emotions of those around you. Good leaders know what spins their wheels and what gets them motivated, and what tasks take a lot of energy and focus to complete. They know how they react to stress, how they work, and when they respond when they are tired, surprised, or under pressure—but most importantly great leaders are able to manage or regulate their natural response and are conscious and mindful of the impact they have on people around them.

Additionally, no matter whether you are naturally extroverted or not, you need to become more extroverted and be engaging with people. It is even as simple as practicing walking the room as a leader and connecting with your people at a personal level—make it about them. If you are typically task-focused, take time to connect with or think about the people's pieces. Equally, if you aren't a natural public speaker, you need to be able to speak to a group from the heart and convey your message with clarity and confidence. Communication is the critical vehicle of inspiration. At its most basic level, help the people who work for you, with you, or around you to be happy. Doing this enables an executive leader to have a leadership presence, as Hillman defined as "an authentic quality of poise and effectiveness that enables an executive to connect with a range of people and influence successful outcomes".

As a final thought, leadership is about perception. Therefore, it's not what you think about yourself as a leader that really matters, but what those below, above, and around you think. It's about growing your understanding of your identity as a leader while developing your reputation. Focusing on your leadership will set you and your business apart from others.

8.5.2 Pillar 2—Agility, Flexibility, and Resilience

Another useful approach to finding strategic relief is to acknowledge the fact that it has become increasingly difficult to formulate a strategy in this constantly changing business environment that it shouldn't even be attempted. Instead, the answer lies in the creation of strategic agility, organizational flexibility, and resilience. The key idea behind being is to take advantage of fundamental shifts faster than the competition. Examples of work which addresses strategic agility in response to a rapidly changing environment include *Fast Strategy: How Strategic Agility Will Help You to Stay Ahead of the Game* by Yves Doz and Mikko Kosonen. Their book explains the three principles required in order to achieve strategic agility which include **strategic sensitivity**, **collective commitment**, and **resource fluidity**. These components of strategic agility are not static but rather constantly being eroded by a company's success, which ironically was likely enabled by being strategically agile at one point. The concept that the same success created by being strategic agile can also destroy the company's strategic agility. This concept is known as the curse of success.

Becoming strategically agile requires three fundamental shifts in the way that top management directs their company. First, they must move away from always looking forward in terms of strategic planning and begin to look at current situations and how their firm is able to make sense of that situation and set a strategic course with that in mind. Second, companies need to move away from only allocating resources to a specific need or task to being capable of having their resources "switch gears" in order to capitalize on a current strategic opportunity. Third, top management needs to set an example of team building instead of one-on-one relationships. Finally, the authors outline four critical levers or tools (cognitive, political, emotional, and organizational) that if used concurrently by management, can help keep or regain strategic agility once it has been lost [9].

8.5.3 Pillar 3—Accountability

A worldwide Gallup poll on employee engagement found that only a startling 15% of employees know the company's priorities and only 6% of employees know their own individual priorities, let alone have seen the company's plan. This is a shocking lack of understanding [8]. The number one thing people wanted was to know what was expected of them at work. Having clear accountability and visible responsibilities makes everyone clear on what needs to be done and will ensure things get done. Accountability creates engagement. This can be aided by the careful design of business **KPIs (Key Performance Indicators)** and linking them to **KBIs (Key Behavioral Indicators)**. To illustrate this, Peter Drucker famously said, "**You can only manage what you measure, and what gets measured gets done**".

Accountability is behavior that allows businesses to successfully execute their strategy, while KPIs are business performance management tools that can support and re-enforce accountability. Hence, the proper linking of the KPIs and KBIs ensures the sustainability of results and business progression toward achieving its strategy. This should also be coupled with visibility. Clear visibility creates accountability. It's a simple but powerful rule. It's important to clearly document who is accountable for the key functional roles in the business and how their performance will be measured.

Every leader needs to clearly identify the top three things the company is working on. It's quite simple—if you can't, you're not leading well. The leader then needs to be seen to lead by example and achieve what they are responsible for and deliver on their promises. The people within the organization also need to know that people will be held accountable for not achieving their goals or KPIs and in turn will start to hold each other accountable. If a team goal attainment is transparent and everyone knows what the other is contributing toward it, the teams become self-managing regarding performance.

8.5.4 Pillar 4—Cadence

We all want to be able to do the things we are meant to do to move our organization forward to achieve our vision, but often we find ourselves putting things off, making excuses, saying "next week/month".

It becomes increasingly difficult when you are swamped with an endless stream of urgent matters, such as losing a key staff member, a key client from the pipeline, or having a safety incident. It becomes too easy to focus on the here and now—when we instead need to keep an eye on the future.

So, if we can't break away from the daily grind and churn to do some work toward achieving our strategy, doing something to make a difference, how can we expect to be somewhere different in the end? It takes a lot of discipline to take the time to reflect on what's going on. What have you achieved? What have you learned? What are the key issues? And what am I going to do about it?

Executing Strategy through Effective Meetings: We often say that we have too many meetings, that they are a waste of time, or that they are ineffective. Why is that, when in reality if done right, meetings help us ensure we execute our business, live our culture and lead effectively. We often find when talking to clients and friends that people get frustrated either by the lack of coordination and direction, lack of accountability to get action, or while their meetings are well-intentioned—they are just a "talk-fest".

Something Business Strategist, Greg Allnutt, learned early on in his military career as a leader was the importance of being able to discuss, plan and execute operations to achieve a result. A key component of this was to have clear meetings with an agenda, where team members contributed ideas, were given tasks, and were then held accountable for implementing them. Later at a more strategic level, he found it was about being able to have robust discussions about strategic initiatives. This was about having a level of trust to have a conflict that enabled healthy and safe challenging of each other's ideas so that they could make the best decisions for the future of the organization. Greg has since found that these ideas are equally important in business—and while it sounds simple—people often have trouble making it happen, confusing the nature of their meetings and so end up frustrated. It's useful to reflect on what we are trying to do and then shape our meetings to the best effect.

8.6 Ten Strategy Stress Tests

Finally, to help executives assess the strength of their strategies before/during their implementation McKinsey team proposed ten tests for strategy. These tests focus on testing the strategy itself (in other words, the output of the strategy-development process), rather than the frameworks, tools, and approaches that generate strategies, for two reasons. First, companies develop the strategy in many different ways, often idiosyncratic to their organizations, people, and markets. Second, many strategies emerge over time rather than from a process of the deliberate formulation [10].

There are ten tests, and all are created equal. The first test is whether the strategy "will beat the market?"—is comprehensive. The remaining nine disaggregate the picture of a market-beating strategy, though it's certainly possible for a strategy to succeed without "passing" all nine of them. In their survey of 2,135 executives on testing business strategy, they found that most of the strategies of the companies pass less than four of the ten tests. Figure 8.8 shows the results of the survey.

Number of tests rated as fully consistent with company strategy, % of respondents

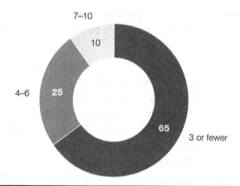

Figure 8.8   Strategy stress tests results

8.6.1 Test 1: Will Your Strategy Beat the Market?

All companies operate in markets surrounded by customers, suppliers, competitors, substitutes, and potential entrants, all seeking to advance their own positions. That process, unimpeded, inexorably drives economic surplus—the gap between the return a company earns and its cost of capital—toward zero.

For a company to beat the market by capturing and retaining an economic surplus, there must be an imperfection that stops or at least slows the working of the market. An imperfection controlled by a company is a competitive advantage. These are by definition scarce and fleeting because markets drive reversion to mean performance. The best companies are emulated by those in the middle of the pack, and the worst exit or undergo significant reform. As each player responds to and learns from the actions of others, best practice becomes commonplace rather than a market-beating strategy. Good strategies emphasize difference—versus your direct competitors, versus potential substitutes, and versus potential entrants.

Market participants play out the drama of competition on a stage beset by randomness. Because the evolution of markets is path-dependent—that is, its current state at any one time is the sum product of all previous events, including a great many random ones—the winners of today are often the accidents of history. Consider the development of the US tire industry. At its peak in the mid-1920s, a frenzy of entry had created almost 300 competitors. Yet by the 1940s, four producers controlled more than 70% of the market [9]. Those winners happened to make retrospectively lucky choices about location and technology, but at the time it was difficult to tell which companies were truly fit for the evolving environment. The histories of many other industries, from aerospace to information technology, show remarkably similar patterns.

To beat the market, therefore, advantages have to be robust and responsive in the face of onrushing market forces. Few companies ask themselves if they are beating the market—the pressures of "just playing along" seem intense enough. But playing along can feel safer than it is. Weaker contenders win surprisingly often in a war when they deploy a divergent strategy, and the same is true in business.

8.6.2 Test 2: Does Your Strategy Tap a True Source of Advantage?

Know your competitive advantage, and you've answered the question of why you make money (and vice versa). Competitive advantage stems from two sources of scarcity: Positional advantages and special capabilities.

Positional advantages are rooted in structurally attractive markets. By definition, such advantages favor incumbents: They create an asymmetry between those inside and those outside high walls.

Special capabilities, the second source of competitive advantage, are scarce resources whose possession confers unique benefits. The most obvious resources, such as drug patents or leases on mineral deposits, are called "privileged, tradable assets"; they can be bought and sold. The second category of special capabilities, "distinctive competencies", consists of things a company does particularly well, such as innovating or managing stakeholders. These capabilities can be just as powerful in creating an advantage but cannot be easily traded.

Too often, companies are cavalier about claiming special capabilities. Such a capability must be critical to a company's profits and exist in abundance within it while being scarce outside. As such, special capabilities tend to be specific in nature and few in number. Companies often err here by mistaking size for scale advantage or overestimating their ability to leverage capabilities across markets. They infer special capabilities from observed performance, often without considering other explanations (such as luck or positional advantage). Companies should test any claimed capability advantage vigorously before pinning their hopes on it. When companies bundle together activities that collectively create an advantage, it becomes more difficult for competitors to identify and replicate their exact source. Consider Aldi, the highly successful discount grocery retailer. To deliver its value proposition of lower prices, Aldi has completely redesigned the typical business system of a supermarket: Only 1,500 or so products rather than 30,000, the stocking of one own-brand or private label rather than hundreds of national brands, and super lean replenishment on pallets and trolleys, thus avoiding the expensive task of hand stacking shelves. Given the enormous changes necessary for any supermarket that wishes to copy the total system, it is extremely difficult to mimic Aldi's value proposition.

Finally, don't forget to take a dynamic view. What can erode positional advantage? Which special capabilities are becoming vulnerable? There is every reason to believe that competitors will exploit points of vulnerability.

8.6.3 Test 3: Is Your Strategy Granular about Where to Compete?

The need to beat the market begs the question of which market. Research shows that the unit of analysis used in determining strategy (essentially, the degree to which a market is segmented) significantly influences resource allocation and thus the likelihood of success: Dividing the same businesses in different ways leads to strikingly different capital allocations. What is the right level of granularity? Push within reason for the finest possible objective segmentation of the market: Think 30 to 50 segments rather than the more typical 5 or so. Too often, by contrast, the business unit as defined by the organizational chart becomes the default for defining markets, reducing from the start the potential scope of strategic thinking.

Defining and understanding these segments correctly is one of the most practical things a company can do to improve its strategy. In fact, 80% of the variance in revenue growth is explained by choices about where to compete, according to research summarized in The Granularity of Growth, leaving only 20% explained by choices about how to compete [11]. Unfortunately, this is the exact opposite of the allocation of time and effort in a typical strategy-development process. Companies should be shifting their attention greatly toward the "where" and should strive to out position competitors by regularly reallocating resources as opportunities shift within and between segments.

8.6.4 Test 4: Does Your Strategy Put You Ahead of Trends?

The emergence of new trends is the norm. But many strategies place too much weight on the continuation of the status quo because they extrapolate from the past three to five years, a time frame too brief to capture the true violence of market forces.

A major innovation or an external shock in regulation, demand, or technology, for example, can drive a rapid, full-scale industry transition. But most trends emerge fairly slowly—so slowly that companies generally fail to respond until a trend hits profit. At this point, it is too late to mount a strategically effective response, let alone shape the change to your advantage. Managers typically delay action, held back by sunk costs, an unwillingness to cannibalize a legacy business, or an attachment to yesterday's formula for success. The cost of delay is steep: Consider the plight of major travel agency chains slow to understand the power of online intermediaries. Conversely, for companies that get ahead of the curve, major market transitions are an opportunity to rethink their commitments in areas ranging from technology to distribution and to tailor their strategies to the new environment.

To do so, strategists must take trend analysis seriously. Always look to the edges. How are early adopters and that small cadre of consumers who seem to be ahead of the curve acting? What are small, innovative entrants doing? What technologies under development could change the game? To see which trends really matter, assess their potential impact on the financial position of your company and articulate the decisions you would make differently if that outcome were certain. For example, don't just stop at an aging population as a trend—work it through to its conclusion. Which consumer behaviors would change? Which particular product lines would be affected? What would be the precise effect on the P&L? And how does that picture line up with today's investment priorities?

8.6.5 Test 5: Does Your Strategy Rest on Privileged Insights?

Data today can be cheap, accessible, and easily assembled into detailed analyses that leave executives with the comfortable feeling of possessing an informed strategy. But much of this is noise, and most of it is widely available to rivals. Furthermore, routinely analyzing readily available data diverts attention from where the insight-creating advantage lies in the weak signals buried in the noise.

In the 1990s, when the ability to burn music onto CDs emerged, no one knew how digitization would play out; MP3s, peer-to-peer file sharing, and streaming web-based media were not on the horizon. But one corporation with a large record label recognized more rapidly than others that the practical advantage of copyright protection could quickly become diluted if consumers began copying material. Early recognition of that possibility allowed the CEO to sell the business at a multiple based on everyone else's assumption that the status quo was unthreatened.

Developing proprietary insights isn't easy. In fact, this is the element of good strategy where most companies stumble. A search for problems can help you get started.

Create a short list of questions whose answers would have major implications for the company's strategy—for example, "What will we regret doing if the development of India hiccups or stalls, and what will we not regret?" In doing so, don't forget to examine the assumptions, explicit and implicit, behind an established business model. Do they still fit the current environment?

Another key is to collect new data through field observations or research rather than recycle the same industry reports everyone else uses. Similarly, seeking novel ways to analyze the data can generate powerful new insights.

Finally, many strategic breakthroughs have their root in a simple but profound customer insight (usually solving an old problem for the customer in a new way). Companies that go out of their way to experience the world from the customer's perspective routinely develop better strategies.

8.6.6 Test 6: Does Your Strategy Embrace Uncertainty?

A central challenge of strategy is that we have to make choices now, but the payoffs occur in a future environment we cannot fully know or control. A critical step in embracing uncertainty is to try to characterize exactly what variety of it you face—a surprisingly rare activity at many companies. Our work over the years has emphasized four levels of uncertainty. Level one offers a reasonably clear view of the future: A range of outcomes tight enough to support a firm decision. At level two, there are a number of identifiable outcomes for which a company should prepare. At level three, the possible outcomes are represented not by a set of points but by a range that can be understood as a probability distribution. Level four features total ambiguity, where even the distribution of outcomes is unknown.

In our experience, companies oscillate between assuming, simplistically, that they are operating at level one (and making bold but unjustified point forecasts) and succumbing to an unnecessarily pessimistic level-four paralysis. In each case, careful analysis of the situation usually redistributes the variables into the middle ground of levels two and three.

Rigorously understanding the uncertainty you face starts with listing the variables that would influence a strategic decision and prioritizing them according to their impact. Focus early analysis on removing as much uncertainty as you can—by, for example, ruling out impossible outcomes and using the underlying economics at work to highlight outcomes that are either mutually reinforcing or unlikely because they would undermine one another in the market. Then apply tools such as scenario analysis to the remaining, irreducible uncertainty, which should be at the heart of your strategy.

8.6.7 Test 7: Does Your Strategy Balance Commitment and Flexibility?

Commitment and flexibility exist in inverse proportion to each other: The greater the commitment you make, the less flexibility remains. This tension is one of the core challenges of strategy. Indeed, strategy can be expressed as making the right trade-offs over time between commitment and flexibility.

Making such trade-offs effectively requires an understanding of which decisions involve commitment. Inside any large company, hundreds of people make thousands of decisions each year. Only a few are strategic: Those that involve commitment through hard-to-reverse investments in long-lasting, company-specific assets. Commitment is the only path to sustainable competitive advantage. In a world of uncertainty, strategy is about not just where and how to compete but also when. Committing too early can be a leap in the dark. Being too late is also dangerous, either because opportunities are perishable or rivals can seize advantage while your company stands on the sidelines. Flexibility is the essential ingredient that allows companies to make commitments when the risk/return trade-off seems most advantageous.

A market-beating strategy will focus on just a few crucial, high-commitment choices to be made now, while leaving flexibility for other such choices to be made over time. In practice, this approach means building your strategy as a portfolio comprising three things: Big bets, or committed positions aimed at gaining significant competitive advantage; no-regrets moves, which will pay off whatever happens; and real options, or actions that involve relatively low costs now but can be elevated to a higher level of commitment as changing conditions warrant. You can build underpriced options into a strategy by, for example, modularizing major capital projects or maintaining the flexibility to switch between different inputs.

8.6.8 Test 8: Is Your Strategy Contaminated by Bias?

It's possible to believe honestly that you have a market-beating strategy when, in fact, you don't. Sometimes, that's because forces beyond your control change. But in other cases, the cause is unintentional fuzzy thinking.

Behavioral economists have identified many characteristics of the brain that are often strengths in a broader, personal environment but that can work against them in the world of business decision-making. The worst offenders include overoptimism (our tendency to hope for the best and believe too much in our own forecasts and abilities), anchoring (tying our valuation of something to an arbitrary reference point), loss aversion (putting too much emphasis on avoiding downsides and so eschewing risks worth taking), the confirmation bias (overweighting information that validates our opinions), herding (taking comfort in following the crowd), and the champion bias (assigning to idea merit that's based on the person proposing it).

Developing multiple hypotheses and potential solutions to choose among is one way to "de-bias" decision-making. Too often, the typical drill is to develop a promising hypothesis and put a lot of effort into building a fact base to validate it. In contrast, it is critical to bring fresh eyes to the issues and to maintain a culture of challenge, in which the obligation to dissent is fostered.

The decision-making process can also be de-biased by, for example, specifying objective decision criteria in advance and examining the possibility of being wrong. Techniques such as the "premortem assessment" (imagining yourself in the future where your decision turns out to have been mistaken and identifying why that might have been so) can also be useful.

8.6.9 Test 9: Is There Conviction to Act on Your Strategy?

This test and the one that follows aren't strictly about the strategy itself but about the investment you've made in implementing it. Many good strategies fall short in implementation because of an absence of conviction in the organization, particularly among the top team, where just one or two nonbelievers can strangle strategic change at birth.

Where a change of strategy is needed, that is usually because changes in the external environment have rendered obsolete the assumptions underlying a company's earlier strategy. To move ahead with implementation, you need a process that openly questions the old assumptions and allows managers to develop a new set of beliefs in tune with the new situation. This goal is not likely to be achieved just via lengthy reports and presentations. Nor will the social processes required to absorb new beliefs—group formation, building shared meaning, exposing and reconciling differences, aligning and accepting accountability—occur in formal meetings.

CEOs and boards should not be fooled by the warm glow they feel after a nice presentation by management. They must make sure that the whole team actually shares the new beliefs that support the strategy. This requirement means taking decision makers on a journey of discovery by creating experiences that will help them viscerally grasp mismatches that may exist between what the new strategy requires and the actions and behavior that have brought them success for many years.

8.6.10 Test 10: Have You Translated Your Strategy into an Action Plan?

In implementing any new strategy, it's imperative to define clearly what you are moving from and where you are moving to with respect to your company's business model, organization, and capabilities. Develop a detailed view of the shifts required to make the move, and ensure that processes and mechanisms, for which individual executives must be accountable, are in place to effect the changes. Quite simply, this is an action plan. Everyone needs to know what to do. Be sure that each major player is matched with the energy to make it happen. And since the totality of the change often represents a major organizational transformation, make sure you and your senior team are drawing on the large body of research and experience offering solid advice on change management—a topic beyond the scope of this chapter!

Finally, don't forget to make sure your ongoing resource allocation processes are aligned with your strategy. If you want to know what it actually is, look where the best people and the most generous budgets are—and be prepared to change these things significantly. Effort spent aligning the budget with the strategy will pay off many times over.

We hope that the ten tests mentioned above will prove a simple and effective antidote: A means of quickly identifying gaps in executives' strategic thinking, opening their minds toward new ways of using strategy to create value, and improving the quality of the strategy development process itself.

8.7 The Future-Today Roadmap

In conclusion, developing and implementing strategies today require a balanced, comprehensive, and integrated end-to-end approach that combines many skills and approaches. Figure 8.9 provides a roadmap for making the Future Happen Today as explained in this book chapters. It requires a good understanding of the **Why** (we need strategy), to get the people of the organization aligned about the real need for the strategy as a means of managing the VUCA world. So, strategy

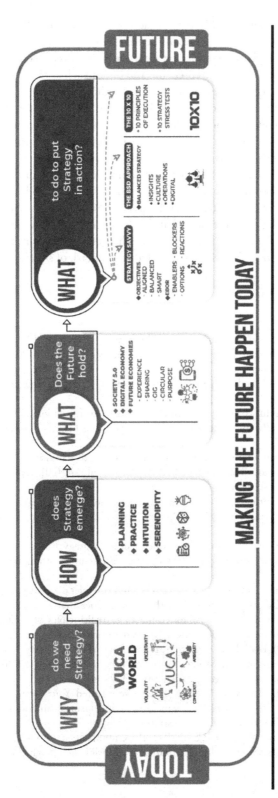

Figure 8.9 Making the Future Happen Today roadmap

can be considered as our insurance policy for proactivity and sustainability. Then, combining different approaches to **How** strategy emerges and evolves, not limiting our efforts on learning and using rigid formal strategic planning tools and techniques. We need to open our minds to the use of more flexible techniques used by entrepreneurs and SMEs such as Strategy-as-Practice and even allow more room for unorthodox approaches such as intuition and serendipity.

Also, we need to keep a very close eye on **What** the future holds and on the evolution of Society 5.0, the digital economy, and the different types of future economies. This close market sensing beyond traditional market studies can open tremendous opportunities for organizations not only to survive but also to thrive. Finally, putting strategy in action requires the use of the existing strategic planning tools in a new way and combining them with the use of methods such as design thinking and innovation management to deliver better strategies.

The proposed new Balanced Strategy Development (BSD) approach that is driven by insights, operations, culture, and digital will ensure that the developed strategies are in tune with the new-age customers and the VUCA world. Asking the tough questions and putting your strategy to the test will ensure success during the difficult and challenging task of strategy execution.

References

1. Sull, D., Homkes, R., and Sull, C. (2015). Why Strategy Execution Unravels—And What to Do About It. *Harvard Business Review*, March 2015. https://hbr.org/2015/03/why-strategy-execution-unravelsand-what-to-do-about-it

2. Ewenstein, B., Smith, W., and Sologar, A. (2015). Changing Change Management. McKinsey Digital, July 2015.

3. Favaro, K. (2015). Big Ideas Mark the Path from Strategy to Execution. *Strategy+Business Magazine*, April 2015. https://www.strategy-business.com/blog/Big-Ideas-Mark-the-Path-from-Strategy-to-Execution?gko=a478b

4. Leinwand, P., and Bäumler, M. (2017). 8 Tough Questions to Ask About Your Company's Strategy. *Harvard Business Review*, November 19, 2017. https://hbr.org/2017/11/8-tough-questions-to-ask-about-your-companys-strategy

5. Leinwand, P., and Rotering, P. (2017). How to Excel and Both Strategy and Executions. *Harvard Business Review*, November 17, 2017. https://hbr.org/2017/11/how-to-excel-at-both-strategy-and-execution

6. Huy, Q. (2017). Five Reasons Most Companies Fail at Strategy Execution. INSEAD Knowledge. https://knowledge.insead.edu/blog/insead-blog/five-reasons-most-companies-fail-at-strategy-execution-4441

7. De Souza, I., Kauffeld, R., and Van Oss, D. (2017). 10 Principles of Strategy through Execution: How to Link where your Company is Headed with What it Does Best. *Strategy+Business Magazine*, 86, Spring 2017. https://www.strategy-business.com/article/10-Principles-of-Strategy-through-Execution

8. Advisory Works. (2016). CEO Guide: The 5 Pillars of Strategy Execution.

9. Badawy, A. M. (2009). Book Review: Fast Strategy: How Strategic Agility Will Help You Stay Ahead of the Game, by Yves Doz and Mikko Kosonen, Wharton School Publishing (2008). *Journal of Engineering and Technology Management*, 26(2009), 342–344.

10. Bradley, C., Hirt, M., and Smit, S. (2011). Have you Tested Your Strategy Lately? *The McKinsey Quarterly*, January 2011. https://www.mckinsey.com/business-functions/strategy-and-corporate-finance/our-insights/have-you-tested-your-strategy-lately

11. Baghai, M., Smit, S., and Viguerie, P. S. (2007). The Granularity of Growth? *The McKinsey Quarterly*, 2071(2), 41–51. https://www.mckinsey.com/featured-insights/employment-and-growth/the-granularity-of-growth

Index

Printed in the United States
by Baker & Taylor Publisher Services